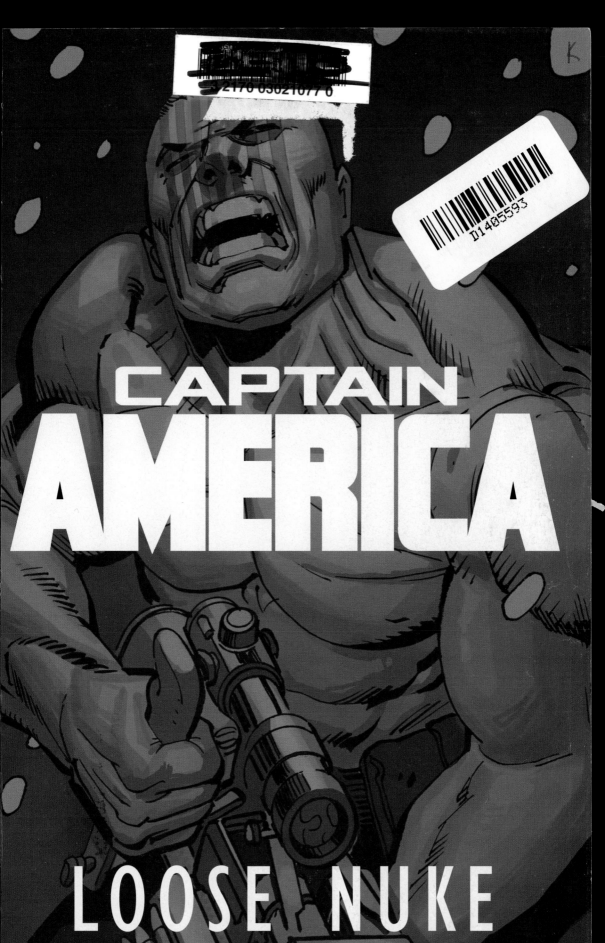

CAPTAIN AMERICA

LOOSE NUKE

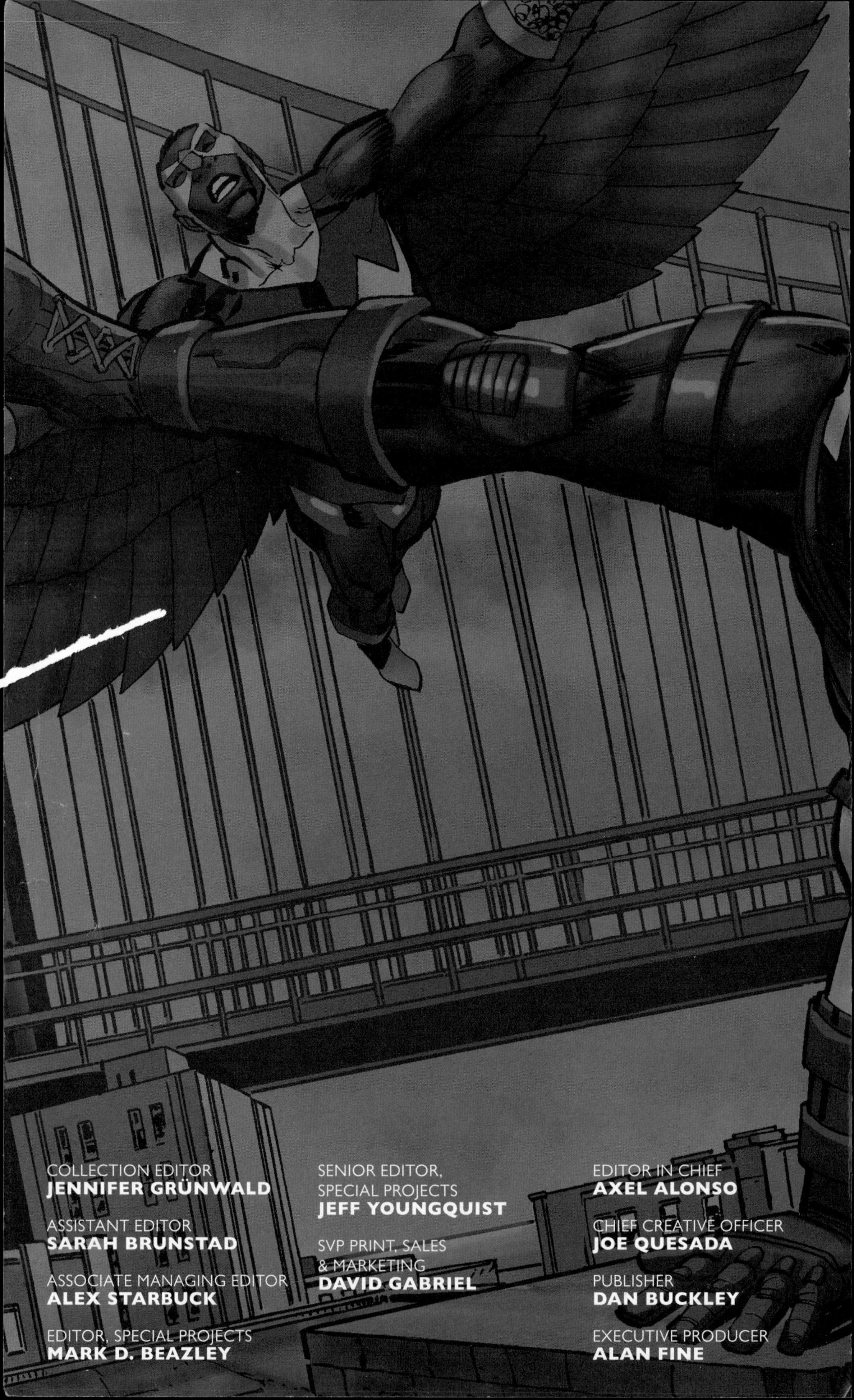

COLLECTION EDITOR
JENNIFER GRÜNWALD

ASSISTANT EDITOR
SARAH BRUNSTAD

ASSOCIATE MANAGING EDITOR
ALEX STARBUCK

EDITOR, SPECIAL PROJECTS
MARK D. BEAZLEY

SENIOR EDITOR, SPECIAL PROJECTS
JEFF YOUNGQUIST

SVP PRINT, SALES & MARKETING
DAVID GABRIEL

EDITOR IN CHIEF
AXEL ALONSO

CHIEF CREATIVE OFFICER
JOE QUESADA

PUBLISHER
DAN BUCKLEY

EXECUTIVE PRODUCER
ALAN FINE

LOOSE NUKE

WRITER
RICK REMENDER

ISSUES #11-12 & #14-15
PENCILER
CARLOS PACHECO

INKERS
KLAUS JANSON (#11-12)
& MARIANO TAIBO (#14-15)

ISSUE #13
ARTIST
NIC KLEIN

COLOR ARTISTS
DEAN WHITE
WITH **RACHELLE ROSENBERG** (#12),
RAIN BEREDO (#15) & **VAL STAPLES** (#15)

LETTERER
VC'S JOE CARAMAGNA

COVER ART
CARLOS PACHECO & DEAN WHITE (#11-14)
AND **JIM CHEUNG** & **LAURA MARTIN** (#15)

ASSISTANT EDITOR
JAKE THOMAS

EDITOR
TOM BREVOORT

CAPTAIN AMERICA CREATED BY JOE SIMON & JACK KIRBY

CAPTAIN AMERICA VOL. 3: LOOSE NUKE. Contains material originally published in magazine form as CAPTAIN AMERICA #11-15. First printing 2014. ISBN# 978-0-7851-8952-7. Published by MARVEL WORLDWIDE, INC., a subsidiary of MARVEL ENTERTAINMENT, LLC. OFFICE OF PUBLICATION: 135 West 50th Street, New York, NY 10020. Copyright © 2013 and 2014 Marvel Characters, Inc. All rights reserved. All characters featured in this issue and the distinctive names and likenesses thereof, and all related indicia are trademarks of Marvel Characters, Inc. No similarity between any of the names, characters, persons, and/or institutions in this magazine with those of any living or dead person or institution is intended, and any such similarity which may exist is purely coincidental. **Printed in the U.S.A.** ALAN FINE, EVP - Office of the President, Marvel Worldwide, Inc. and EVP & CMO Marvel Characters B.V.; DAN BUCKLEY, Publisher & President - Print, Animation & Digital Divisions; JOE QUESADA, Chief Creative Officer; TOM BREVOORT, SVP of Publishing; DAVID BOGART, SVP of Operations & Procurement, Publishing; C.B. CEBULSKI, SVP of Creator & Content Development; DAVID GABRIEL, SVP Print, Sales & Marketing; JIM O'KEEFE, VP of Operations & Logistics; DAN CARR, Executive Director of Publishing Technology; SUSAN CRESPI, Editorial Operations Manager; ALEX MORALES, Publishing Operations Manager; STAN LEE, Chairman Emeritus. For information regarding advertising in Marvel Comics or on Marvel.com, please contact Niza Disla, Director of Marvel Partnerships, at ndisla@marvel.com. For Marvel subscription inquiries, please call 800-217-9158. **Manufactured between 10/10/2014 and 11/17/2014 by R.R. DONNELLEY, INC., SALEM, VA, USA.**

10 9 8 7 6 5 4 3 2 1

During WWII, a secret military experiment turned scrawny Steve Rogers into America's first super-soldier, Captain America. Near the end of the war, Rogers was presumed dead in an explosion over the English Channel.

Decades later, Captain America was found frozen in ice and revived. Steve Rogers awakened to a world he never imagined, a man out of time. He again took up the mantle of Captain America, defending the U.S. and the world from threats of all kinds.

PREVIOUSLY...

At long last, Captain America returned from Dimension Z, battered and weary but alive. With him was Jet Black, Arnim Zola's daughter and Cap's unexpected ally. After a years-long one-man war against his nemesis, Steve finally defeated Zola with Jet's help but at a heavy price: in the final confrontation, Steve lost both his adopted son, Ian, and his lover, Sharon Carter.

After 12 years in Dimension Z, Steve Rogers must reenter a world where he was only gone a moment, once again making him a man out of time.

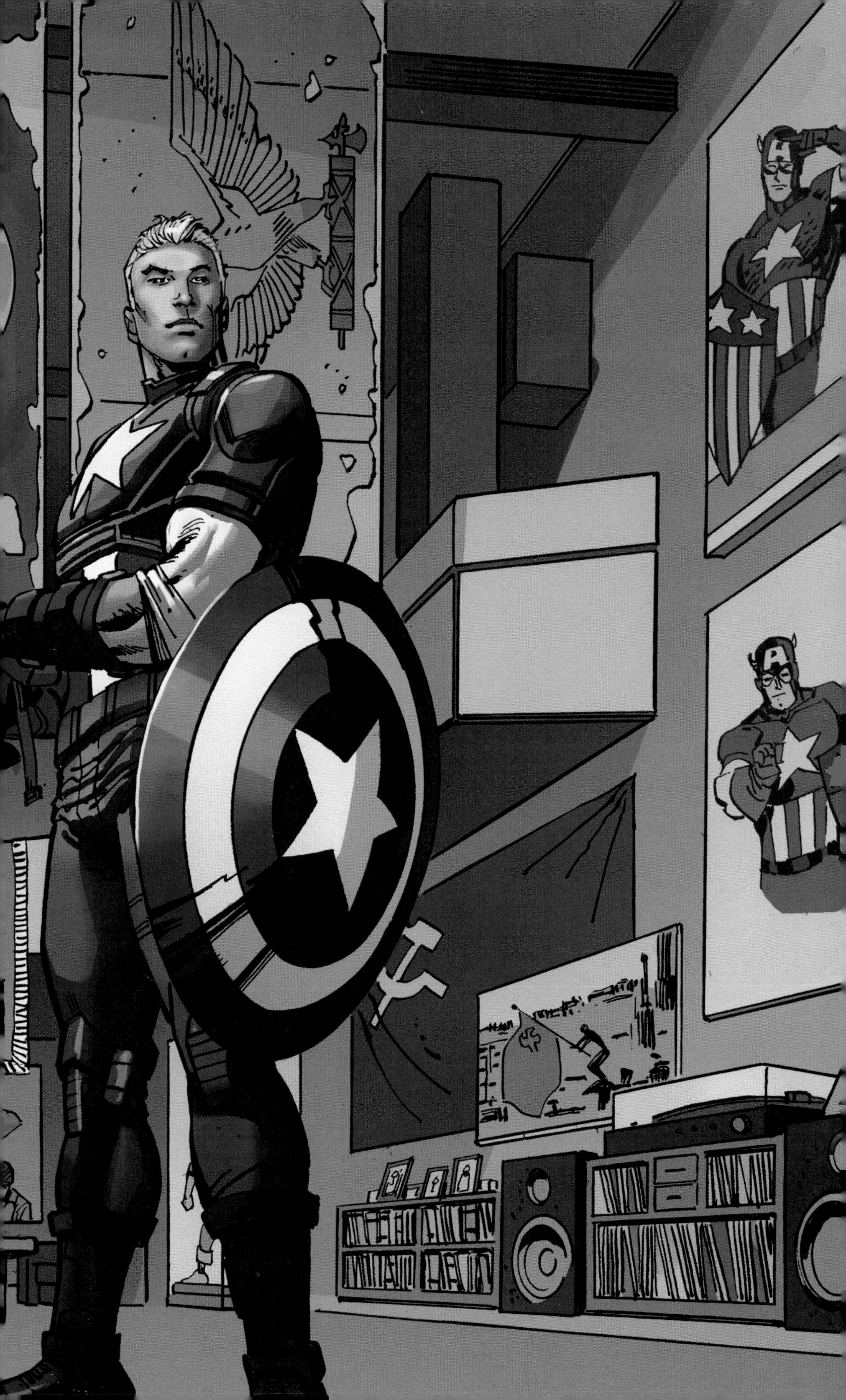

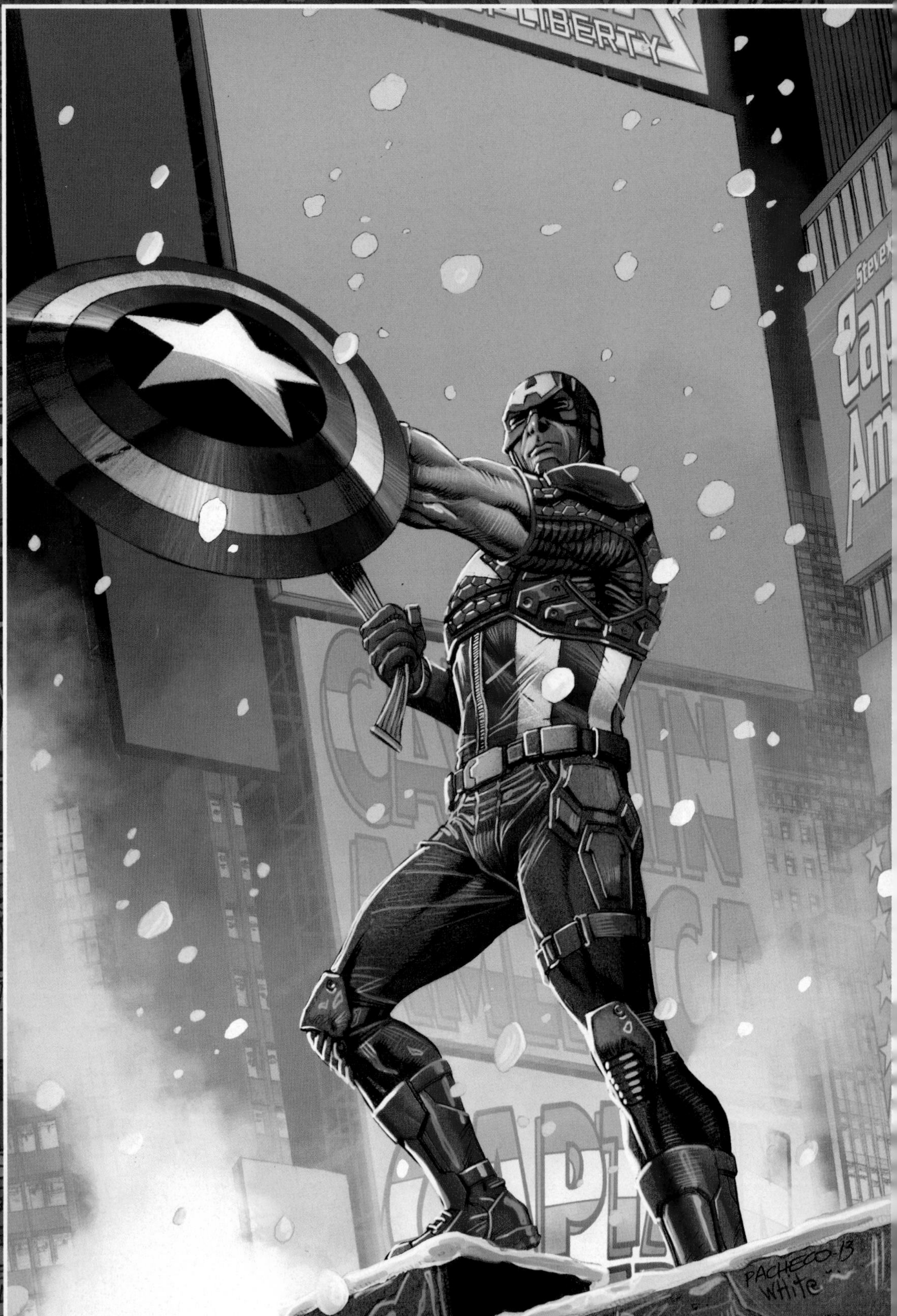
LIBERTY
Steve
PACHECO-13
White

ELEVEN

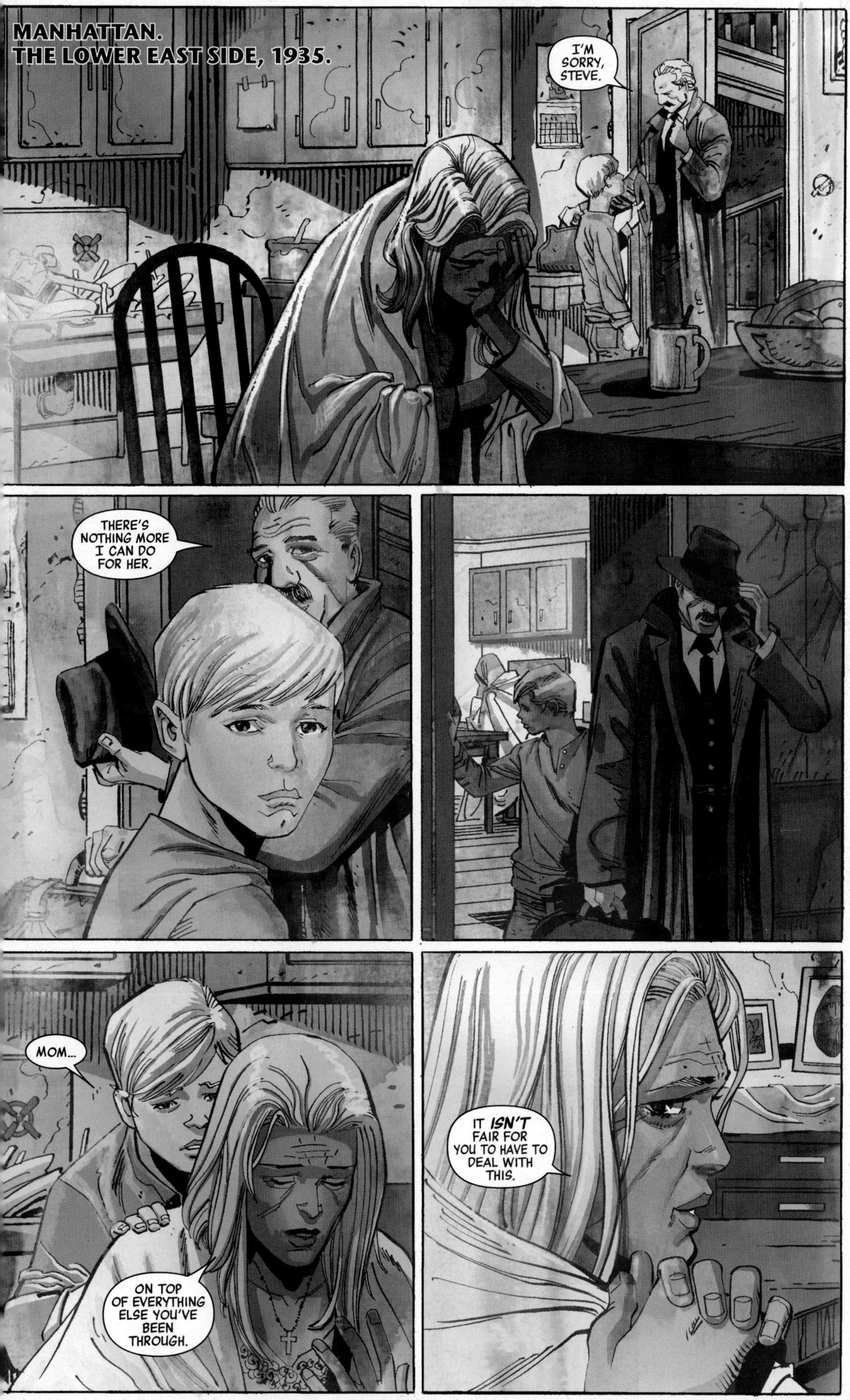
MANHATTAN.
THE LOWER EAST SIDE, 1935.
I'M SORRY, STEVE.
THERE'S NOTHING MORE I CAN DO FOR HER.
MOM...
ON TOP OF EVERYTHING ELSE YOU'VE BEEN THROUGH.
IT ISN'T FAIR FOR YOU TO HAVE TO DEAL WITH THIS.

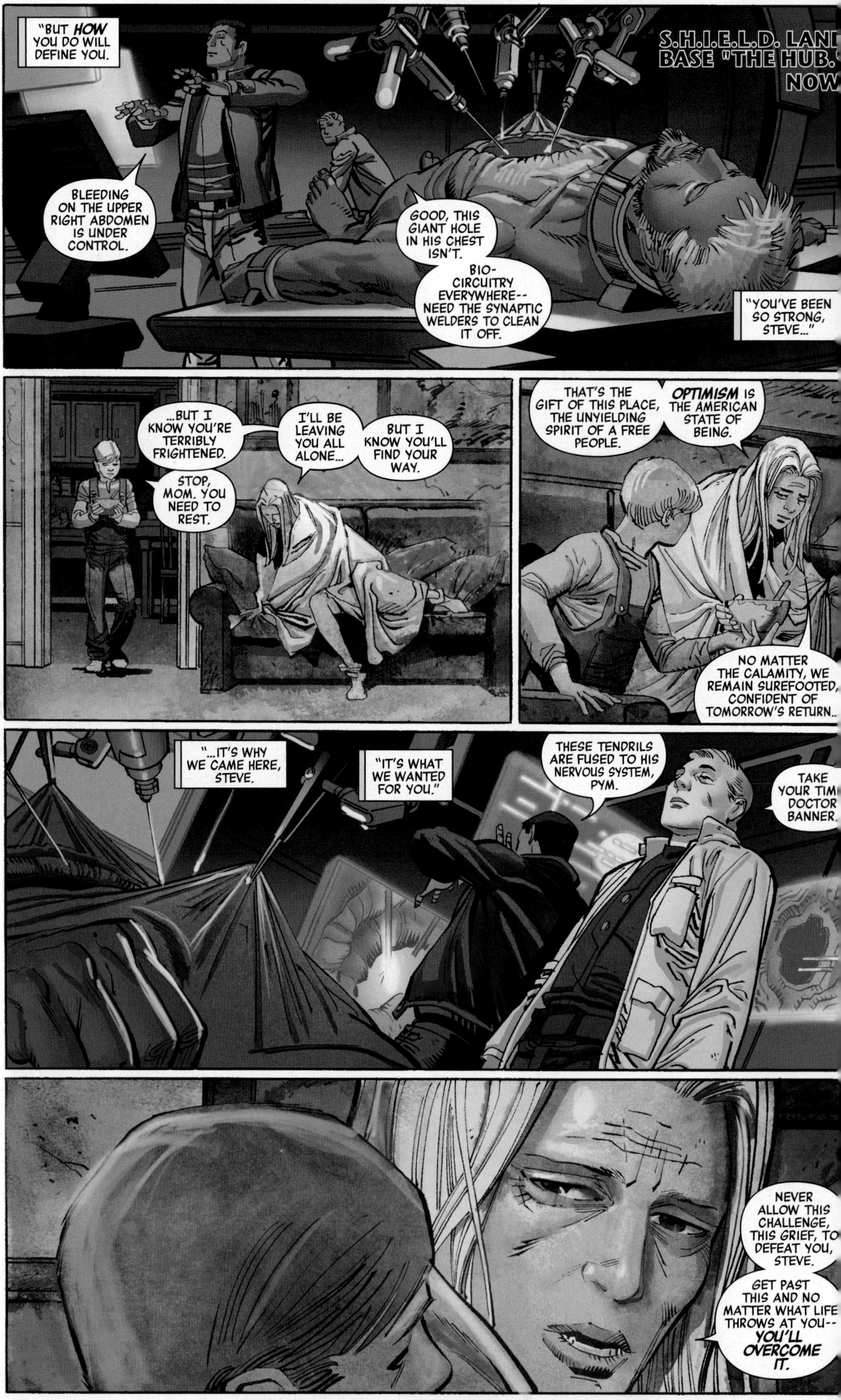
"BUT HOW YOU DO WILL DEFINE YOU.
S.H.I.E.L.D. LAND BASE "THE HUB." NOW
BLEEDING ON THE UPPER RIGHT ABDOMEN IS UNDER CONTROL.
GOOD, THIS GIANT HOLE IN HIS CHEST ISN'T.
BIO-CIRCUITRY EVERYWHERE--NEED THE SYNAPTIC WELDERS TO CLEAN IT OFF.
"YOU'VE BEEN SO STRONG, STEVE..."
...BUT I KNOW YOU'RE TERRIBLY FRIGHTENED.
I'LL BE LEAVING YOU ALL ALONE...
BUT I KNOW YOU'LL FIND YOUR WAY.
STOP, MOM. YOU NEED TO REST.
THAT'S THE GIFT OF THIS PLACE, THE UNYIELDING SPIRIT OF A FREE PEOPLE.
OPTIMISM IS THE AMERICAN STATE OF BEING.
NO MATTER THE CALAMITY, WE REMAIN SUREFOOTED, CONFIDENT OF TOMORROW'S RETURN...
"...IT'S WHY WE CAME HERE, STEVE.
"IT'S WHAT WE WANTED FOR YOU."
THESE TENDRILS ARE FUSED TO HIS NERVOUS SYSTEM, PYM.
TAKE YOUR TIME DOCTOR BANNER.
NEVER ALLOW THIS CHALLENGE, THIS GRIEF, TO DEFEAT YOU, STEVE.
GET PAST THIS AND NO MATTER WHAT LIFE THROWS AT YOU--YOU'LL OVERCOME IT.

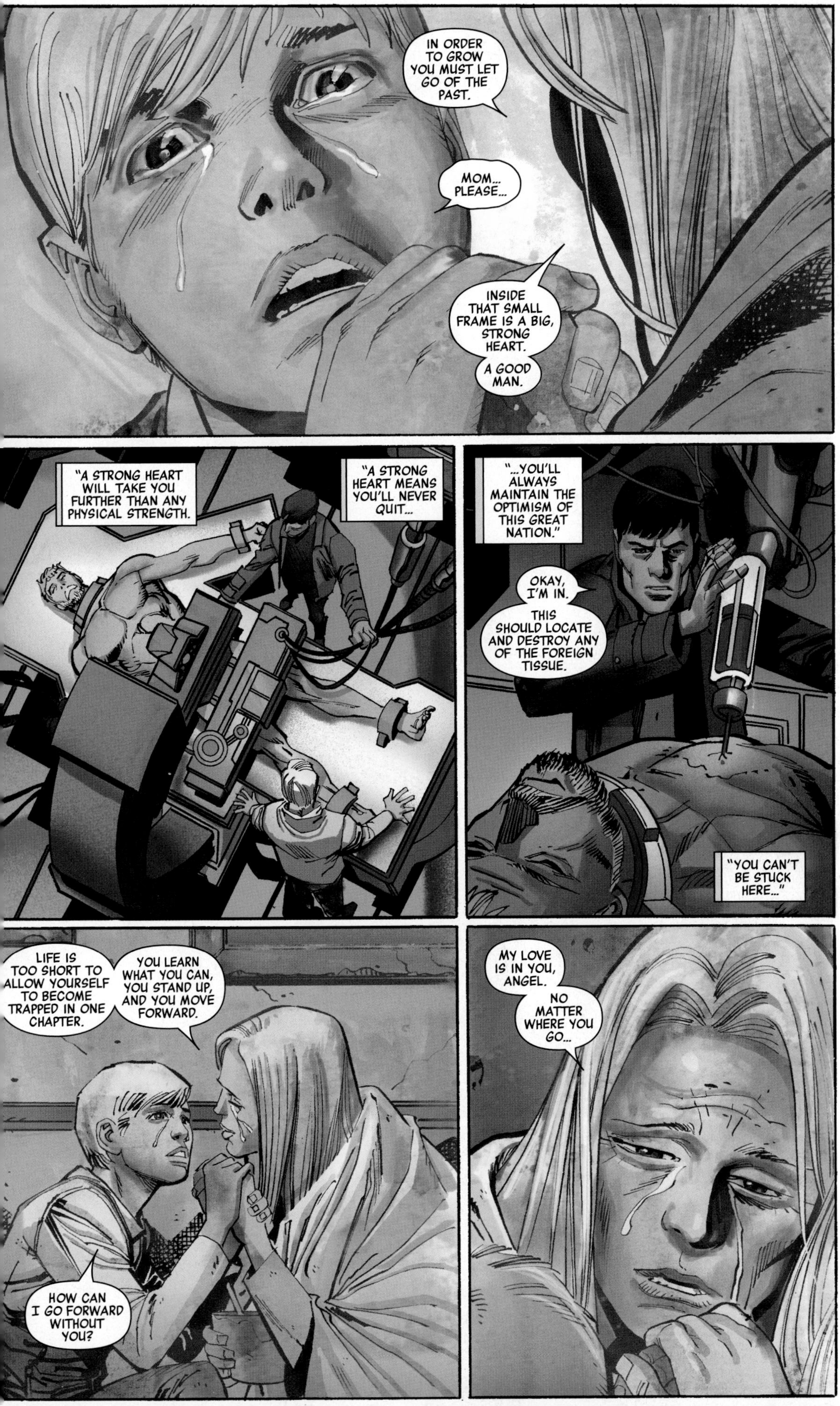
IN ORDER TO GROW YOU MUST LET GO OF THE PAST.
MOM... PLEASE...
INSIDE THAT SMALL FRAME IS A BIG, STRONG HEART.
A GOOD MAN.
"A STRONG HEART WILL TAKE YOU FURTHER THAN ANY PHYSICAL STRENGTH.
"A STRONG HEART MEANS YOU'LL NEVER QUIT...
"...YOU'LL ALWAYS MAINTAIN THE OPTIMISM OF THIS GREAT NATION."
OKAY, I'M IN.
THIS SHOULD LOCATE AND DESTROY ANY OF THE FOREIGN TISSUE.
"YOU CAN'T BE STUCK HERE..."
LIFE IS TOO SHORT TO ALLOW YOURSELF TO BECOME TRAPPED IN ONE CHAPTER.
YOU LEARN WHAT YOU CAN, YOU STAND UP, AND YOU MOVE FORWARD.
HOW CAN I GO FORWARD WITHOUT YOU?
MY LOVE IS IN YOU, ANGEL.
NO MATTER WHERE YOU GO...

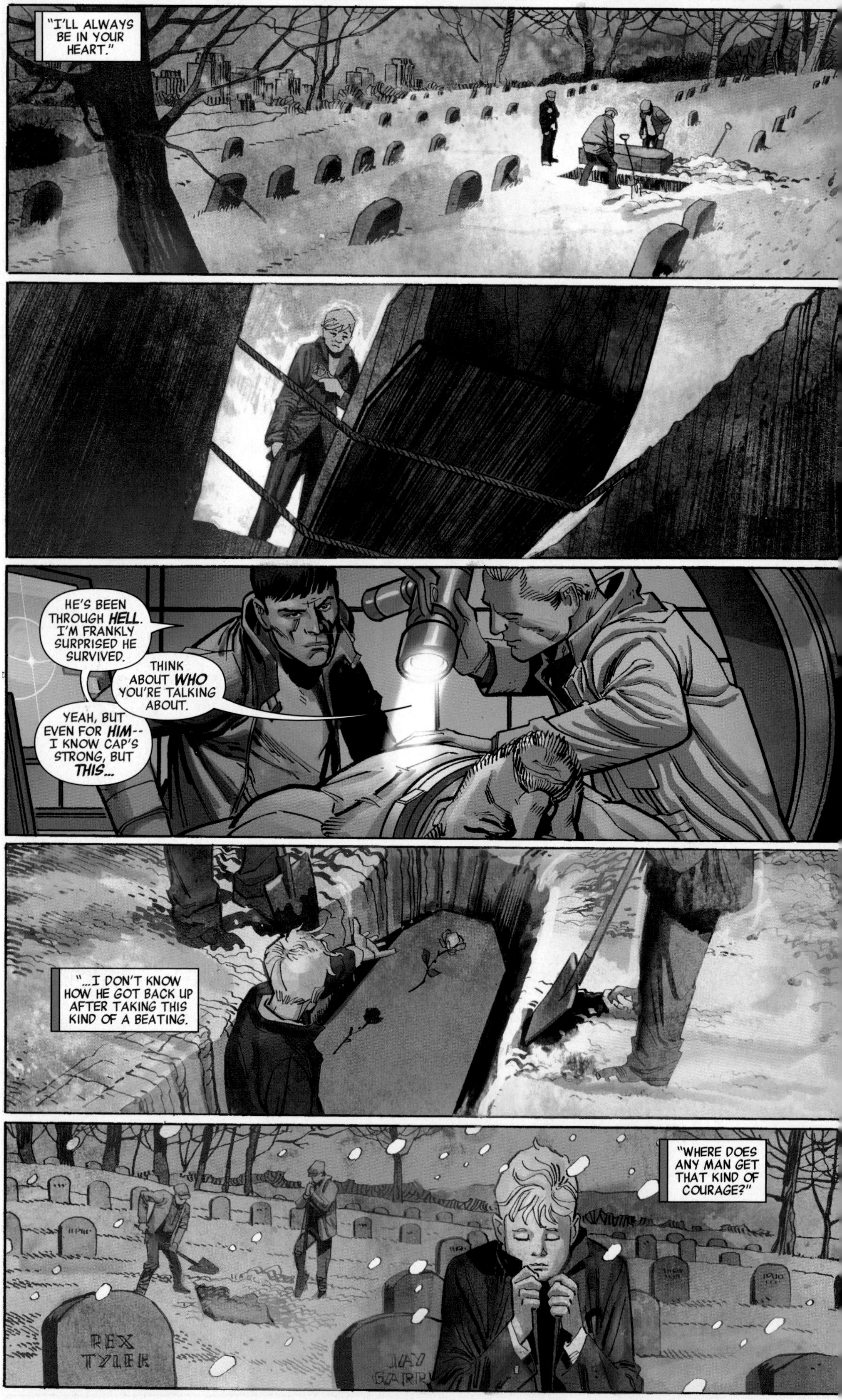
"I'LL ALWAYS BE IN YOUR HEART."
HE'S BEEN THROUGH HELL. I'M FRANKLY SURPRISED HE SURVIVED.
THINK ABOUT WHO YOU'RE TALKING ABOUT.
YEAH, BUT EVEN FOR HIM-- I KNOW CAP'S STRONG, BUT THIS...
"...I DON'T KNOW HOW HE GOT BACK UP AFTER TAKING THIS KIND OF A BEATING.
"WHERE DOES ANY MAN GET THAT KIND OF COURAGE?"
REX TYLER

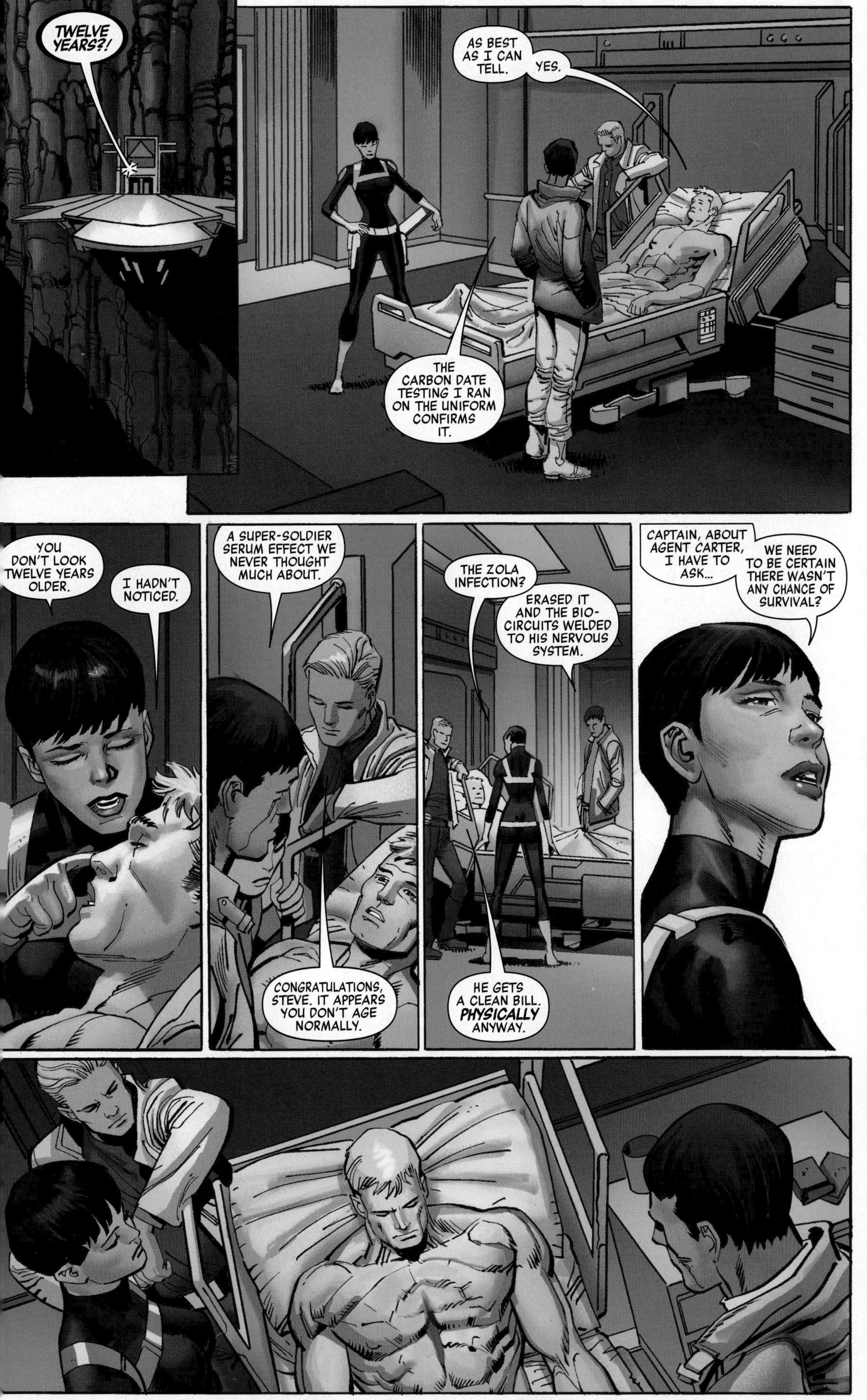
TWELVE YEARS?!
AS BEST AS I CAN TELL.
YES.
THE CARBON DATE TESTING I RAN ON THE UNIFORM CONFIRMS IT.
YOU DON'T LOOK TWELVE YEARS OLDER.
I HADN'T NOTICED.
A SUPER-SOLDIER SERUM EFFECT WE NEVER THOUGHT MUCH ABOUT.
CONGRATULATIONS, STEVE. IT APPEARS YOU DON'T AGE NORMALLY.
THE ZOLA INFECTION?
ERASED IT AND THE BIO-CIRCUITS WELDED TO HIS NERVOUS SYSTEM.
HE GETS A CLEAN BILL. PHYSICALLY ANYWAY.
CAPTAIN, ABOUT AGENT CARTER, I HAVE TO ASK...
WE NEED TO BE CERTAIN THERE WASN'T ANY CHANCE OF SURVIVAL?

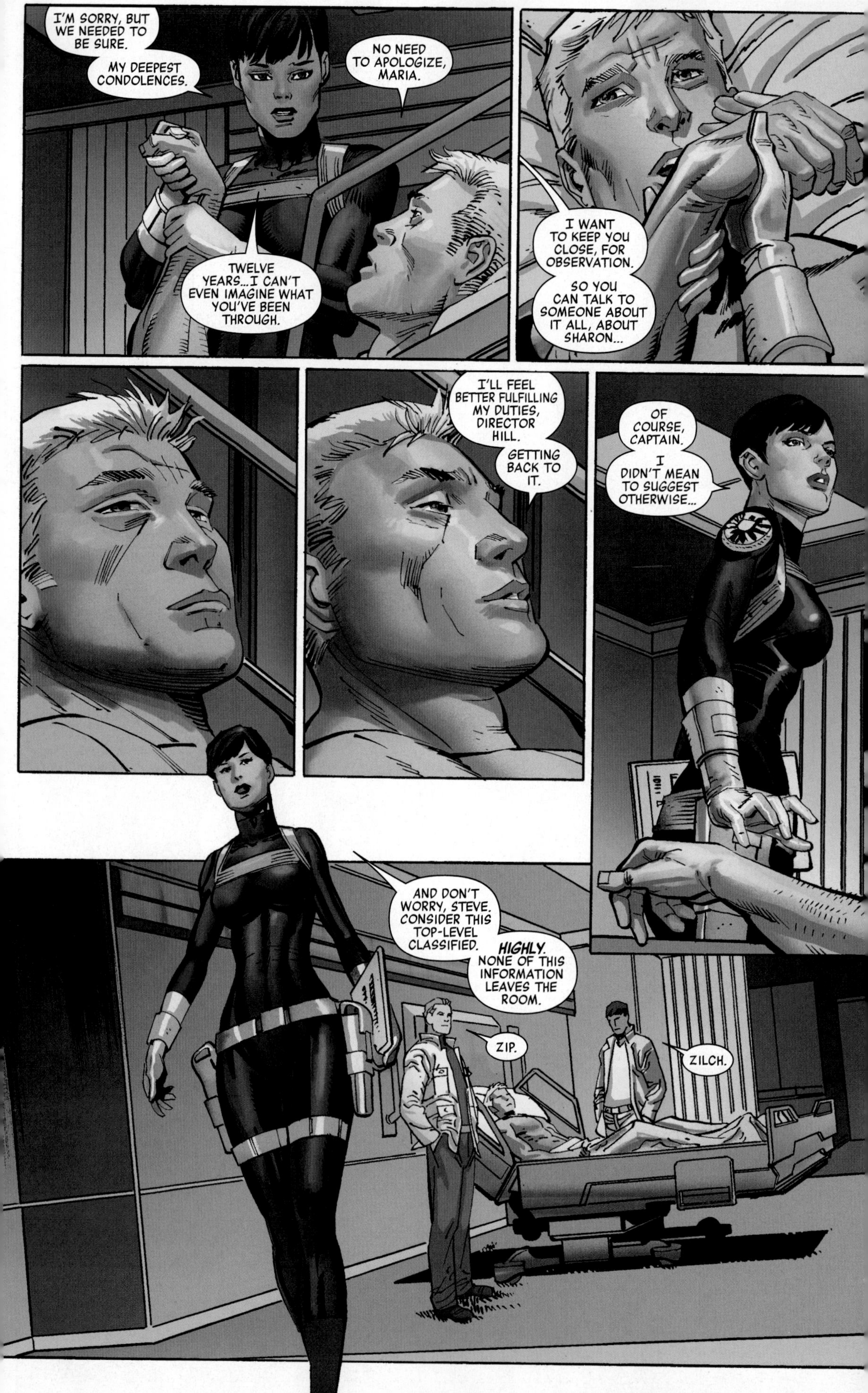
I'M SORRY, BUT WE NEEDED TO BE SURE.
MY DEEPEST CONDOLENCES.
NO NEED TO APOLOGIZE, MARIA.
TWELVE YEARS...I CAN'T EVEN IMAGINE WHAT YOU'VE BEEN THROUGH.
I WANT TO KEEP YOU CLOSE, FOR OBSERVATION.
SO YOU CAN TALK TO SOMEONE ABOUT IT ALL, ABOUT SHARON...
I'LL FEEL BETTER FULFILLING MY DUTIES, DIRECTOR HILL.
GETTING BACK TO IT.
OF COURSE, CAPTAIN.
I DIDN'T MEAN TO SUGGEST OTHERWISE...
AND DON'T WORRY, STEVE. CONSIDER THIS TOP-LEVEL CLASSIFIED.
HIGHLY. NONE OF THIS INFORMATION LEAVES THE ROOM.
ZIP.
ZILCH.

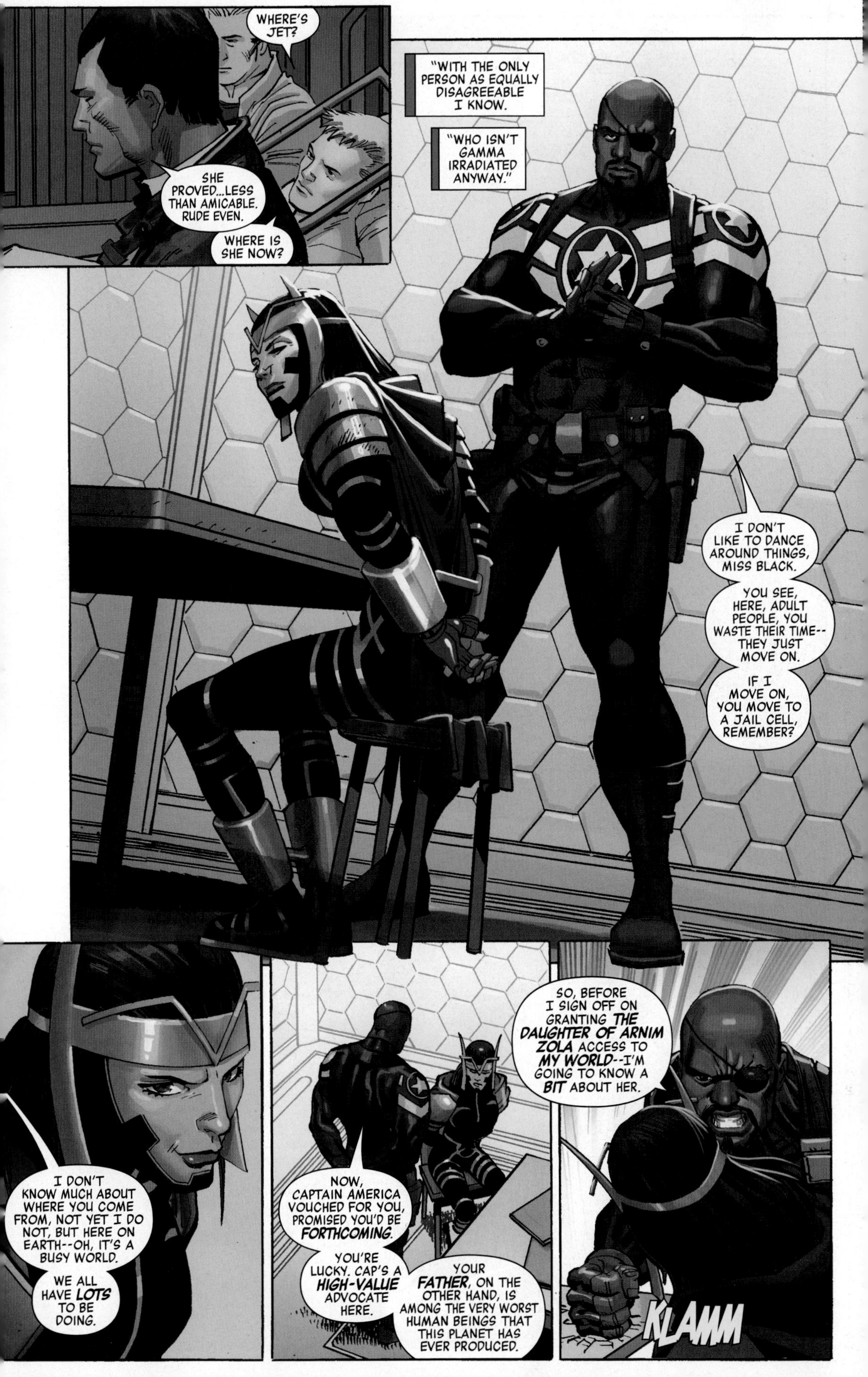
WHERE'S JET?
SHE PROVED...LESS THAN AMICABLE. RUDE EVEN.
WHERE IS SHE NOW?
"WITH THE ONLY PERSON AS EQUALLY DISAGREEABLE I KNOW.
"WHO ISN'T GAMMA IRRADIATED ANYWAY."
I DON'T LIKE TO DANCE AROUND THINGS, MISS BLACK.
YOU SEE, HERE, ADULT PEOPLE, YOU WASTE THEIR TIME-- THEY JUST MOVE ON.
IF I MOVE ON, YOU MOVE TO A JAIL CELL, REMEMBER?
I DON'T KNOW MUCH ABOUT WHERE YOU COME FROM, NOT YET I DO NOT, BUT HERE ON EARTH--OH, IT'S A BUSY WORLD.
WE ALL HAVE LOTS TO BE DOING.
NOW, CAPTAIN AMERICA VOUCHED FOR YOU, PROMISED YOU'D BE FORTHCOMING.
YOU'RE LUCKY. CAP'S A HIGH-VALUE ADVOCATE HERE.
YOUR FATHER, ON THE OTHER HAND, IS AMONG THE VERY WORST HUMAN BEINGS THAT THIS PLANET HAS EVER PRODUCED.
SO, BEFORE I SIGN OFF ON GRANTING THE DAUGHTER OF ARNIM ZOLA ACCESS TO MY WORLD--I'M GOING TO KNOW A BIT ABOUT HER.
KLAMM

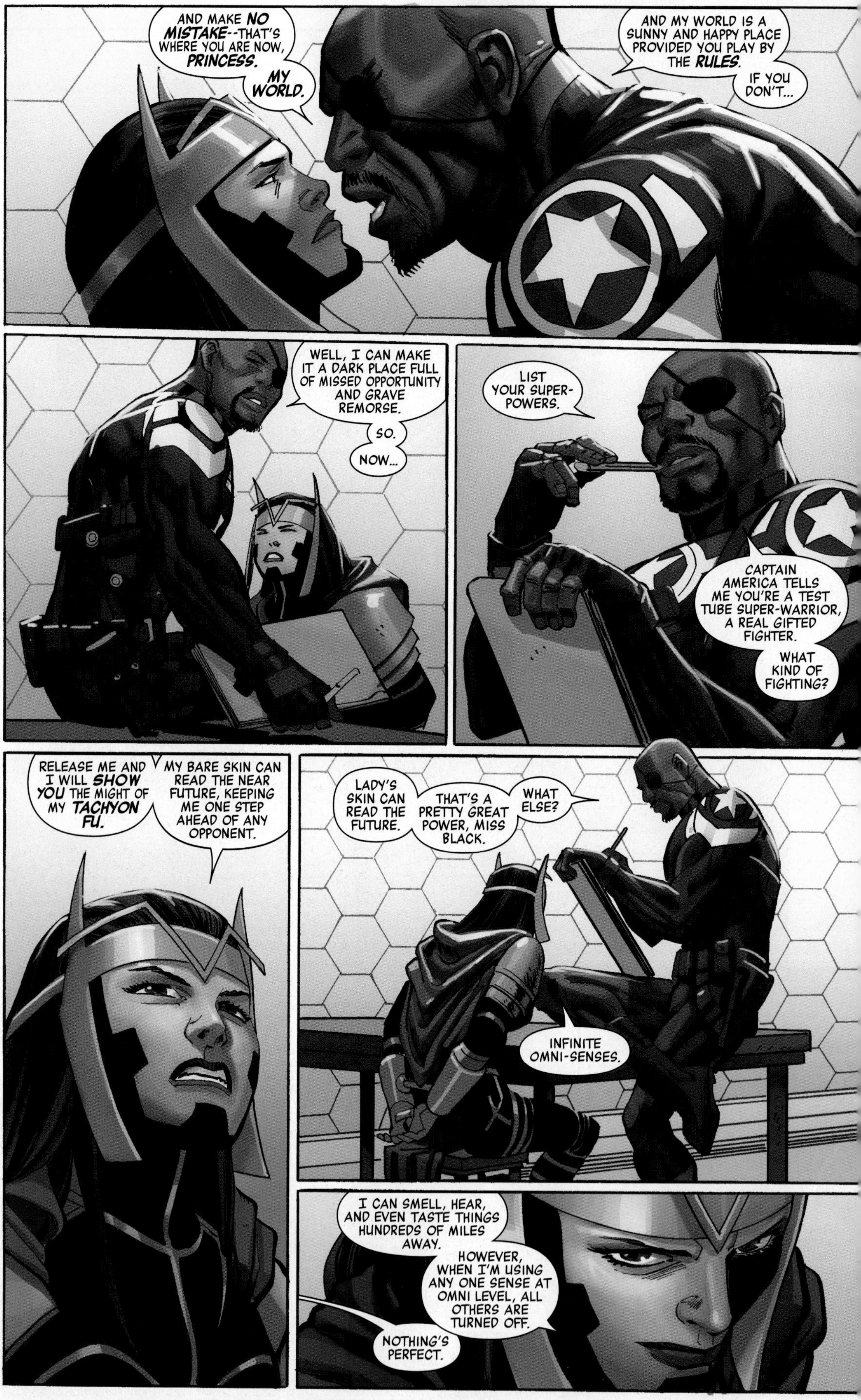

AND MAKE NO MISTAKE--THAT'S WHERE YOU ARE NOW, PRINCESS.
MY WORLD.
AND MY WORLD IS A SUNNY AND HAPPY PLACE PROVIDED YOU PLAY BY THE RULES.
IF YOU DON'T...
WELL, I CAN MAKE IT A DARK PLACE FULL OF MISSED OPPORTUNITY AND GRAVE REMORSE.
SO.
NOW...
LIST YOUR SUPER-POWERS.
CAPTAIN AMERICA TELLS ME YOU'RE A TEST TUBE SUPER-WARRIOR, A REAL GIFTED FIGHTER.
WHAT KIND OF FIGHTING?
RELEASE ME AND I WILL SHOW YOU THE MIGHT OF MY TACHYON FU.
MY BARE SKIN CAN READ THE NEAR FUTURE, KEEPING ME ONE STEP AHEAD OF ANY OPPONENT.
LADY'S SKIN CAN READ THE FUTURE.
THAT'S A PRETTY GREAT POWER, MISS BLACK.
WHAT ELSE?
INFINITE OMNI-SENSES.
I CAN SMELL, HEAR, AND EVEN TASTE THINGS HUNDREDS OF MILES AWAY.
HOWEVER, WHEN I'M USING ANY ONE SENSE AT OMNI LEVEL, ALL OTHERS ARE TURNED OFF.
NOTHING'S PERFECT.

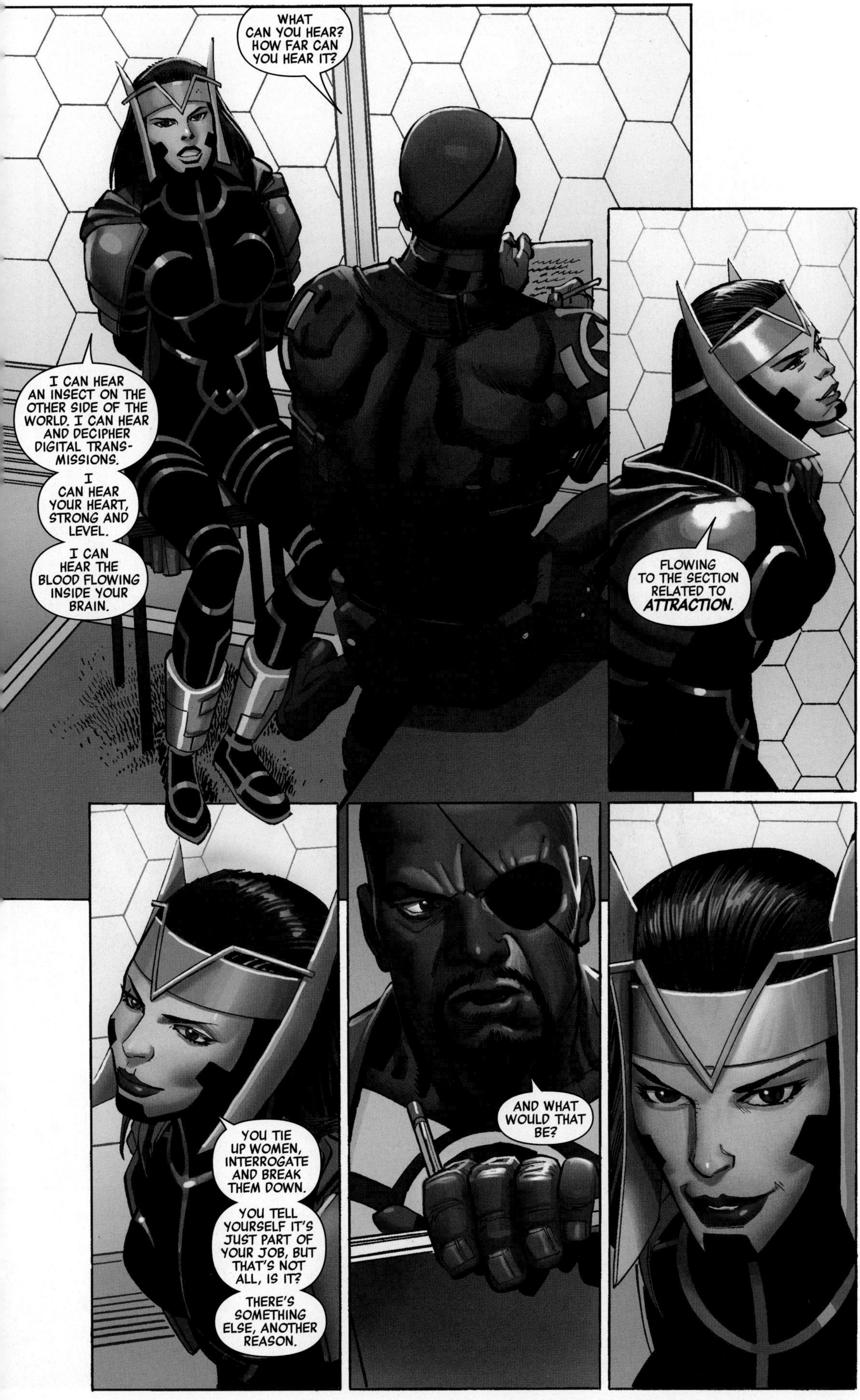
WHAT CAN YOU HEAR? HOW FAR CAN YOU HEAR IT?
I CAN HEAR AN INSECT ON THE OTHER SIDE OF THE WORLD. I CAN HEAR AND DECIPHER DIGITAL TRANS-MISSIONS.
I CAN HEAR YOUR HEART, STRONG AND LEVEL.
I CAN HEAR THE BLOOD FLOWING INSIDE YOUR BRAIN.
FLOWING TO THE SECTION RELATED TO *ATTRACTION*.
YOU TIE UP WOMEN, INTERROGATE AND BREAK THEM DOWN.
YOU TELL YOURSELF IT'S JUST PART OF YOUR JOB, BUT THAT'S NOT ALL, IS IT?
THERE'S SOMETHING ELSE, ANOTHER REASON.
AND WHAT WOULD THAT BE?

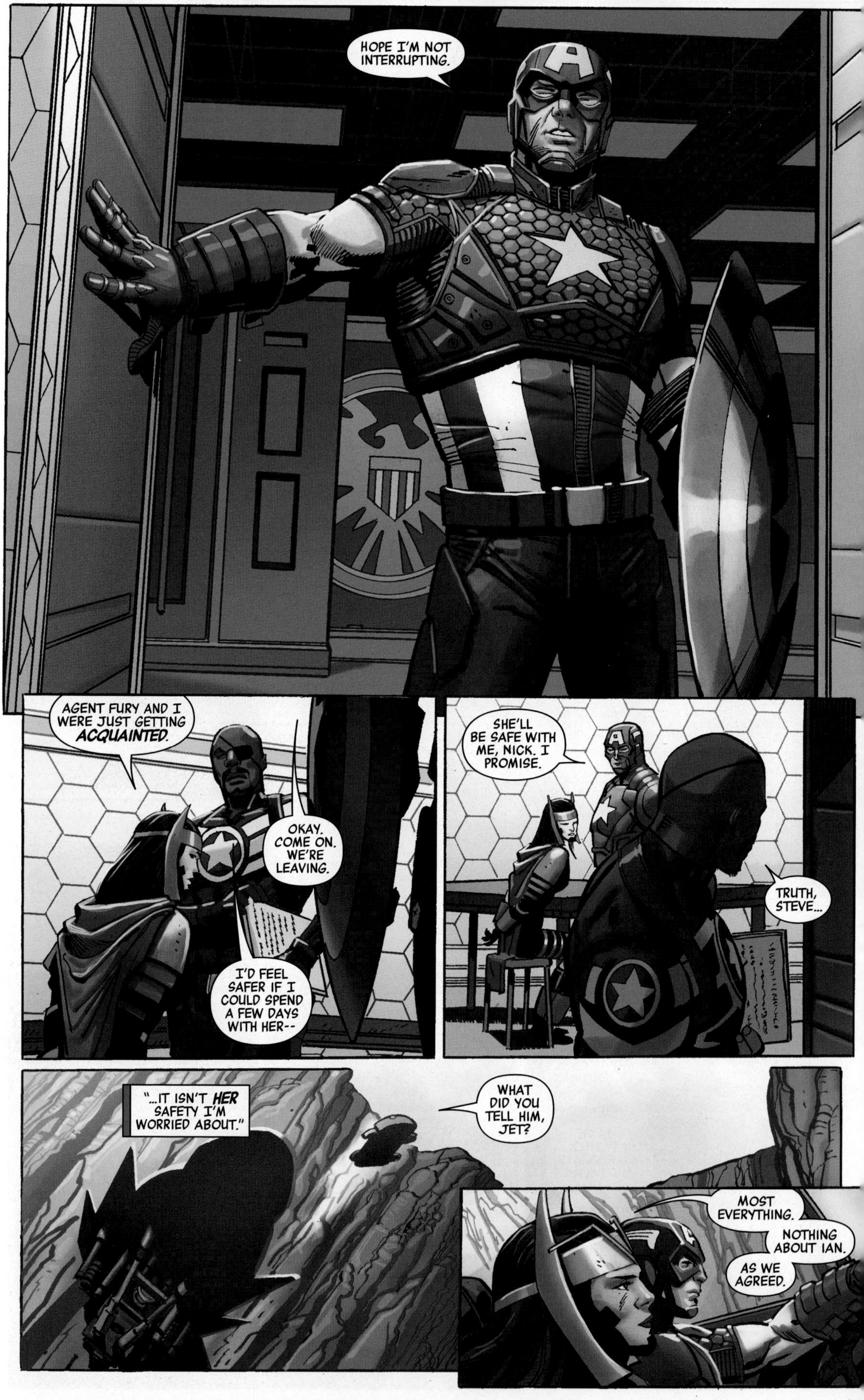
HOPE I'M NOT INTERRUPTING.
AGENT FURY AND I WERE JUST GETTING ACQUAINTED.
OKAY. COME ON. WE'RE LEAVING.
I'D FEEL SAFER IF I COULD SPEND A FEW DAYS WITH HER--
SHE'LL BE SAFE WITH ME, NICK. I PROMISE.
TRUTH, STEVE...
"...IT ISN'T HER SAFETY I'M WORRIED ABOUT."
WHAT DID YOU TELL HIM, JET?
MOST EVERYTHING.
NOTHING ABOUT IAN.
AS WE AGREED.

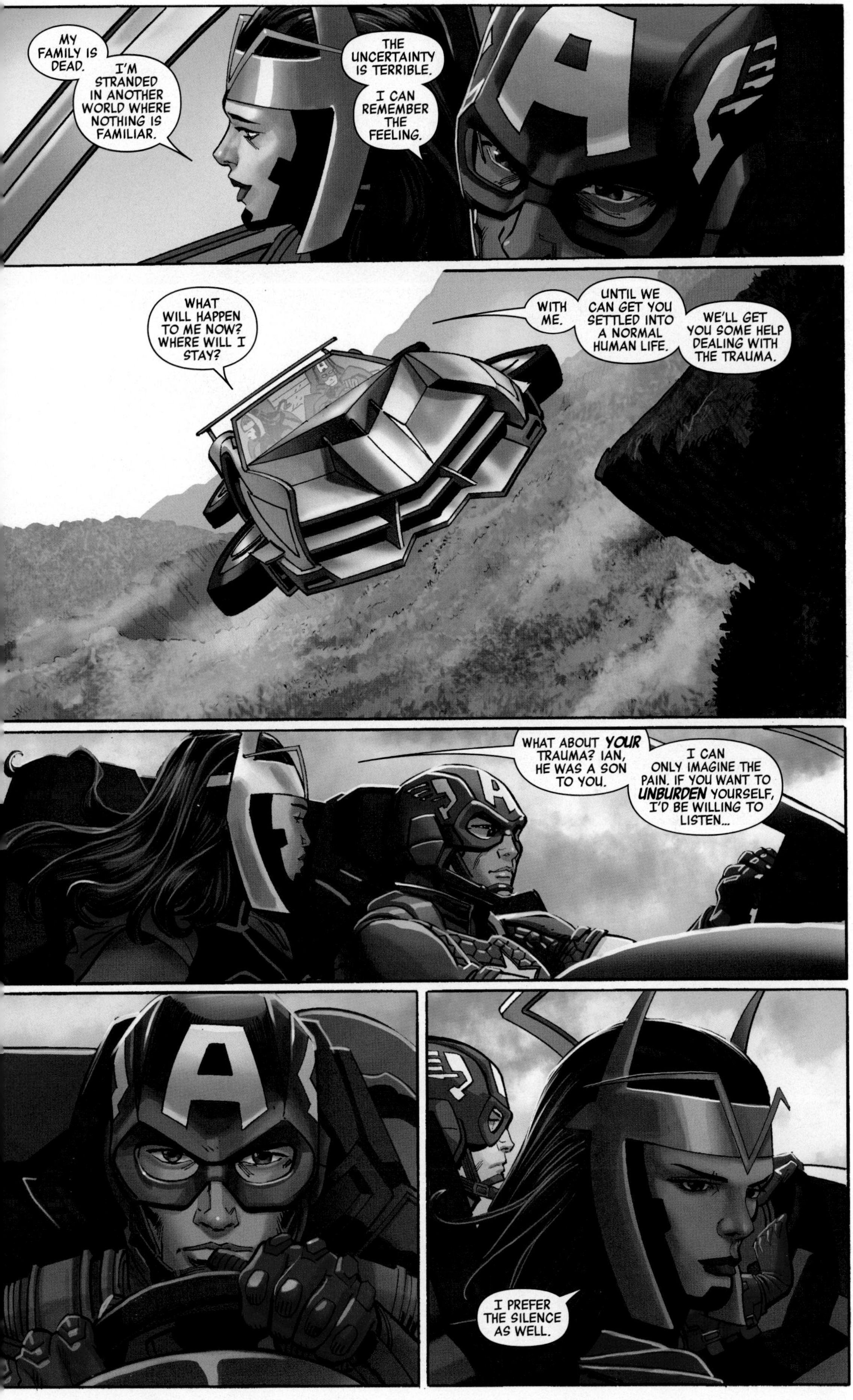
MY FAMILY IS DEAD.
I'M STRANDED IN ANOTHER WORLD WHERE NOTHING IS FAMILIAR.
THE UNCERTAINTY IS TERRIBLE.
I CAN REMEMBER THE FEELING.
WHAT WILL HAPPEN TO ME NOW? WHERE WILL I STAY?
WITH ME.
UNTIL WE CAN GET YOU SETTLED INTO A NORMAL HUMAN LIFE.
WE'LL GET YOU SOME HELP DEALING WITH THE TRAUMA.
WHAT ABOUT YOUR TRAUMA? IAN, HE WAS A SON TO YOU.
I CAN ONLY IMAGINE THE PAIN. IF YOU WANT TO UNBURDEN YOURSELF, I'D BE WILLING TO LISTEN...
I PREFER THE SILENCE AS WELL.

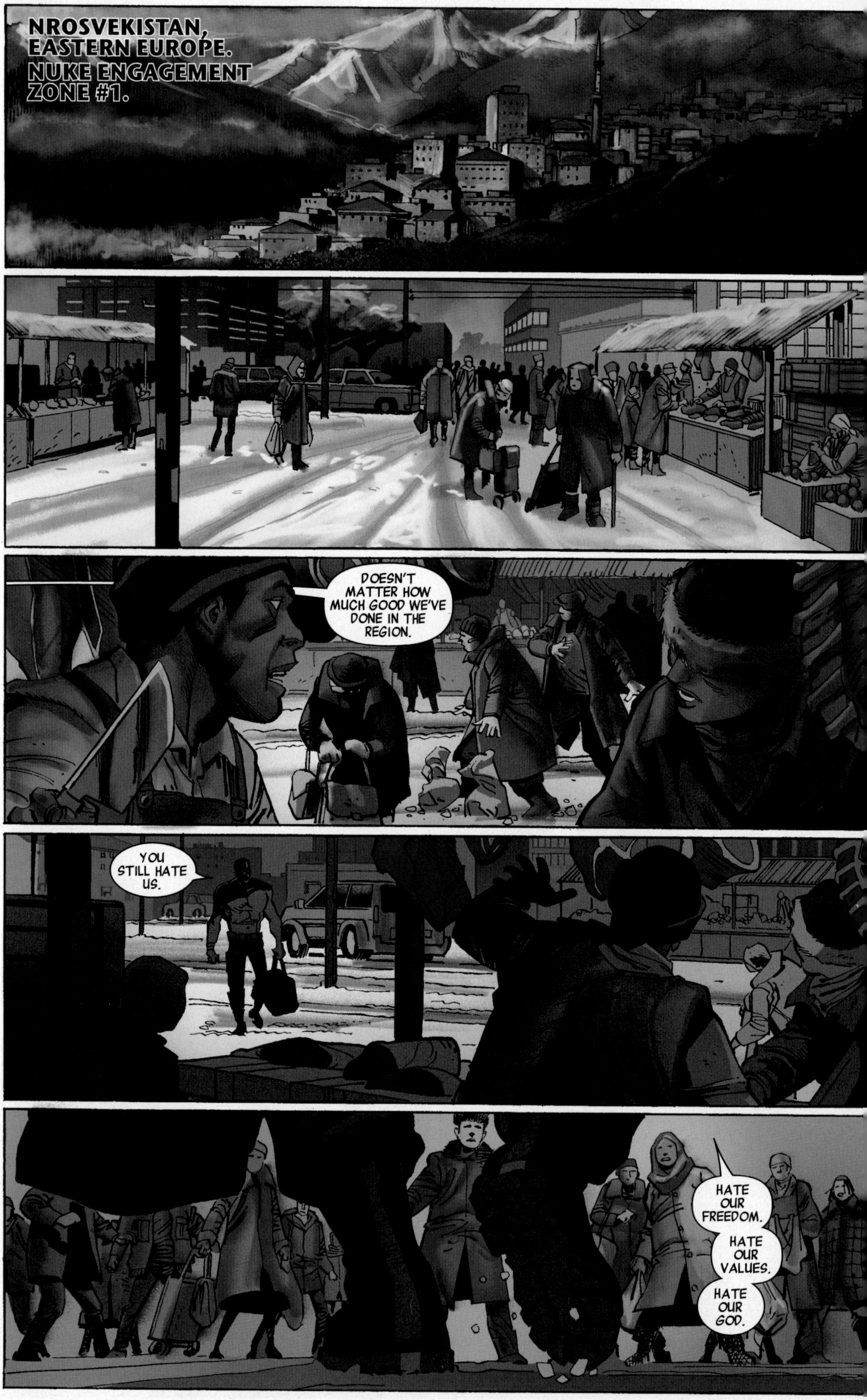
NROSVEKISTAN, EASTERN EUROPE.
NUKE ENGAGEMENT ZONE #1.
DOESN'T MATTER HOW MUCH GOOD WE'VE DONE IN THE REGION.
YOU STILL HATE US.
HATE OUR FREEDOM.
HATE OUR VALUES.
HATE OUR GOD.

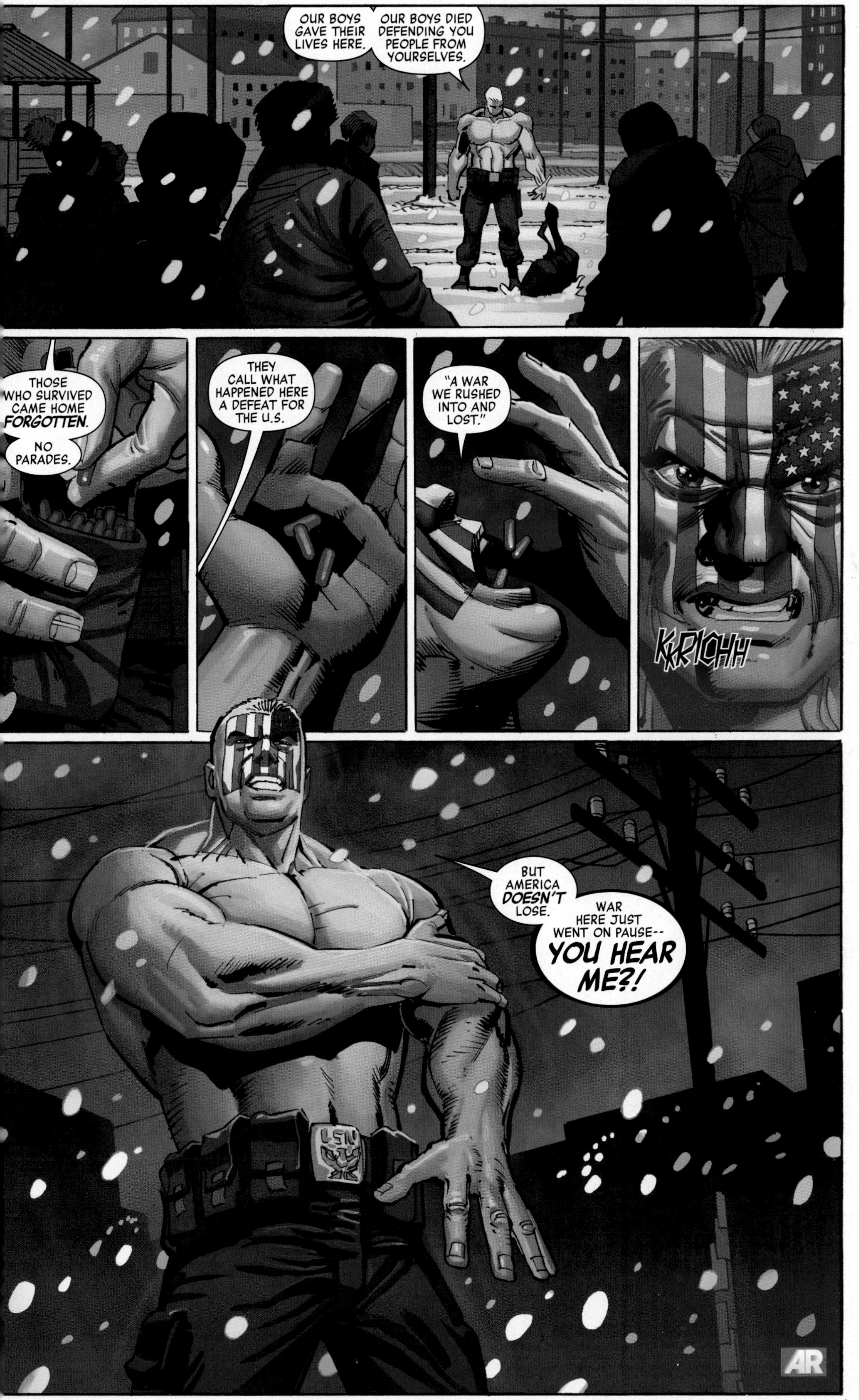
OUR BOYS GAVE THEIR LIVES HERE.
OUR BOYS DIED DEFENDING YOU PEOPLE FROM YOURSELVES.
THOSE WHO SURVIVED CAME HOME ***FORGOTTEN***.
NO PARADES.
THEY CALL WHAT HAPPENED HERE A DEFEAT FOR THE U.S.
"A WAR WE RUSHED INTO AND LOST."
KKKRICHHH
BUT AMERICA ***DOESN'T*** LOSE.
WAR HERE JUST WENT ON PAUSE--
YOU HEAR ME?!
AR

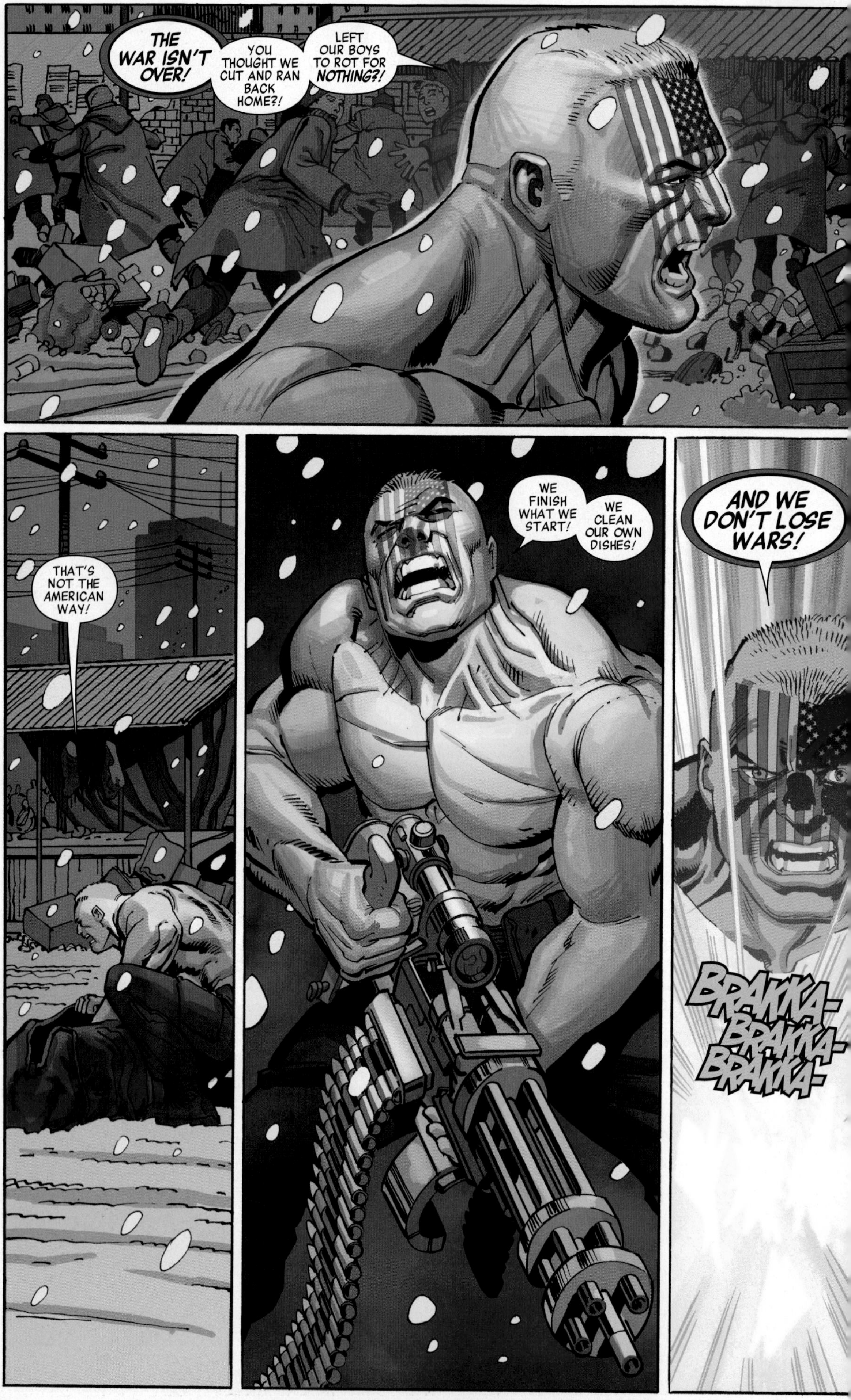
THE WAR ISN'T OVER!
YOU THOUGHT WE CUT AND RAN BACK HOME?!
LEFT OUR BOYS TO ROT FOR NOTHING?!
THAT'S NOT THE AMERICAN WAY!
WE FINISH WHAT WE START!
WE CLEAN OUR OWN DISHES!
AND WE DON'T LOSE WARS!
BRAKKA-BRAKKA-BRAKKA-

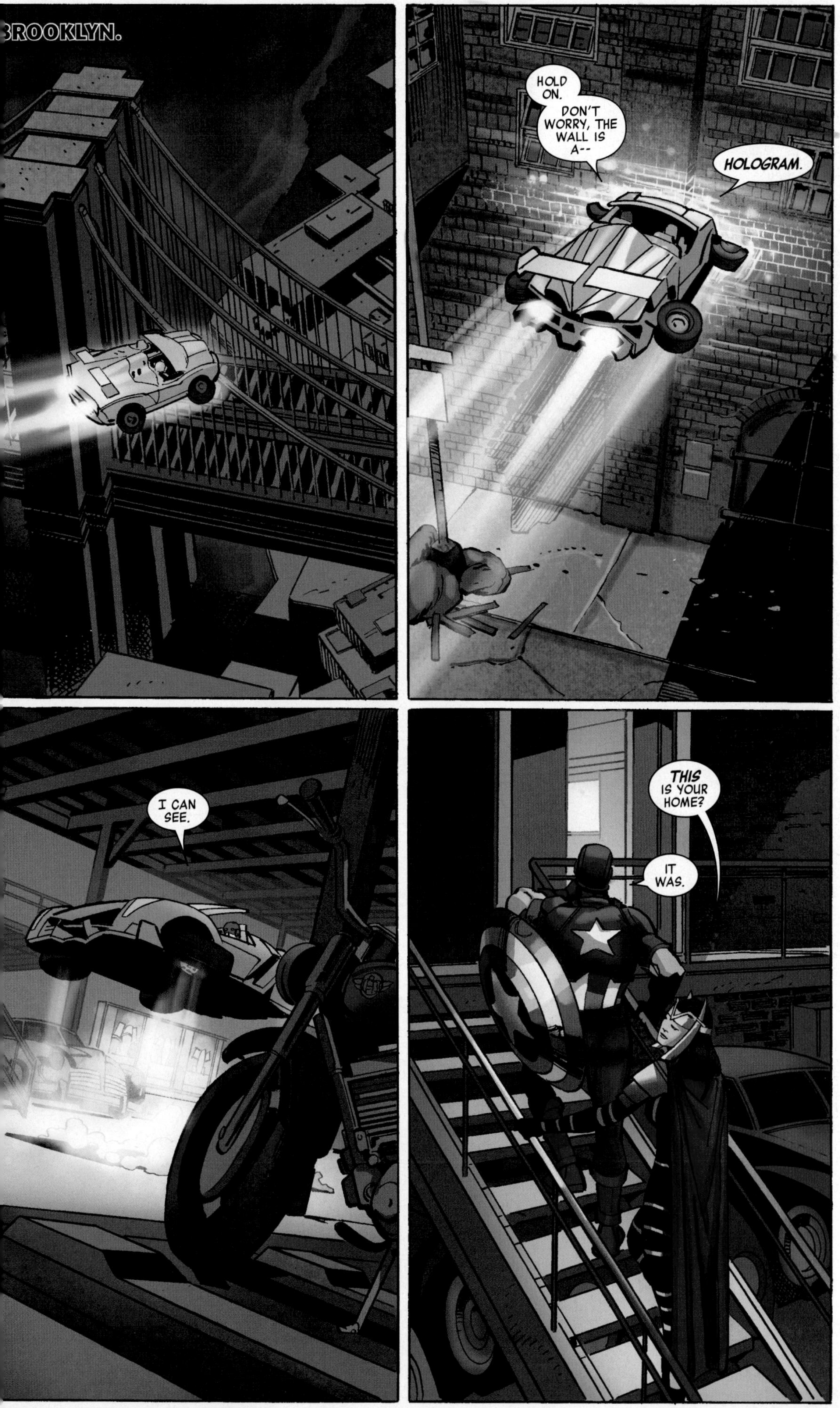
BROOKLYN.
HOLD ON.
DON'T WORRY, THE WALL IS A--
HOLOGRAM.
I CAN SEE.
THIS IS YOUR HOME?
IT WAS.

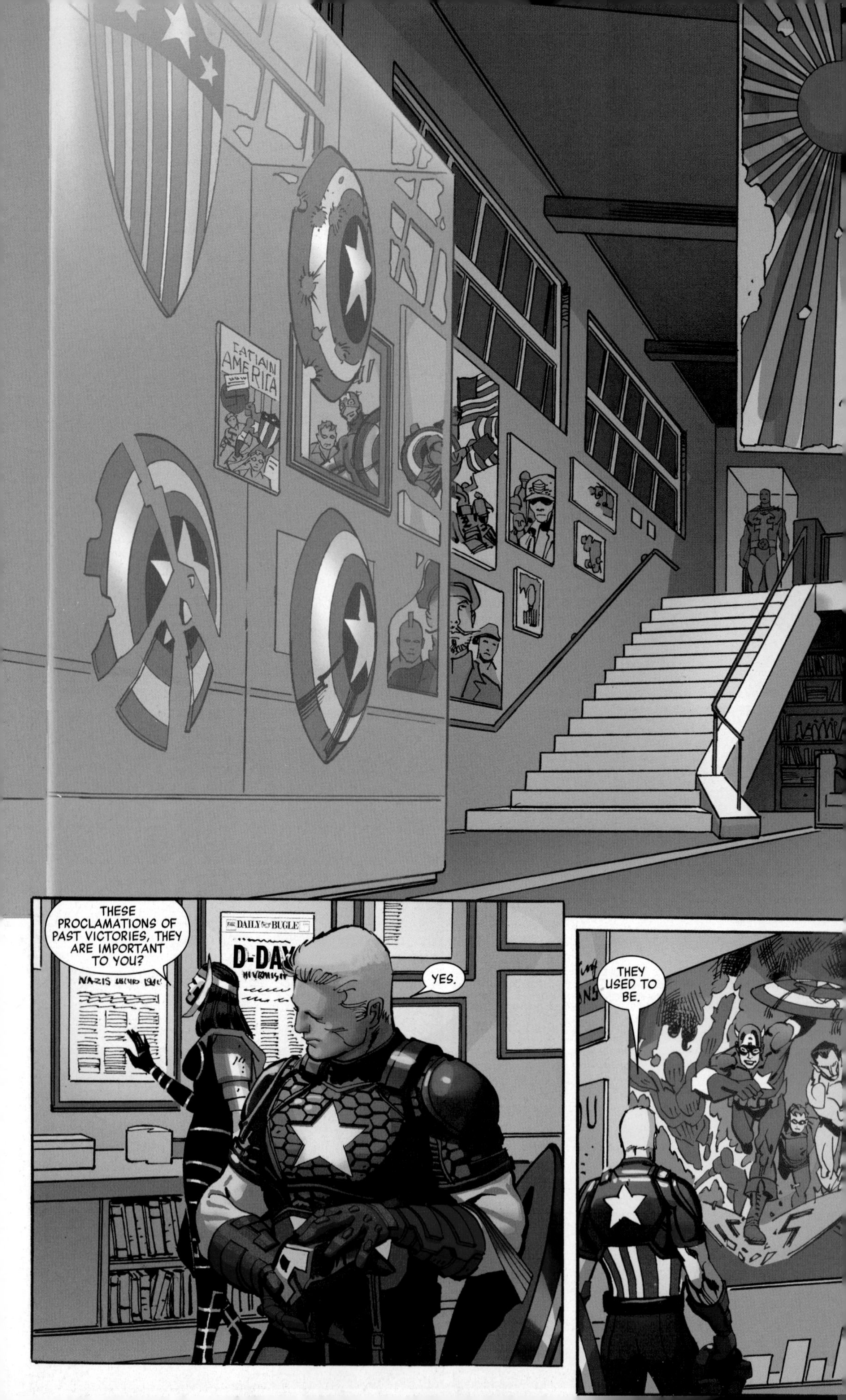

CAPTAIN AMERICA
DAILY BUGLE
D-DAY
NAZIS
THESE PROCLAMATIONS OF PAST VICTORIES, THEY ARE IMPORTANT TO YOU?
YES.
THEY USED TO BE.

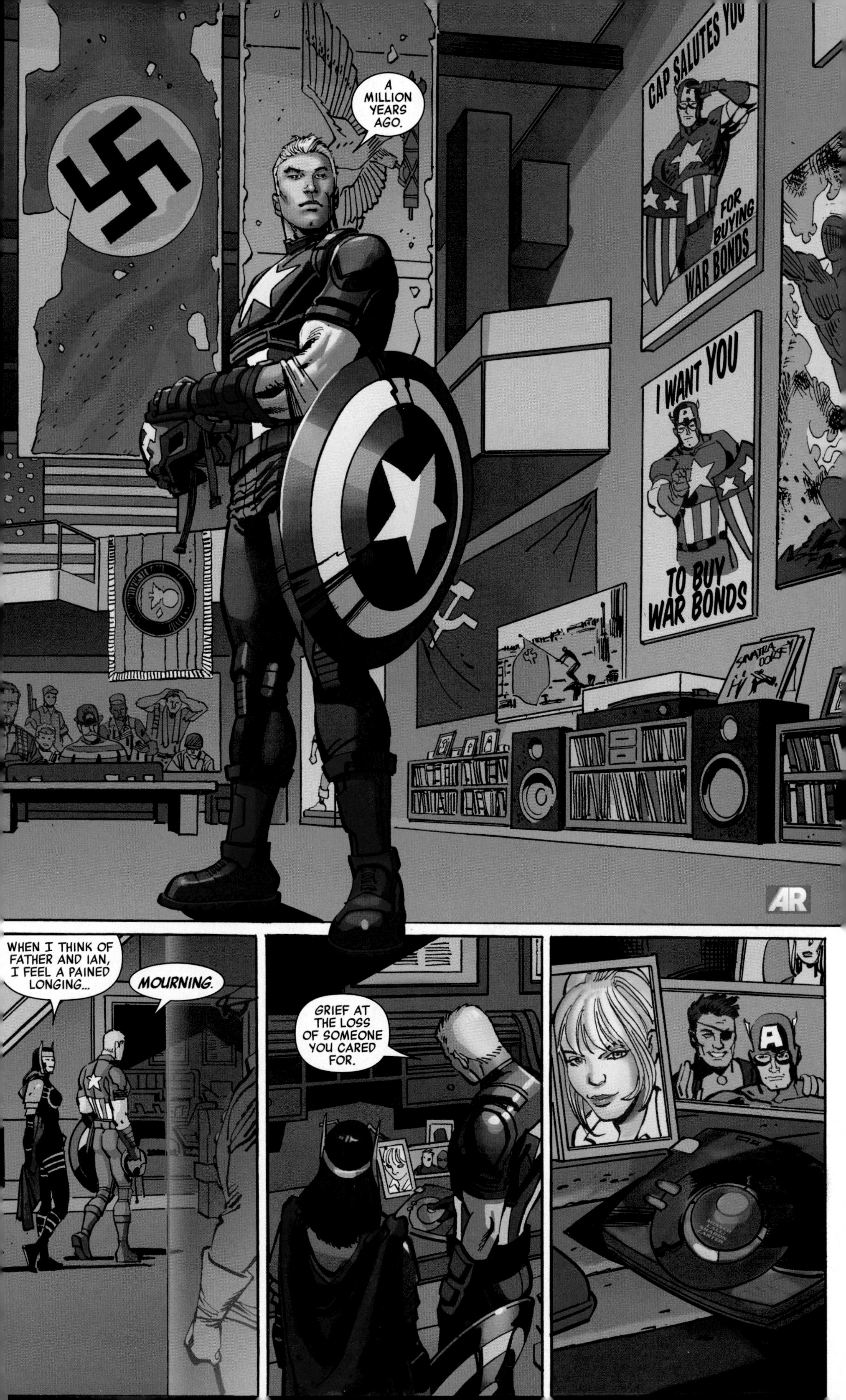
A MILLION YEARS AGO.
CAP SALUTES YOU FOR BUYING WAR BONDS
I WANT YOU TO BUY WAR BONDS
WHEN I THINK OF FATHER AND IAN, I FEEL A PAINED LONGING...
MOURNING.
GRIEF AT THE LOSS OF SOMEONE YOU CARED FOR.

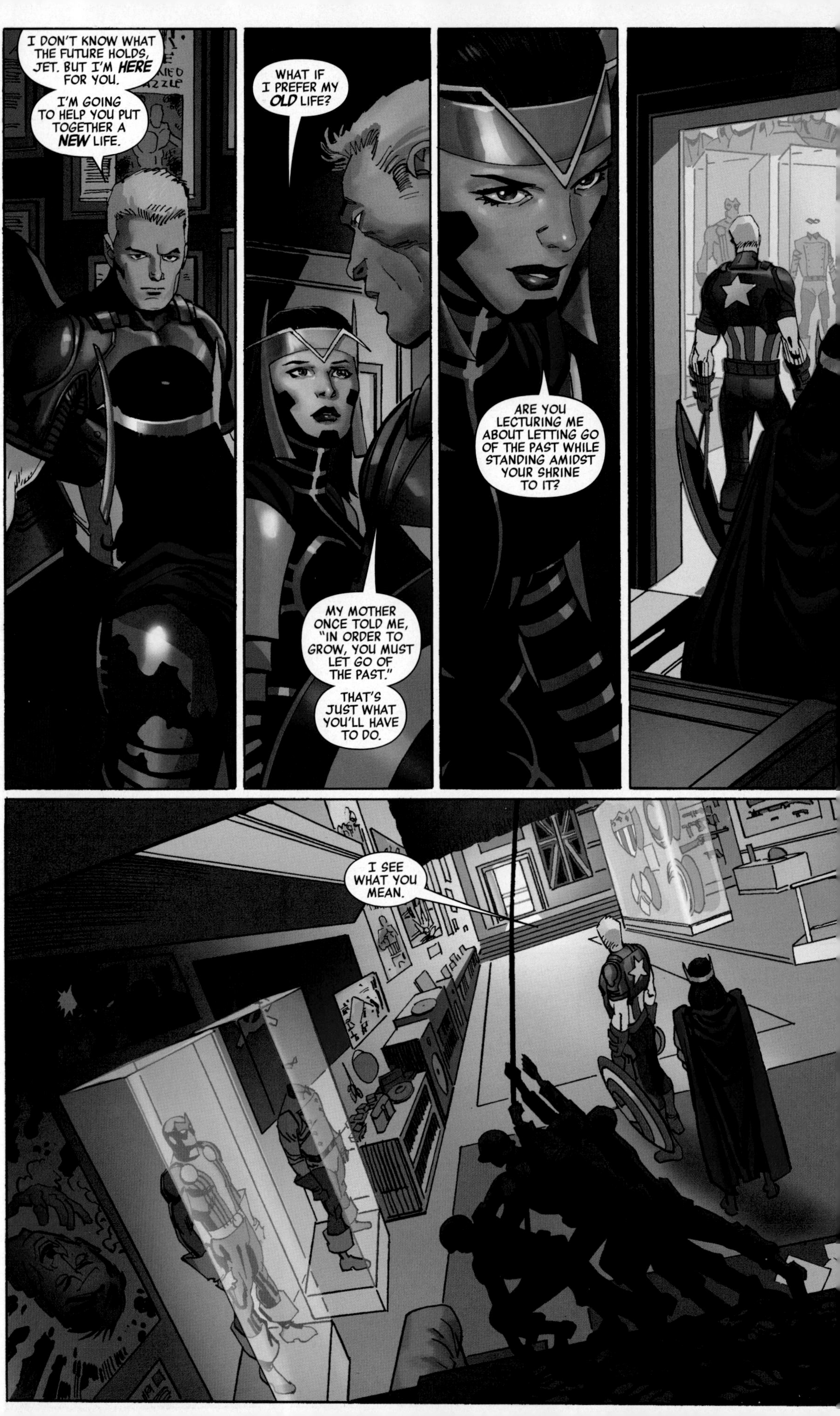
I DON'T KNOW WHAT THE FUTURE HOLDS, JET. BUT I'M HERE FOR YOU.
I'M GOING TO HELP YOU PUT TOGETHER A NEW LIFE.
WHAT IF I PREFER MY OLD LIFE?
MY MOTHER ONCE TOLD ME, "IN ORDER TO GROW, YOU MUST LET GO OF THE PAST."
THAT'S JUST WHAT YOU'LL HAVE TO DO.
ARE YOU LECTURING ME ABOUT LETTING GO OF THE PAST WHILE STANDING AMIDST YOUR SHRINE TO IT?
I SEE WHAT YOU MEAN.

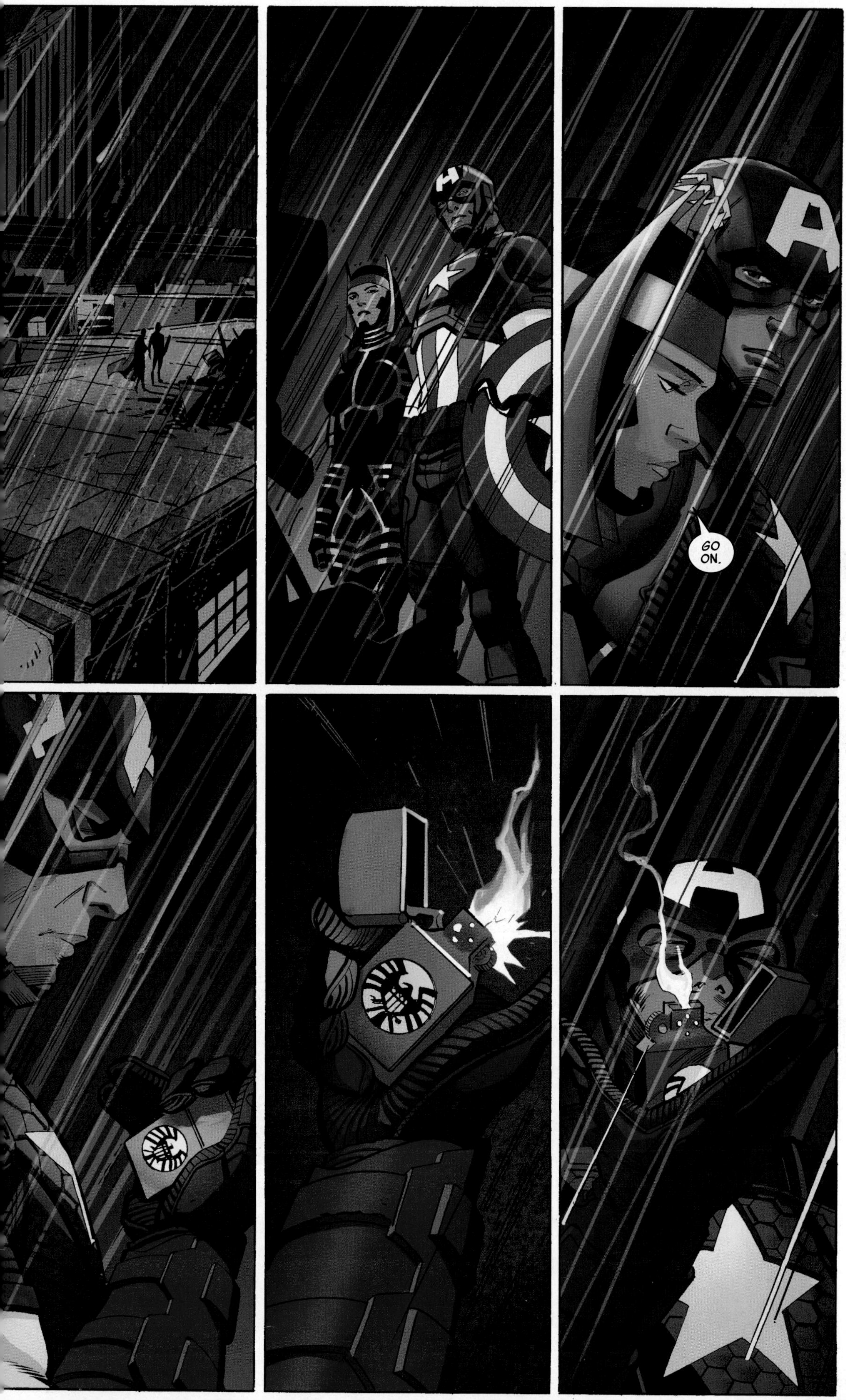
GO ON.

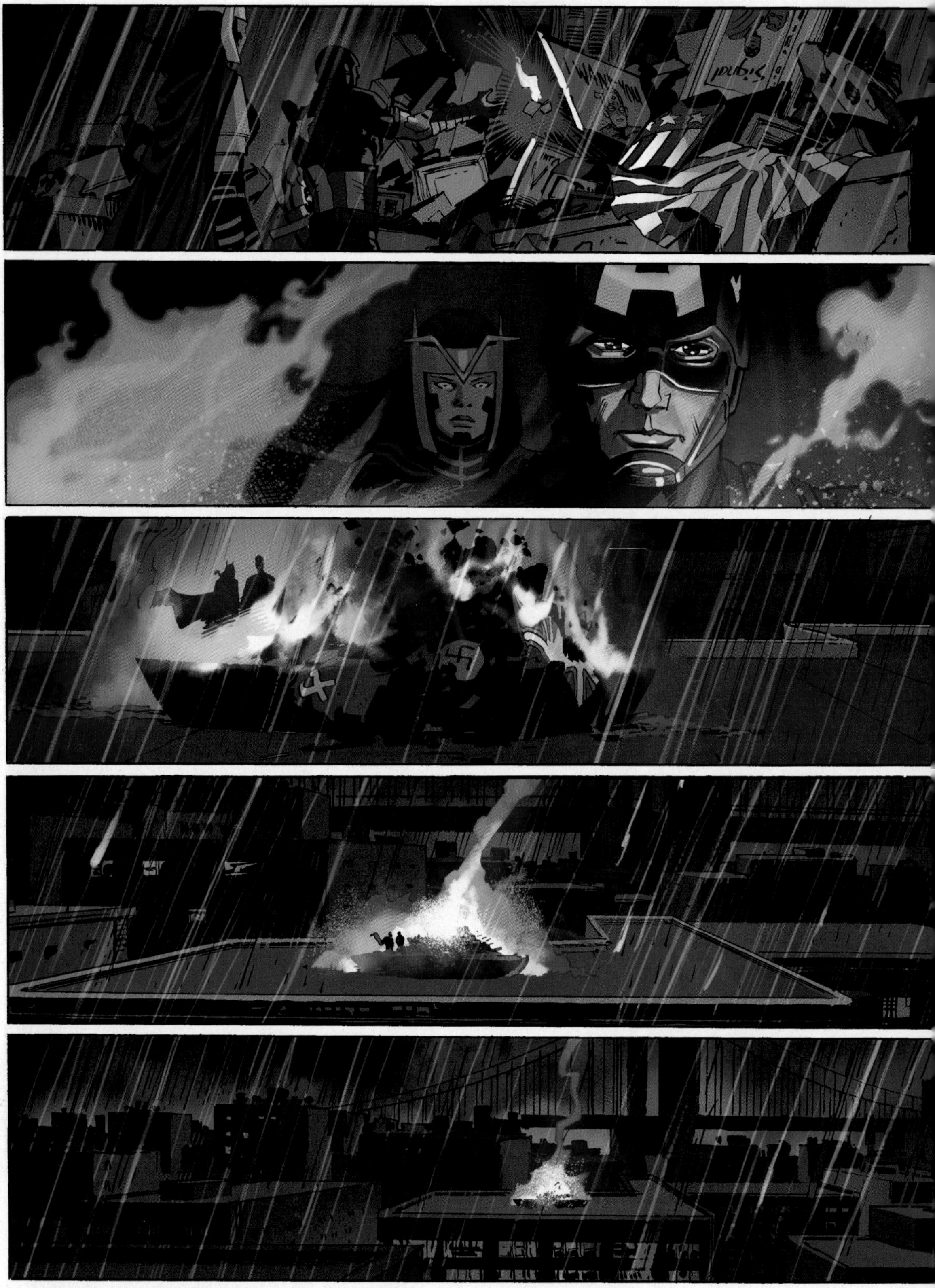

A FIRE IN THE RAIN

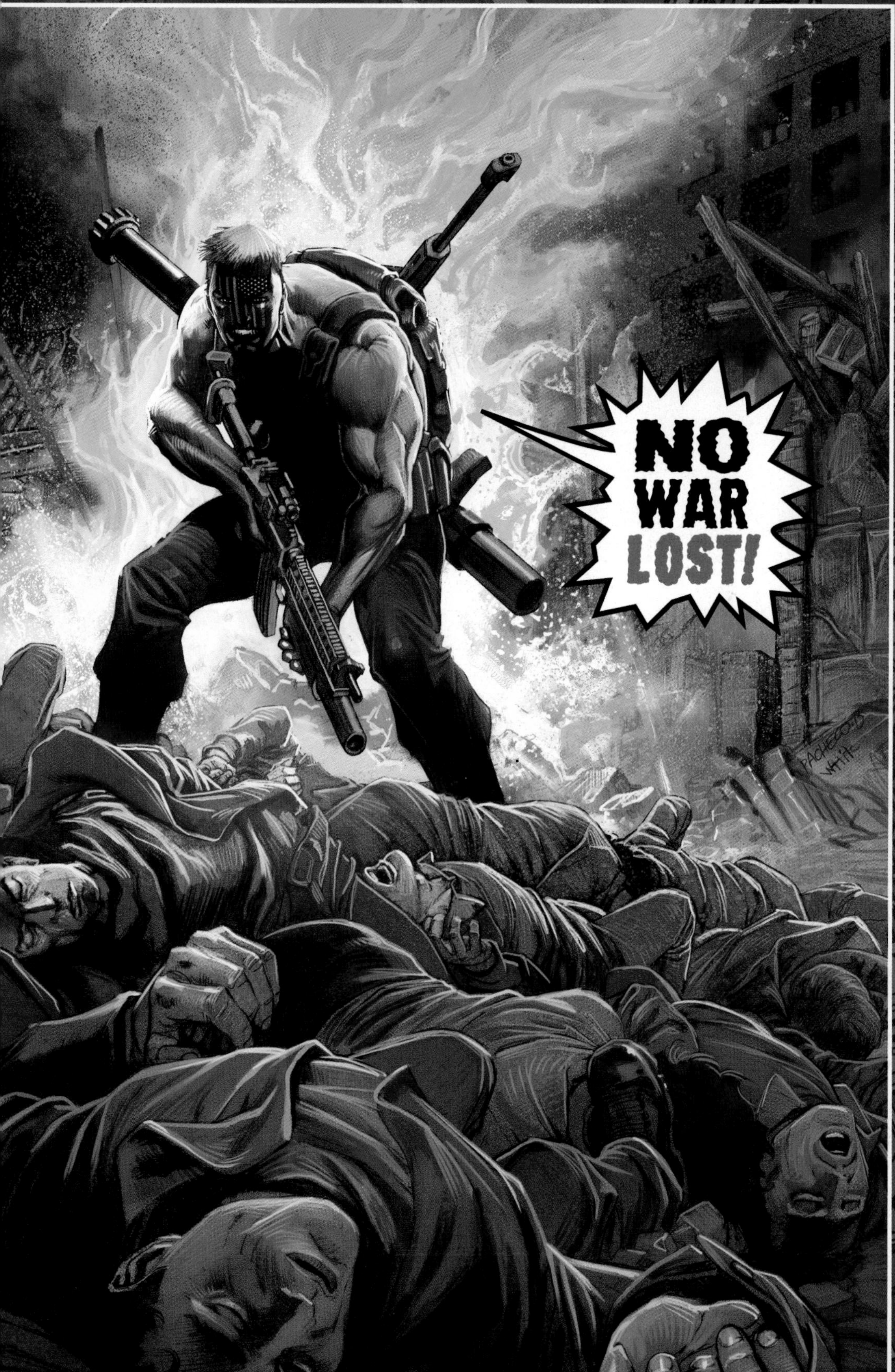
NO WAR LOST!
PACHECO
VAHP

TWELVE

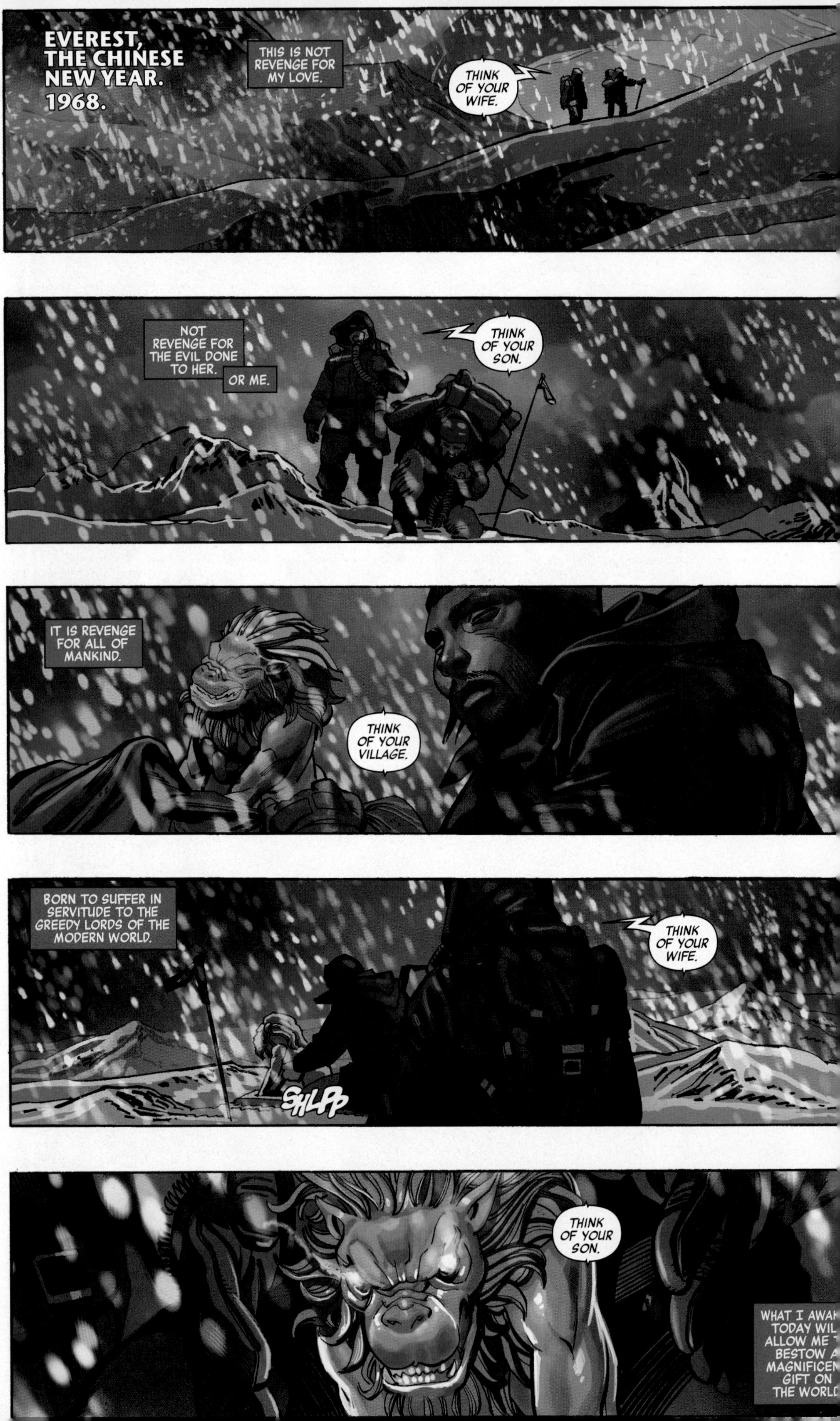
EVEREST, THE CHINESE NEW YEAR. 1968.
THIS IS NOT REVENGE FOR MY LOVE.
THINK OF YOUR WIFE.
NOT REVENGE FOR THE EVIL DONE TO HER.
OR ME.
THINK OF YOUR SON.
IT IS REVENGE FOR ALL OF MANKIND.
THINK OF YOUR VILLAGE.
BORN TO SUFFER IN SERVITUDE TO THE GREEDY LORDS OF THE MODERN WORLD.
THINK OF YOUR WIFE.
SHLPP
THINK OF YOUR SON.
WHAT I AWAK TODAY WIL ALLOW ME T BESTOW A MAGNIFICEN GIFT ON THE WORLD

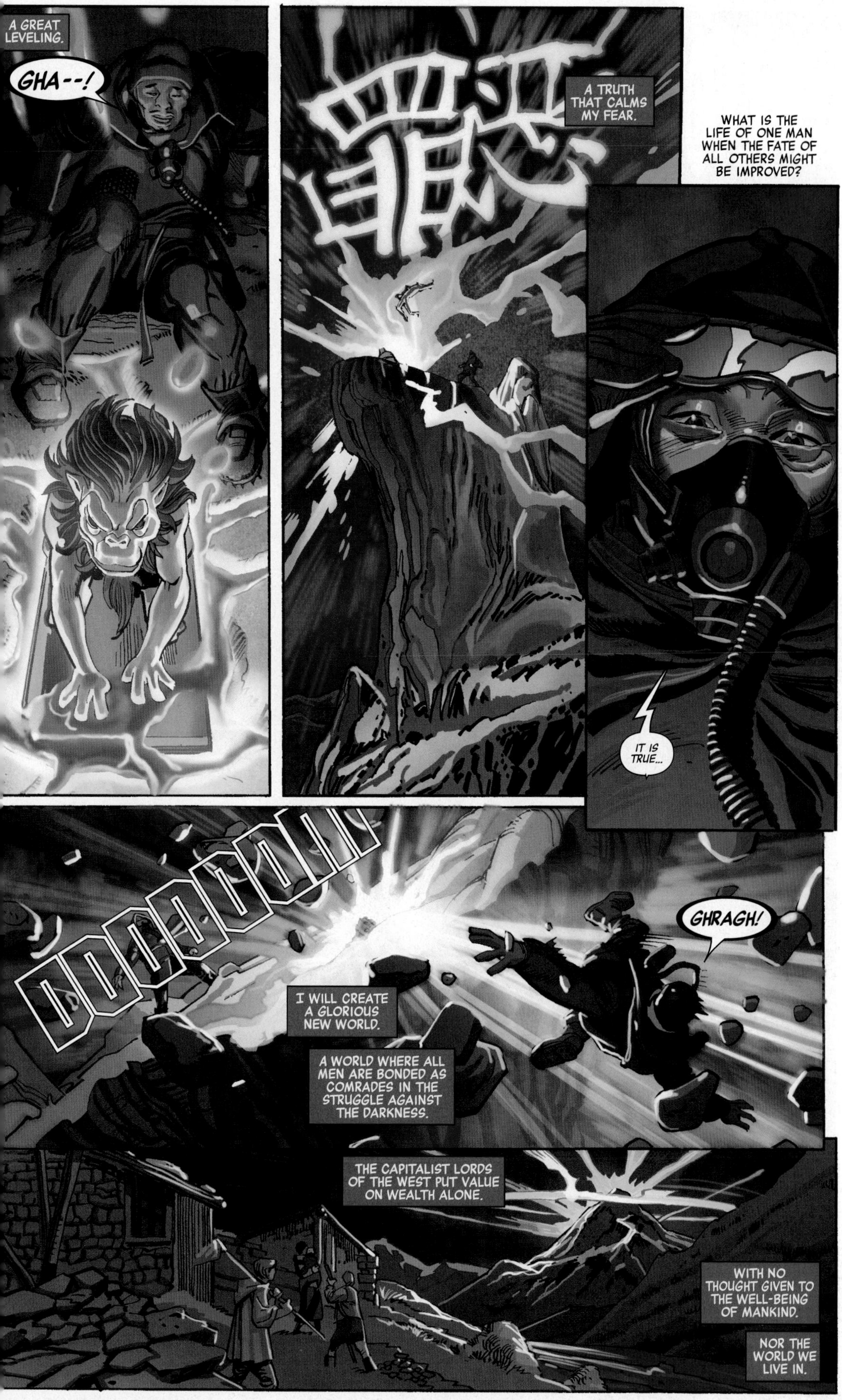
A GREAT LEVELING.
GHA--!
A TRUTH THAT CALMS MY FEAR.
WHAT IS THE LIFE OF ONE MAN WHEN THE FATE OF ALL OTHERS MIGHT BE IMPROVED?
IT IS TRUE...
GHRAGH!
I WILL CREATE A GLORIOUS NEW WORLD.
A WORLD WHERE ALL MEN ARE BONDED AS COMRADES IN THE STRUGGLE AGAINST THE DARKNESS.
THE CAPITALIST LORDS OF THE WEST PUT VALUE ON WEALTH ALONE.
WITH NO THOUGHT GIVEN TO THE WELL-BEING OF MANKIND.
NOR THE WORLD WE LIVE IN.

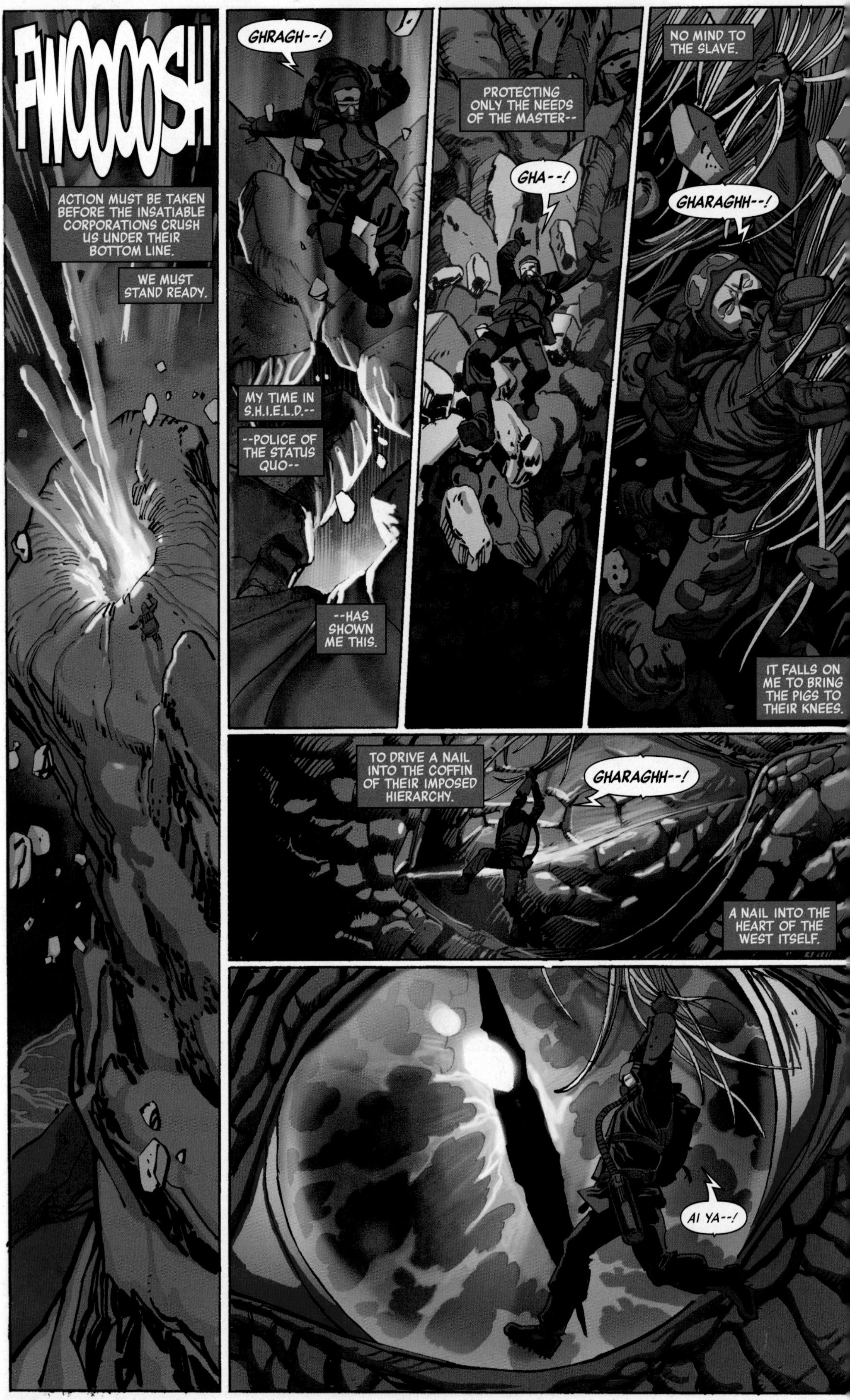
FWOOOOSH
ACTION MUST BE TAKEN BEFORE THE INSATIABLE CORPORATIONS CRUSH US UNDER THEIR BOTTOM LINE.
WE MUST STAND READY.
GHRAGH--!
MY TIME IN S.H.I.E.L.D.--
--POLICE OF THE STATUS QUO--
--HAS SHOWN ME THIS.
PROTECTING ONLY THE NEEDS OF THE MASTER--
GHA--!
NO MIND TO THE SLAVE.
GHARAGHH--!
IT FALLS ON ME TO BRING THE PIGS TO THEIR KNEES.
TO DRIVE A NAIL INTO THE COFFIN OF THEIR IMPOSED HIERARCHY.
GHARAGHH--!
A NAIL INTO THE HEART OF THE WEST ITSELF.
AI YA--!

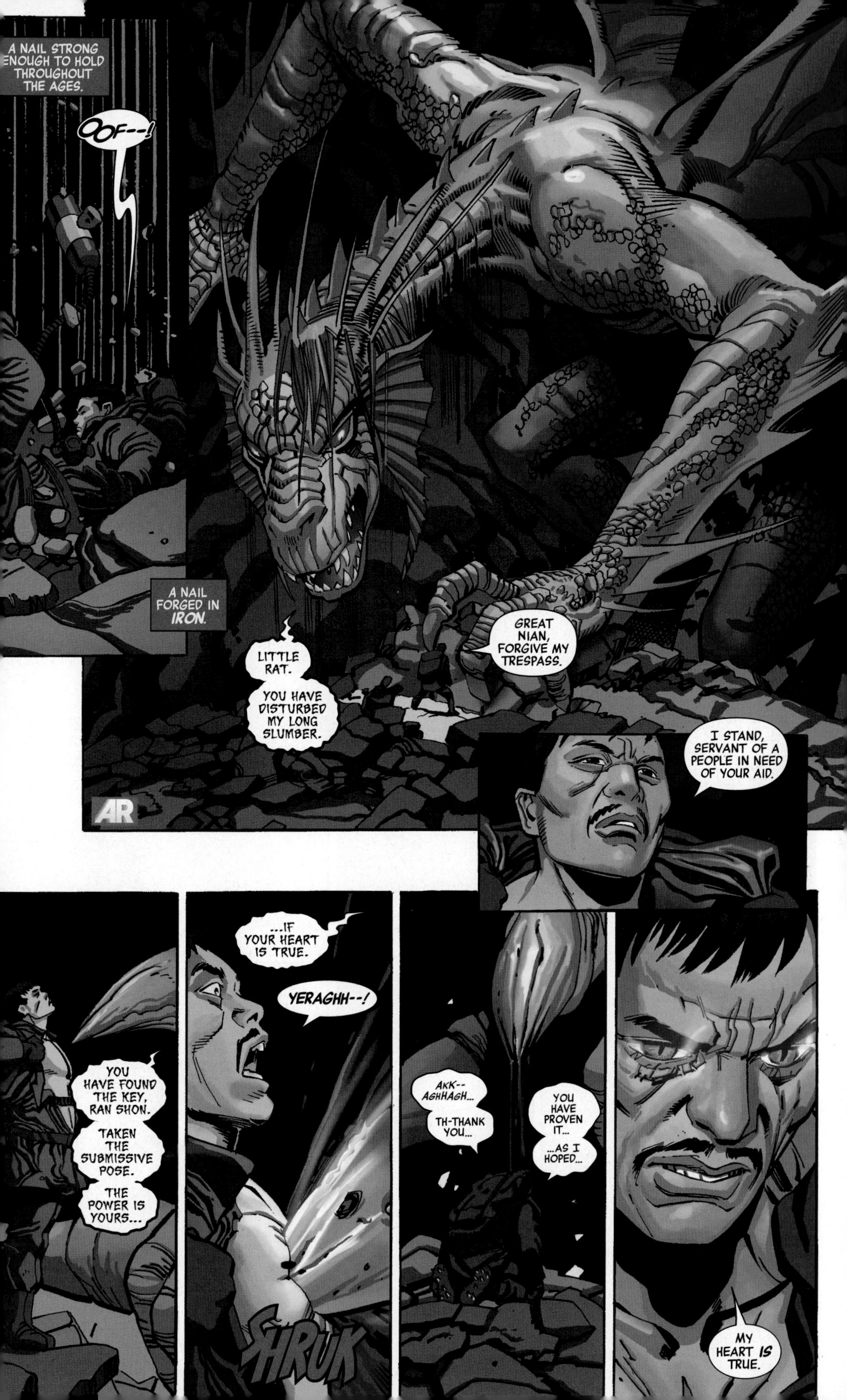
A NAIL STRONG ENOUGH TO HOLD THROUGHOUT THE AGES.
OOF--!
A NAIL FORGED IN IRON.
LITTLE RAT.
YOU HAVE DISTURBED MY LONG SLUMBER.
GREAT NIAN, FORGIVE MY TRESPASS.
I STAND, SERVANT OF A PEOPLE IN NEED OF YOUR AID.
YOU HAVE FOUND THE KEY, RAN SHON.
TAKEN THE SUBMISSIVE POSE.
THE POWER IS YOURS...
...IF YOUR HEART IS TRUE.
YERAGHH--!
SHRUK
AKK-- AGHHAGH...
TH-THANK YOU...
YOU HAVE PROVEN IT...
...AS I HOPED...
MY HEART IS TRUE.

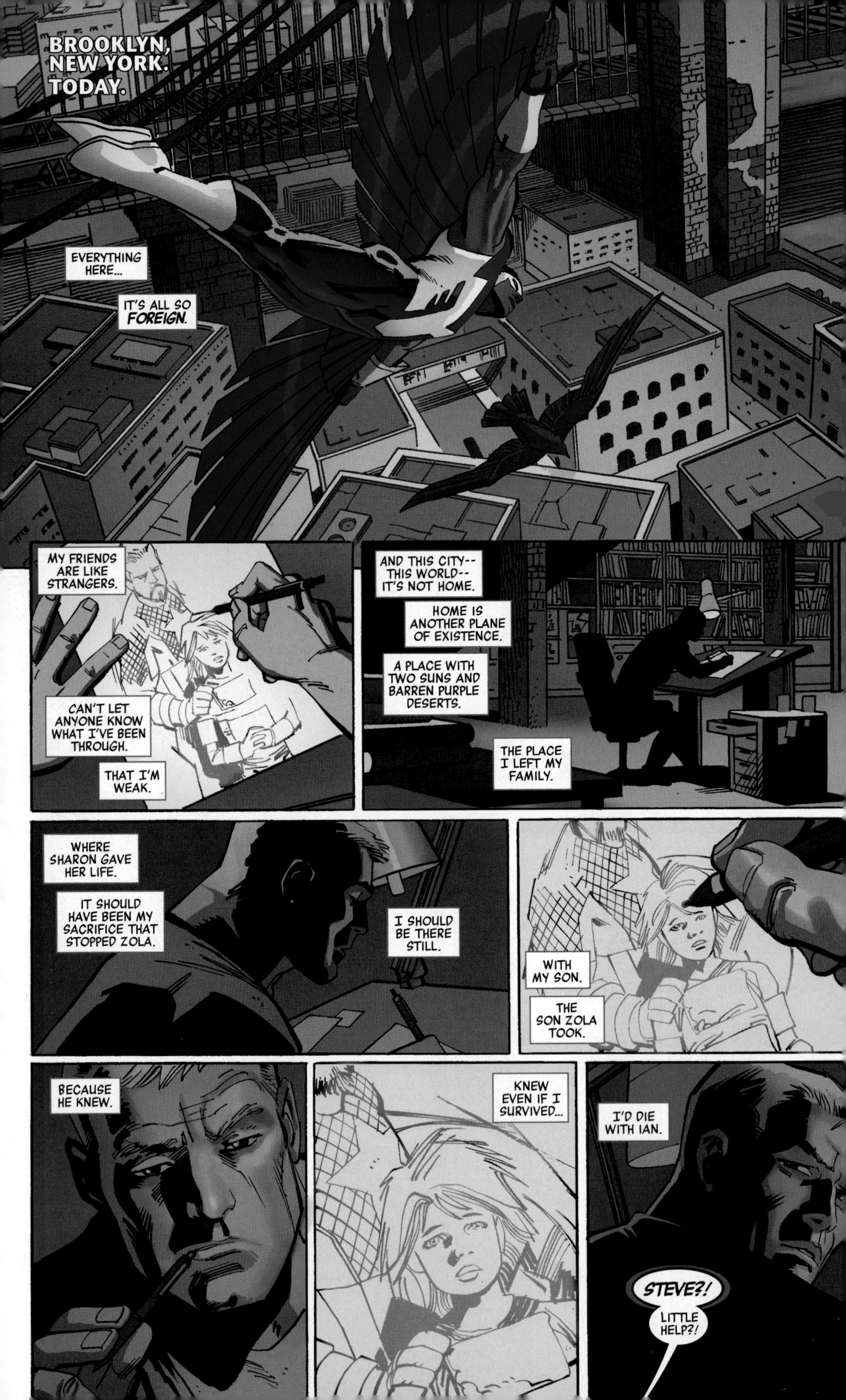
BROOKLYN, NEW YORK. TODAY.
EVERYTHING HERE...
IT'S ALL SO FOREIGN.
MY FRIENDS ARE LIKE STRANGERS.
CAN'T LET ANYONE KNOW WHAT I'VE BEEN THROUGH.
THAT I'M WEAK.
AND THIS CITY-- THIS WORLD-- IT'S NOT HOME.
HOME IS ANOTHER PLANE OF EXISTENCE.
A PLACE WITH TWO SUNS AND BARREN PURPLE DESERTS.
THE PLACE I LEFT MY FAMILY.
WHERE SHARON GAVE HER LIFE.
IT SHOULD HAVE BEEN MY SACRIFICE THAT STOPPED ZOLA.
I SHOULD BE THERE STILL.
WITH MY SON.
THE SON ZOLA TOOK.
BECAUSE HE KNEW.
KNEW EVEN IF I SURVIVED...
I'D DIE WITH IAN.
STEVE?!
LITTLE HELP?!

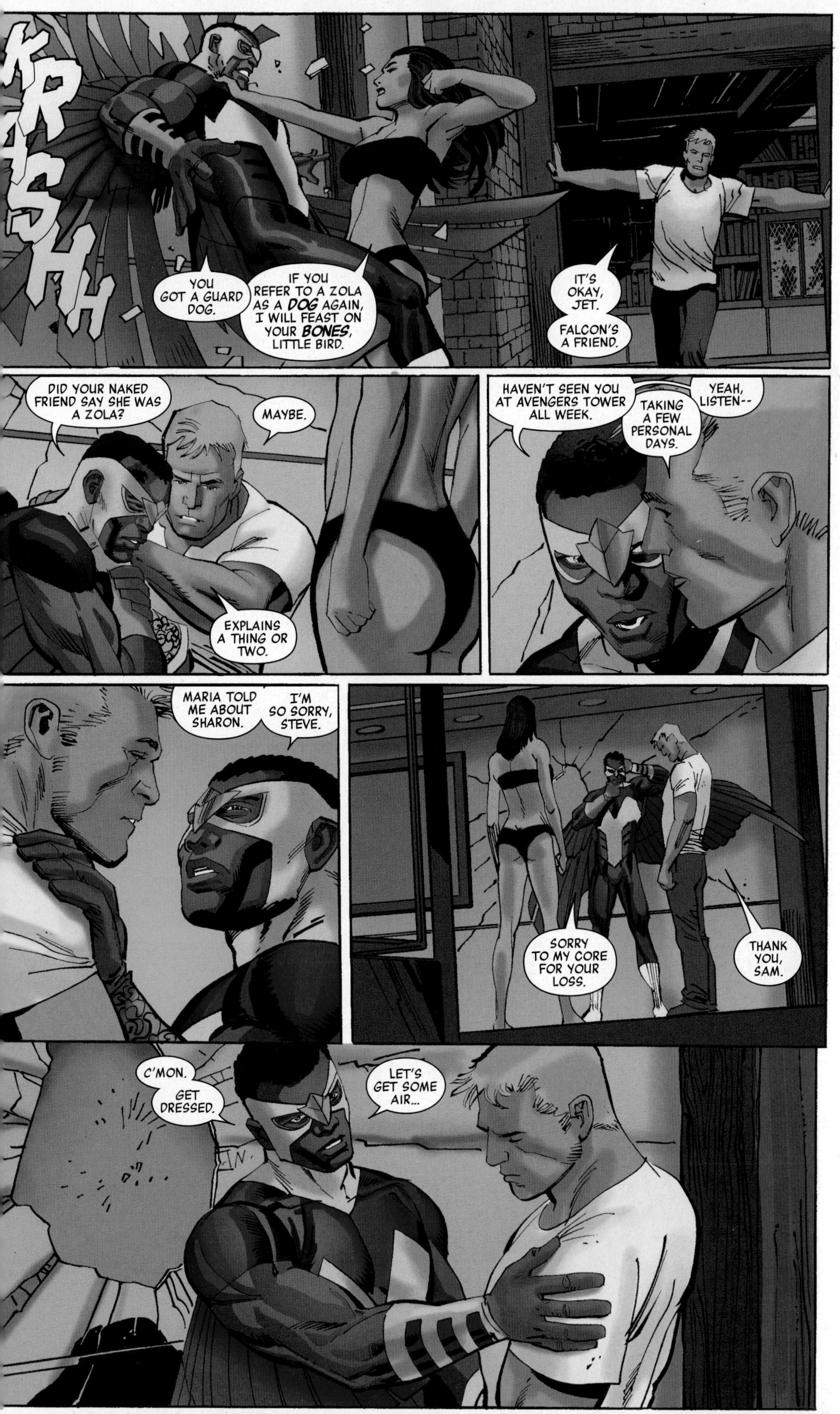
KRASHH
YOU GOT A GUARD DOG.
IF YOU REFER TO A ZOLA AS A *DOG* AGAIN, I WILL FEAST ON YOUR *BONES*, LITTLE BIRD.
IT'S OKAY, JET.
FALCON'S A FRIEND.
DID YOUR NAKED FRIEND SAY SHE WAS A ZOLA?
MAYBE.
EXPLAINS A THING OR TWO.
HAVEN'T SEEN YOU AT AVENGERS TOWER ALL WEEK.
TAKING A FEW PERSONAL DAYS.
YEAH, LISTEN--
MARIA TOLD ME ABOUT SHARON.
I'M SO SORRY, STEVE.
SORRY TO MY CORE FOR YOUR LOSS.
THANK YOU, SAM.
C'MON.
GET DRESSED.
LET'S GET SOME AIR...

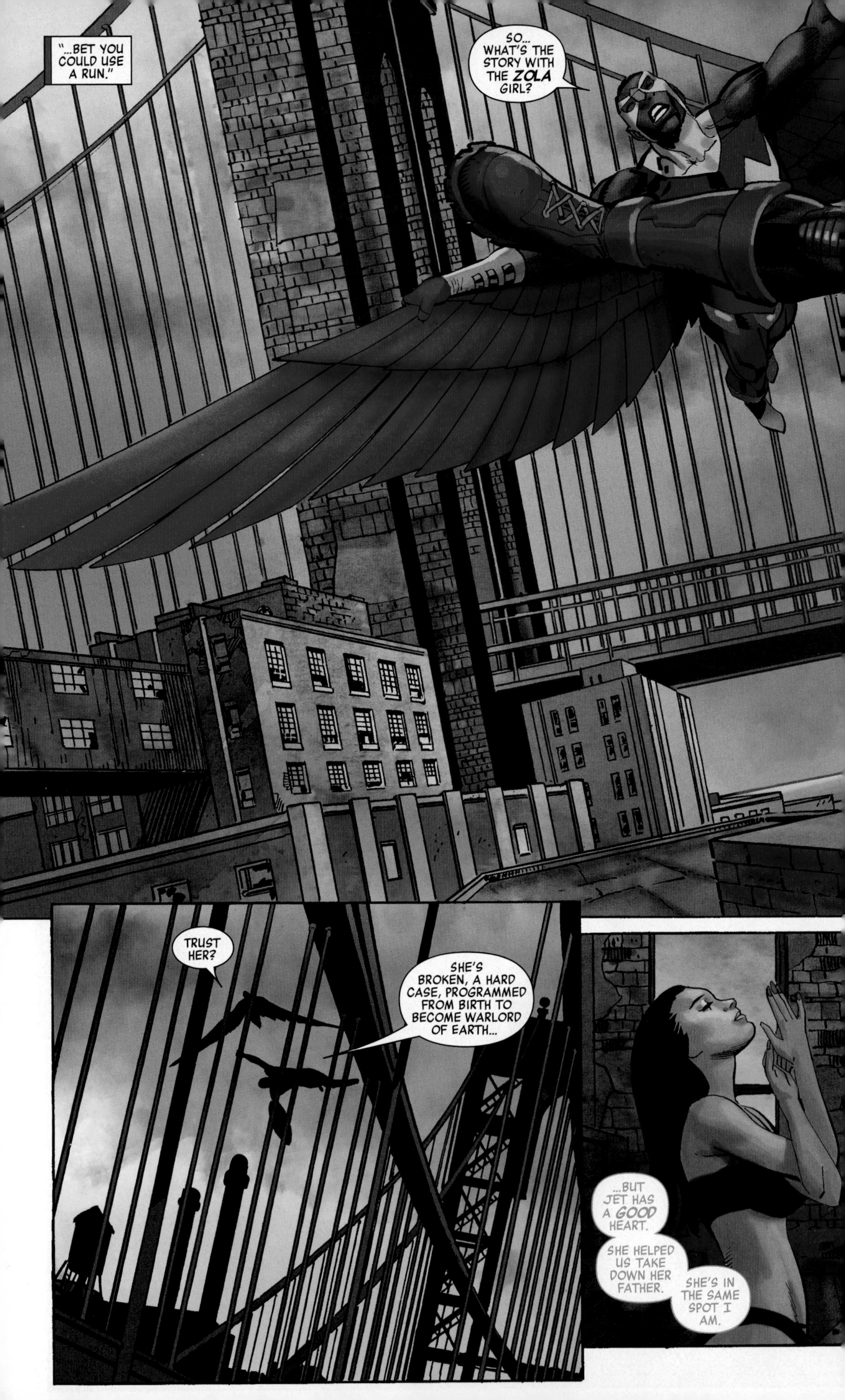
"...BET YOU COULD USE A RUN."
SO... WHAT'S THE STORY WITH THE ZOLA GIRL?
TRUST HER?
SHE'S BROKEN, A HARD CASE, PROGRAMMED FROM BIRTH TO BECOME WARLORD OF EARTH...
...BUT JET HAS A GOOD HEART.
SHE HELPED US TAKE DOWN HER FATHER.
SHE'S IN THE SAME SPOT I AM.

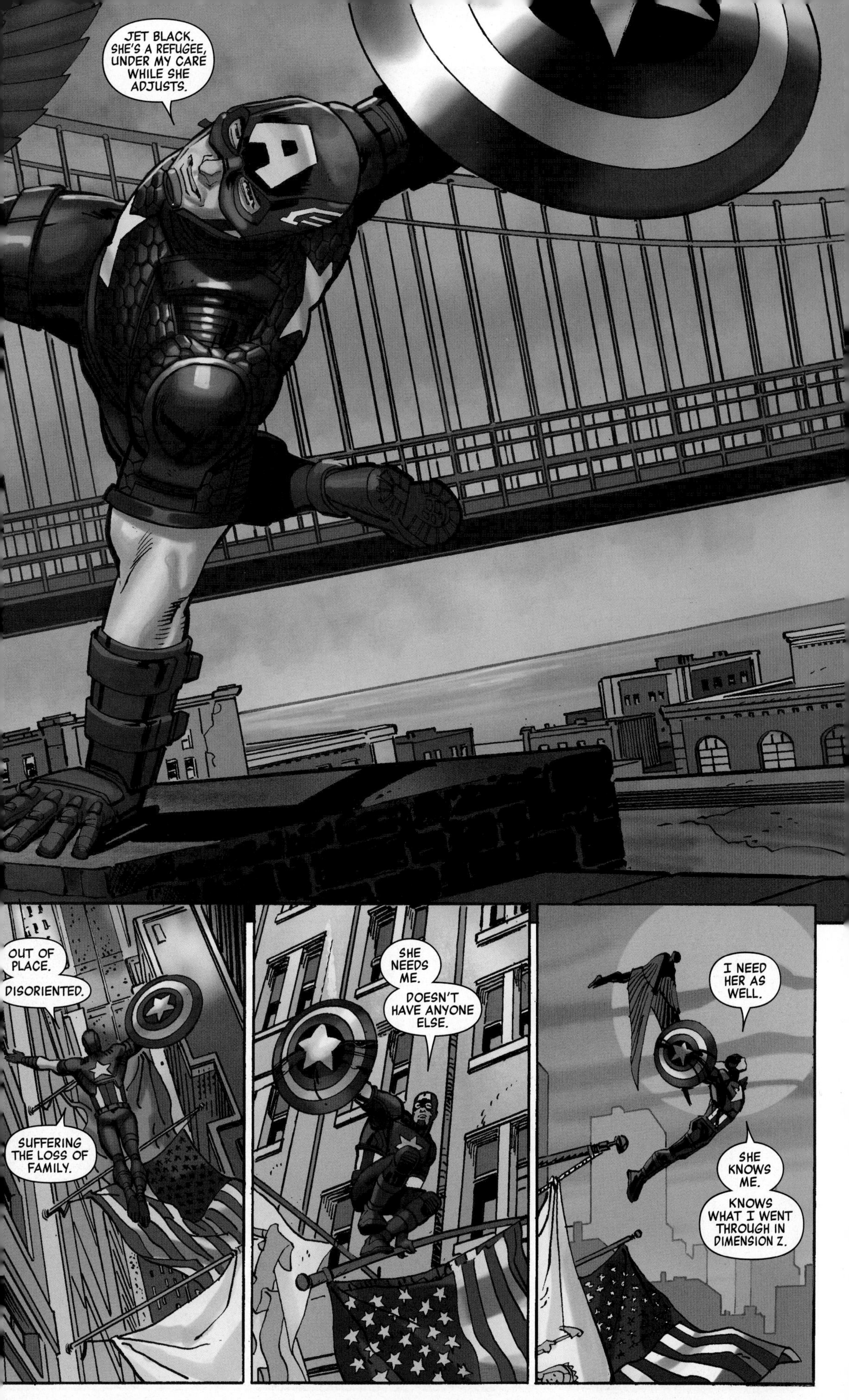

JET BLACK. SHE'S A REFUGEE, UNDER MY CARE WHILE SHE ADJUSTS.
OUT OF PLACE.
DISORIENTED.
SUFFERING THE LOSS OF FAMILY.
SHE NEEDS ME.
DOESN'T HAVE ANYONE ELSE.
I NEED HER AS WELL.
SHE KNOWS ME.
KNOWS WHAT I WENT THROUGH IN DIMENSION Z.

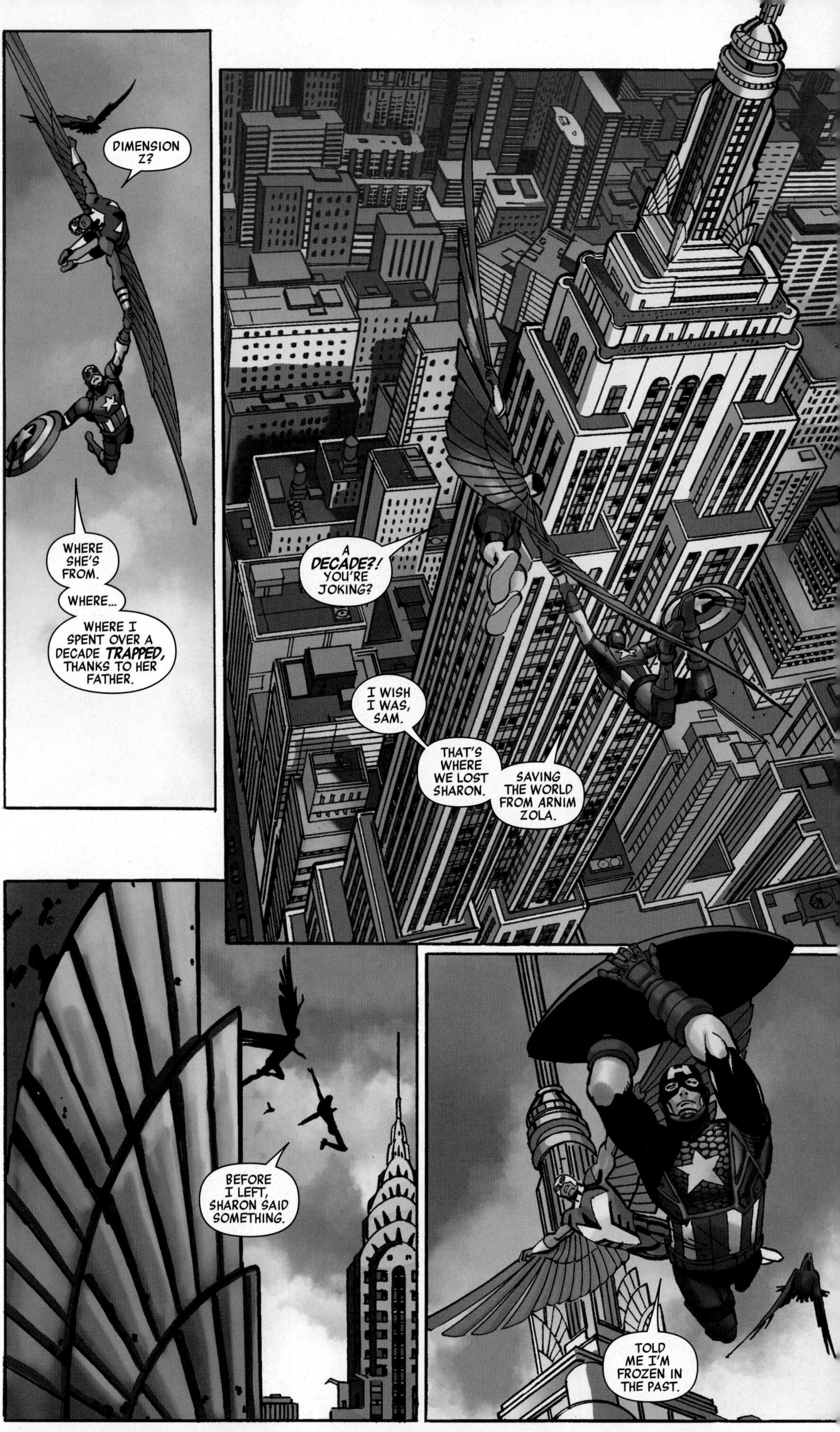
DIMENSION Z?
WHERE SHE'S FROM.
WHERE...
WHERE I SPENT OVER A DECADE TRAPPED, THANKS TO HER FATHER.
A DECADE?! YOU'RE JOKING?
I WISH I WAS, SAM.
THAT'S WHERE WE LOST SHARON.
SAVING THE WORLD FROM ARNIM ZOLA.
BEFORE I LEFT, SHARON SAID SOMETHING.
TOLD ME I'M FROZEN IN THE PAST.

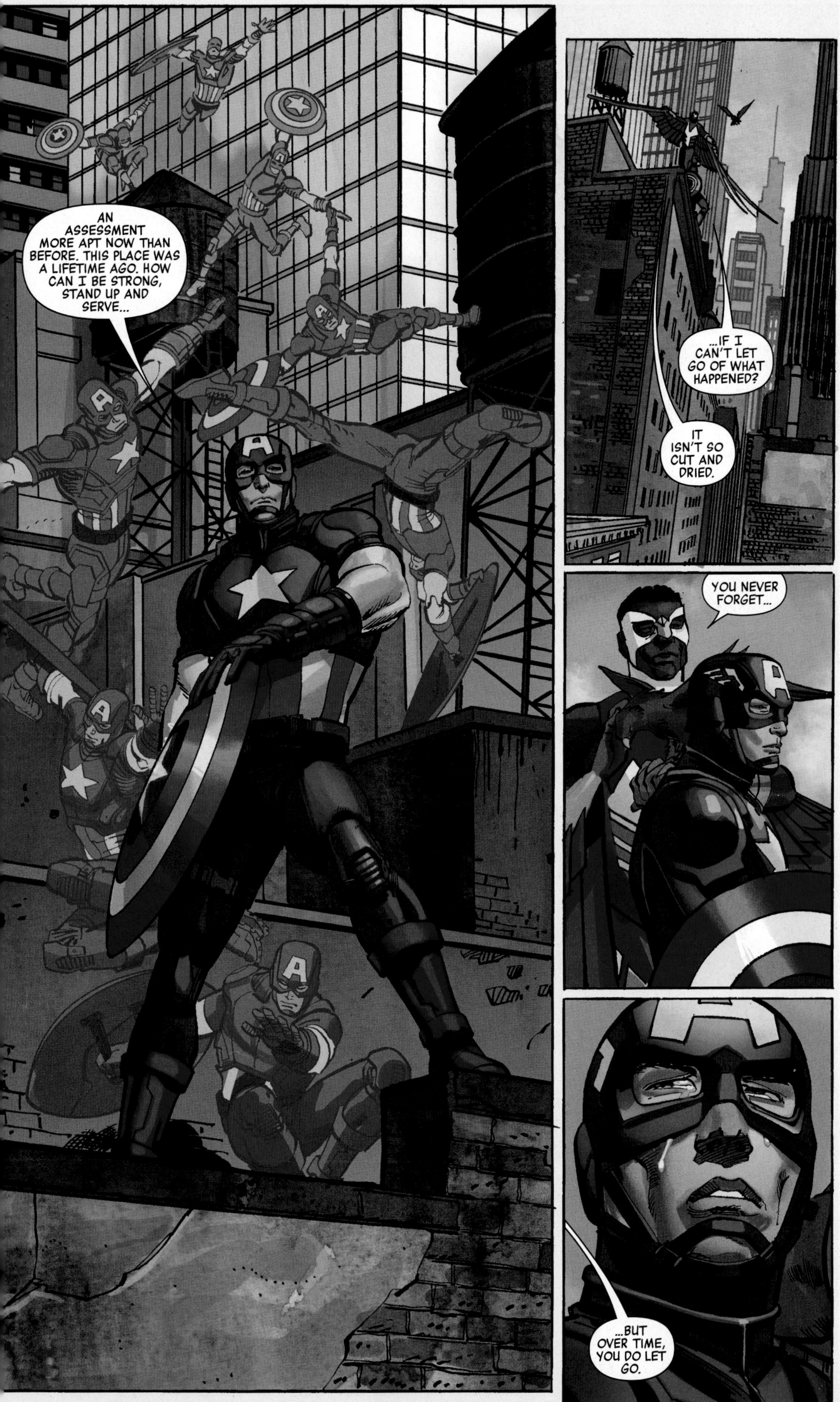
AN ASSESSMENT MORE APT NOW THAN BEFORE. THIS PLACE WAS A LIFETIME AGO. HOW CAN I BE STRONG, STAND UP AND SERVE...
...IF I CAN'T LET GO OF WHAT HAPPENED?
IT ISN'T SO CUT AND DRIED.
YOU NEVER FORGET...
...BUT OVER TIME, YOU DO LET GO.

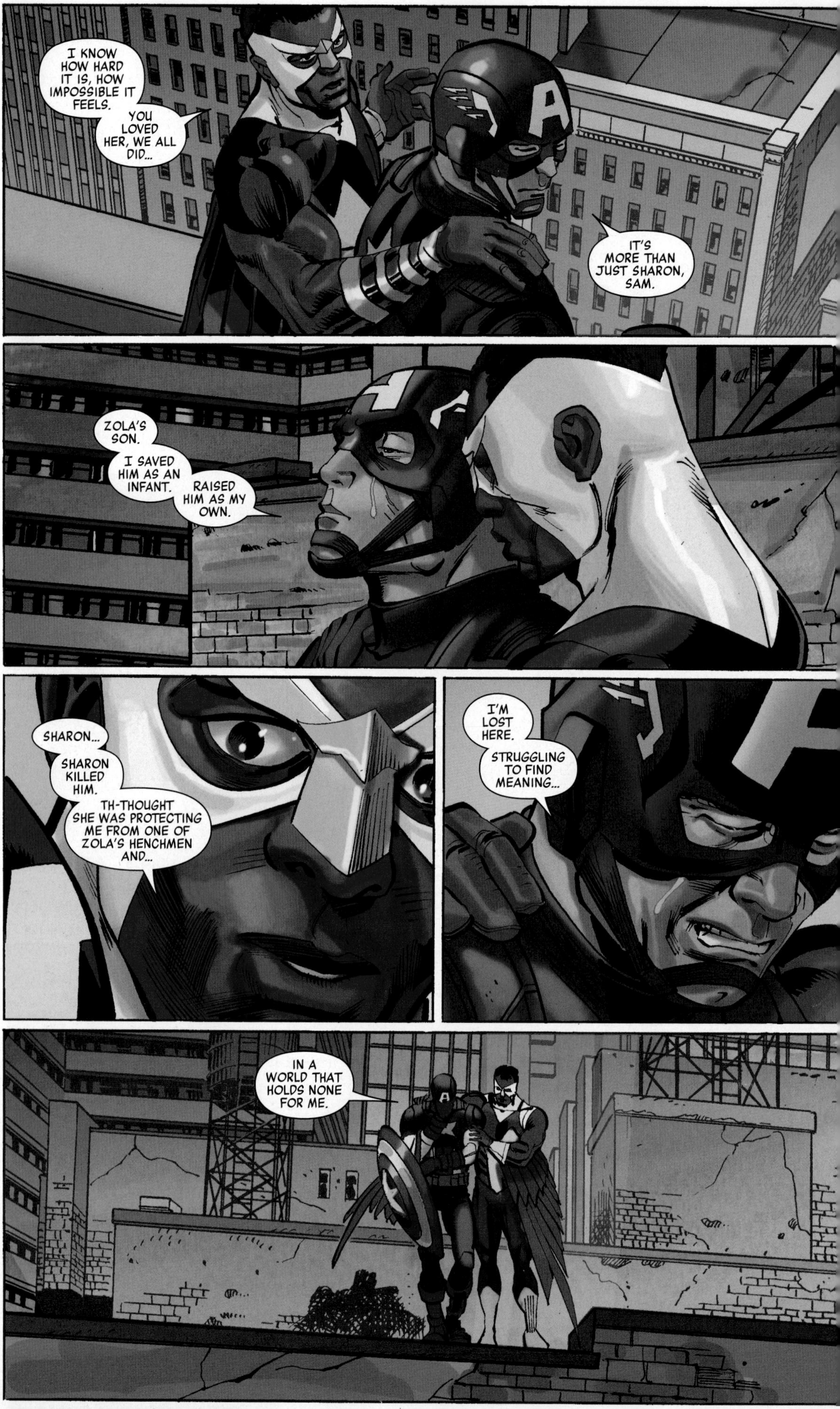
I KNOW HOW HARD IT IS, HOW IMPOSSIBLE IT FEELS.
YOU LOVED HER, WE ALL DID...
IT'S MORE THAN JUST SHARON, SAM.
ZOLA'S SON.
I SAVED HIM AS AN INFANT.
RAISED HIM AS MY OWN.
SHARON...
SHARON KILLED HIM.
TH-THOUGHT SHE WAS PROTECTING ME FROM ONE OF ZOLA'S HENCHMEN AND...
I'M LOST HERE.
STRUGGLING TO FIND MEANING...
IN A WORLD THAT HOLDS NONE FOR ME.

PROSVEKISTAN, EASTERN EUROPE. NUKE ENGAGEMENT ZONE 2.

THE DAILY BUGLE'S AS TIGHT AS A DRUM THESE DAYS.

I'D MAKE MORE PANHANDLING.

ROBBIE ISN'T PAYING A RED CENT UNLESS I DELIVER A SCOOP.

NEW FACE OF FREELANCE JOURNALISM.

YOU DIG IT UP FAST, YOU GET PAID--

KLIKK

KLIKK

--COME IN AN HOUR BEHIND THE NEXT GUY--

--AND YOU DON'T.

BUT THIS?

KLIKK

THIS IS GONNA COST YOU, ROBBIE.

JUST AS SOON AS I CAN LINK TO THE SATELLITE AND GET YOU A TASTE.

PHONE'S SCRAMBLED. NO INTERNET EITHER.

KLIKK

SOMEONE DOESN'T WANT THIS GETTING OUT.

HOW THE HELL IS IT ALL CONNECTED?

DOZENS OF THE WORLD'S RICHEST PEOPLE HAVE BEEN DISAPPEARING.

AND EVERY TRAIL LEADS HERE.

WUPWUPPWUPPWUPP!

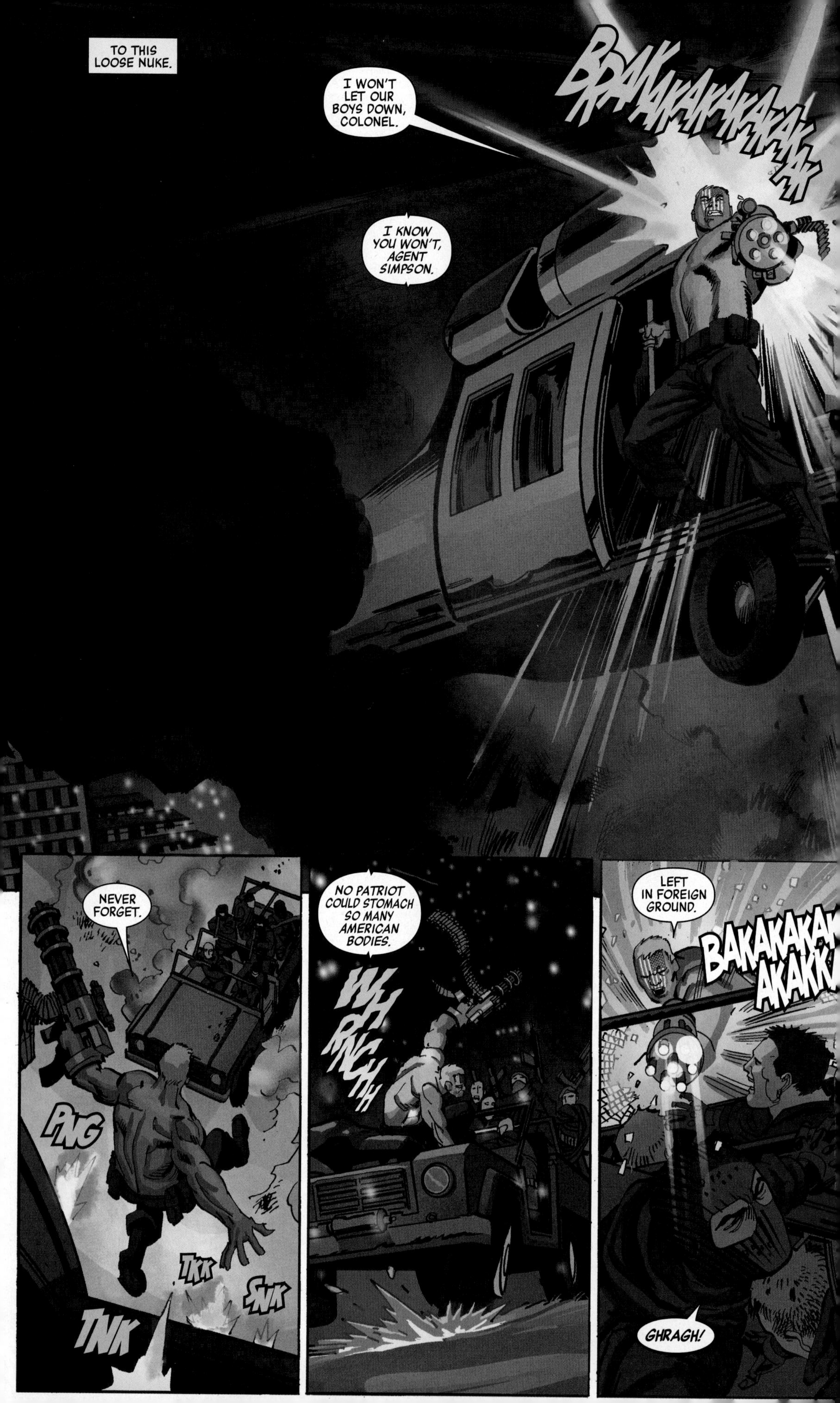

TO THIS LOOSE NUKE.
I WON'T LET OUR BOYS DOWN, COLONEL.
BRAKAKAKAKAKAKAKAK
I KNOW YOU WON'T, AGENT SIMPSON.
NEVER FORGET.
PNG
TKK
SNK
TNK
NO PATRIOT COULD STOMACH SO MANY AMERICAN BODIES.
WHRNCH
LEFT IN FOREIGN GROUND.
BAKAKAKAK AKAKK
GHRAGH!

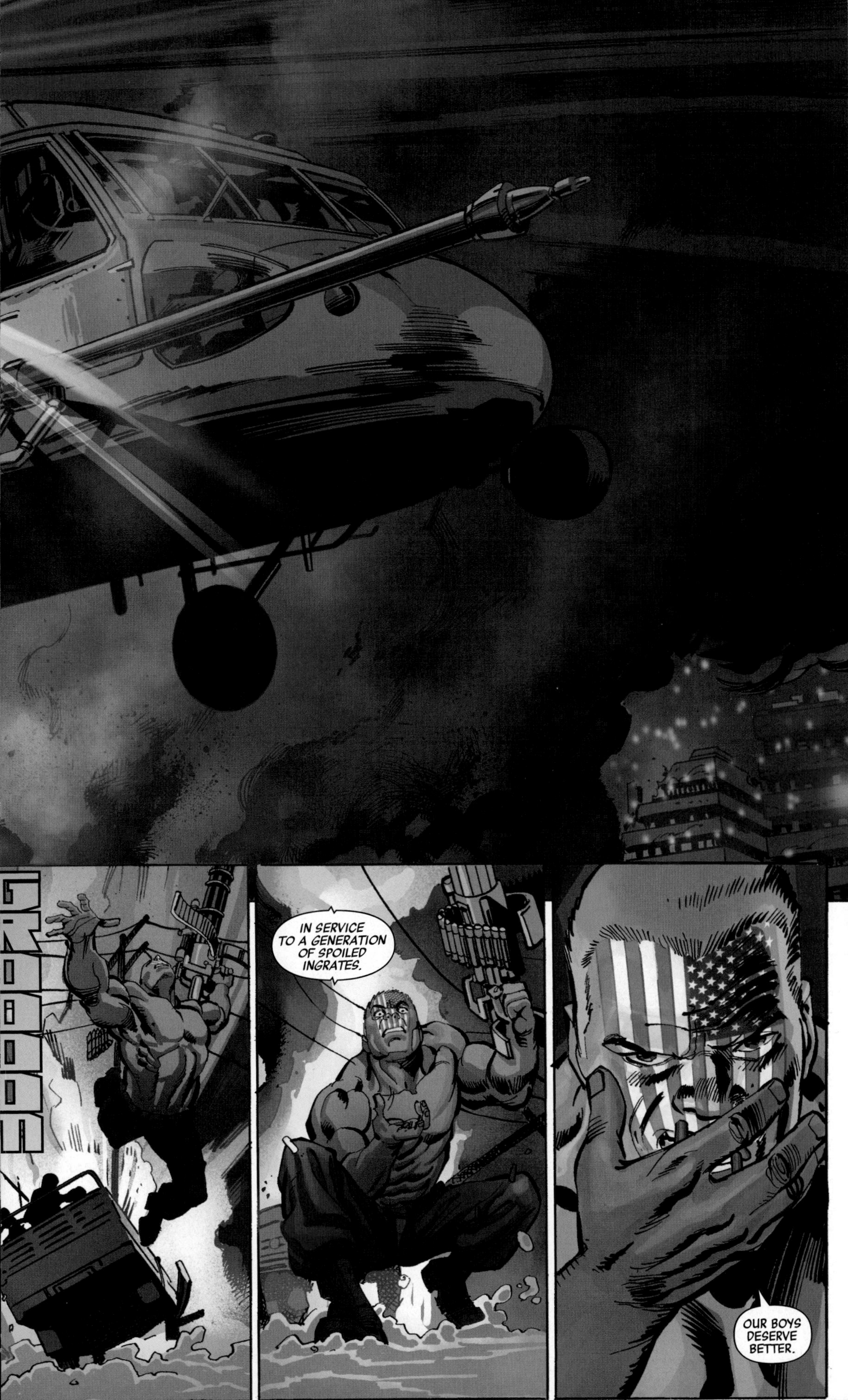
IN SERVICE TO A GENERATION OF SPOILED INGRATES.
OUR BOYS DESERVE BETTER.

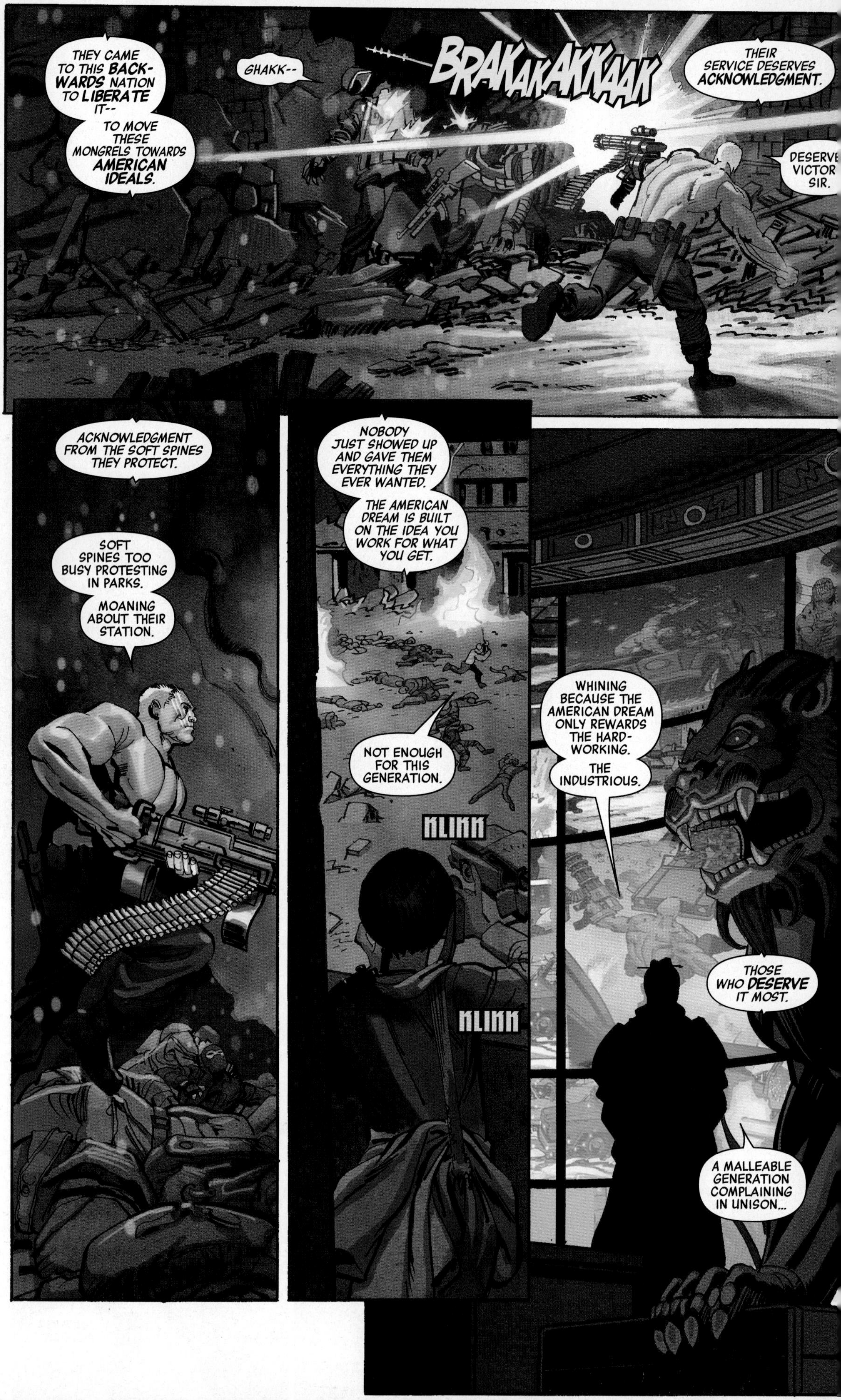

THEY CAME TO THIS BACK-WARDS NATION TO LIBERATE IT--
TO MOVE THESE MONGRELS TOWARDS AMERICAN IDEALS.
GHAKK--
BRAKAKAKKAAK
THEIR SERVICE DESERVES ACKNOWLEDGMENT.
DESERVE VICTOR SIR.
ACKNOWLEDGMENT FROM THE SOFT SPINES THEY PROTECT.
SOFT SPINES TOO BUSY PROTESTING IN PARKS.
MOANING ABOUT THEIR STATION.
NOBODY JUST SHOWED UP AND GAVE THEM EVERYTHING THEY EVER WANTED.
THE AMERICAN DREAM IS BUILT ON THE IDEA YOU WORK FOR WHAT YOU GET.
NOT ENOUGH FOR THIS GENERATION.
KLIKK
KLIKK
WHINING BECAUSE THE AMERICAN DREAM ONLY REWARDS THE HARD-WORKING.
THE INDUSTRIOUS.
THOSE WHO DESERVE IT MOST.
A MALLEABLE GENERATION COMPLAINING IN UNISON...

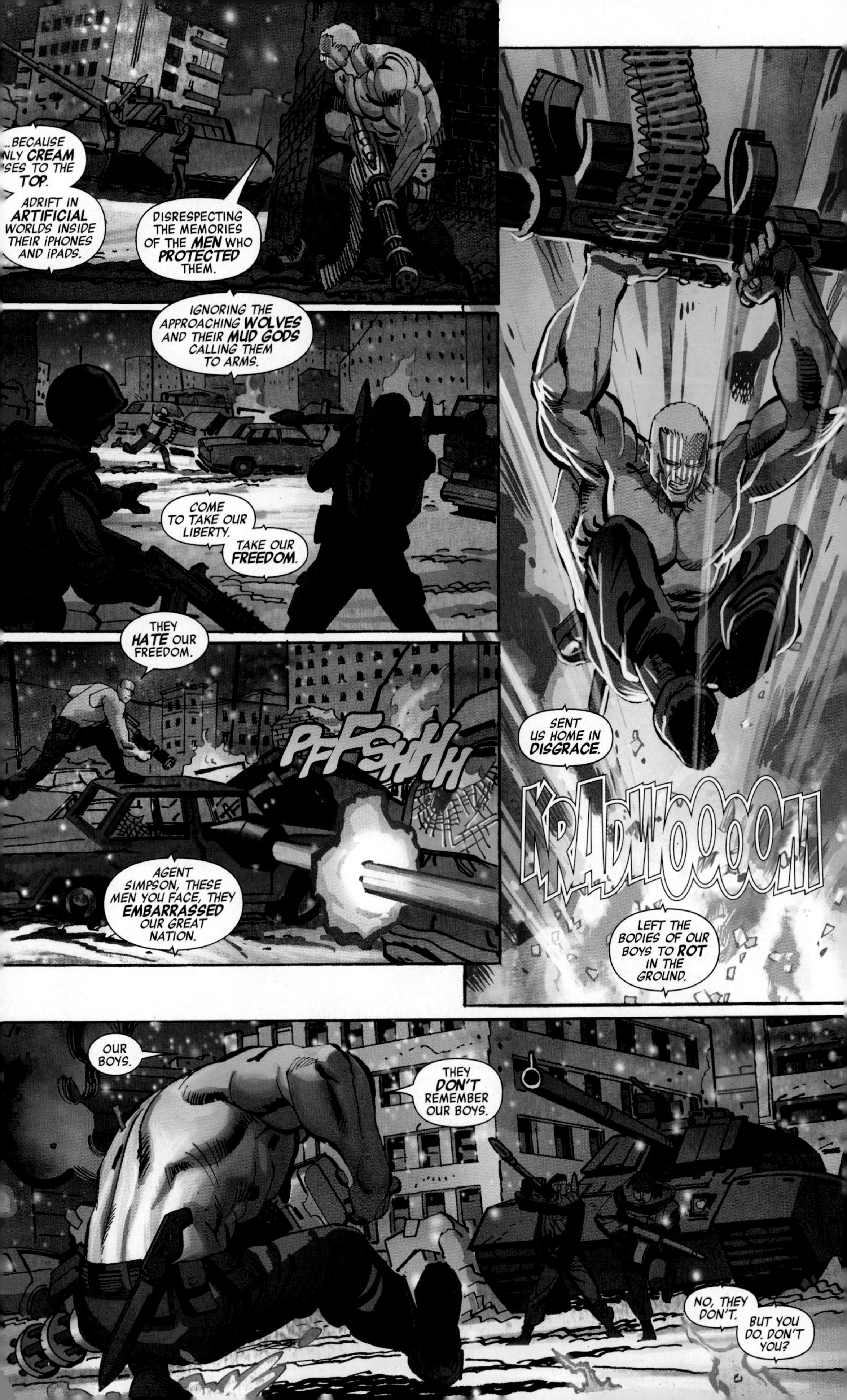
..BECAUSE
NLY CREAM
SES TO THE
TOP.
ADRIFT IN ARTIFICIAL WORLDS INSIDE THEIR iPHONES AND iPADS.
DISRESPECTING THE MEMORIES OF THE MEN WHO PROTECTED THEM.
IGNORING THE APPROACHING WOLVES AND THEIR MUD GODS CALLING THEM TO ARMS.
COME TO TAKE OUR LIBERTY.
TAKE OUR FREEDOM.
THEY HATE OUR FREEDOM.
PFFSHHH
AGENT SIMPSON, THESE MEN YOU FACE, THEY EMBARRASSED OUR GREAT NATION.
SENT US HOME IN DISGRACE.
KRADWOOOOOM
LEFT THE BODIES OF OUR BOYS TO ROT IN THE GROUND.
OUR BOYS.
THEY DON'T REMEMBER OUR BOYS.
NO, THEY DON'T.
BUT YOU DO. DON'T YOU?

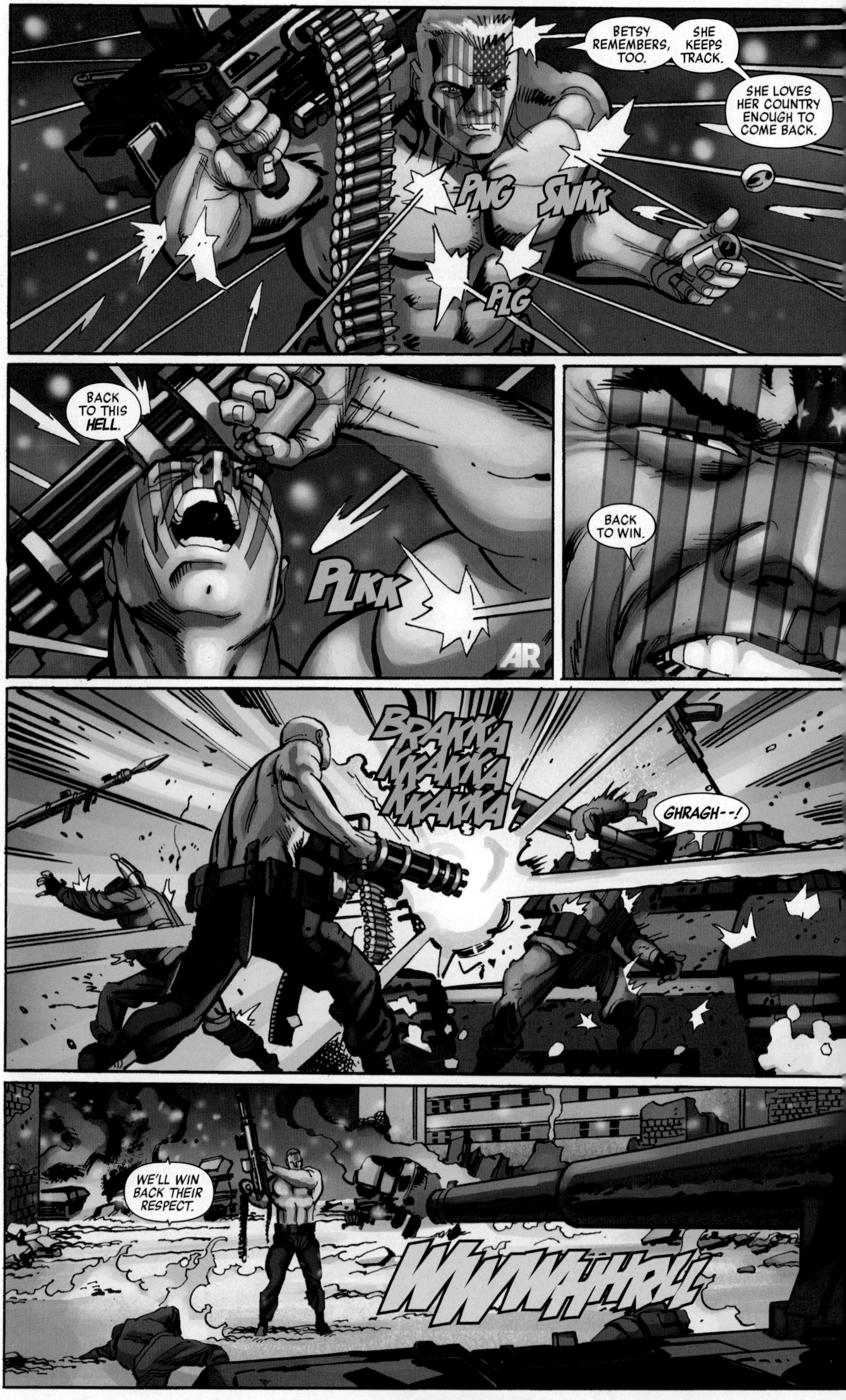
BETSY REMEMBERS, TOO.
SHE KEEPS TRACK.
SHE LOVES HER COUNTRY ENOUGH TO COME BACK.
PNG
SNKK
PLG
BACK TO THIS HELL.
PLKK
BACK TO WIN.
BRAKKA KKAKKA KKAKKA
GHRAGH--!
WE'LL WIN BACK THEIR RESPECT.
WWWAHHRLL

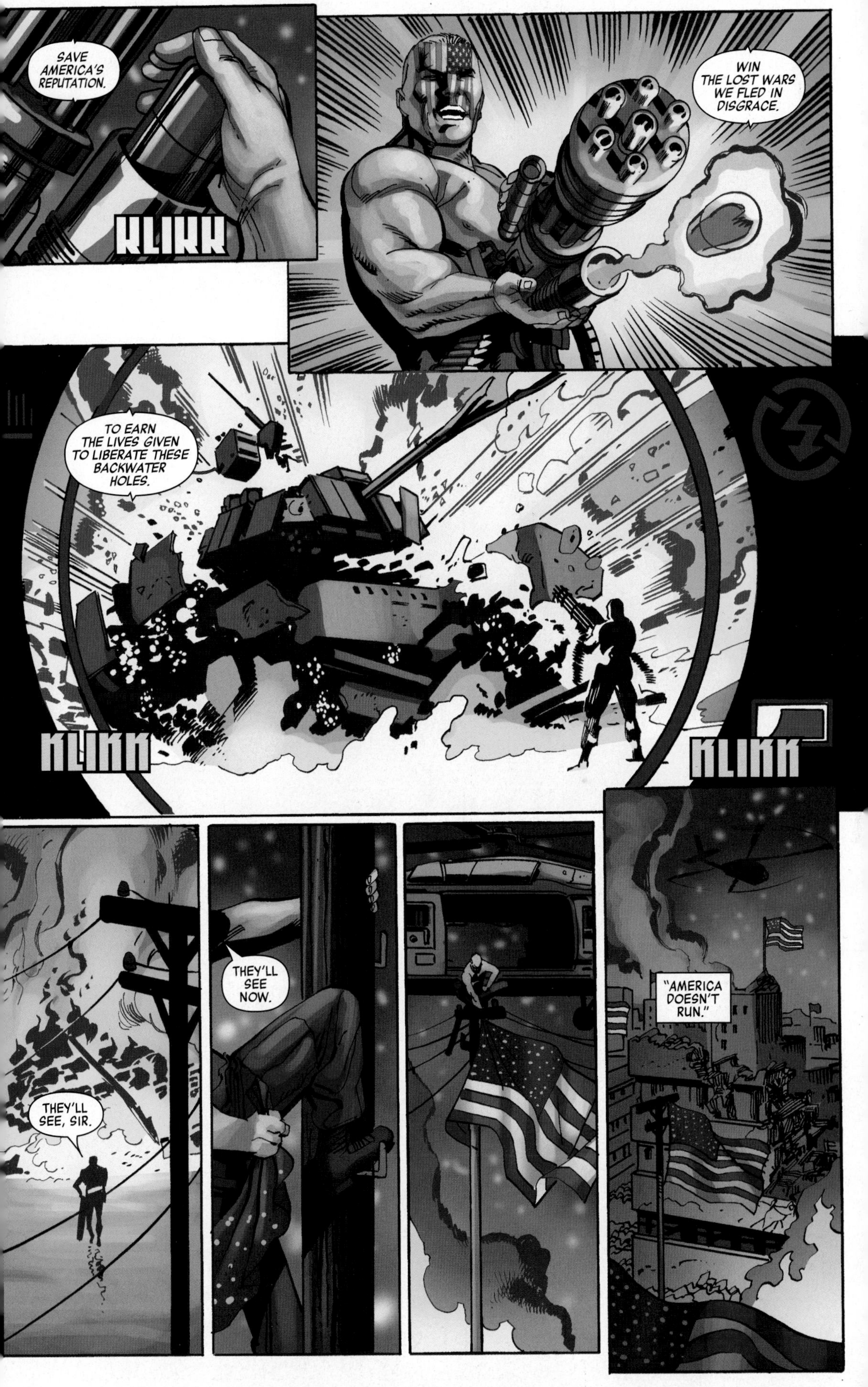
SAVE AMERICA'S REPUTATION.
KLIKK
WIN THE LOST WARS WE FLED IN DISGRACE.
TO EARN THE LIVES GIVEN TO LIBERATE THESE BACKWATER HOLES.
KLIKK
KLIKK
THEY'LL SEE, SIR.
THEY'LL SEE NOW.
"AMERICA DOESN'T RUN."

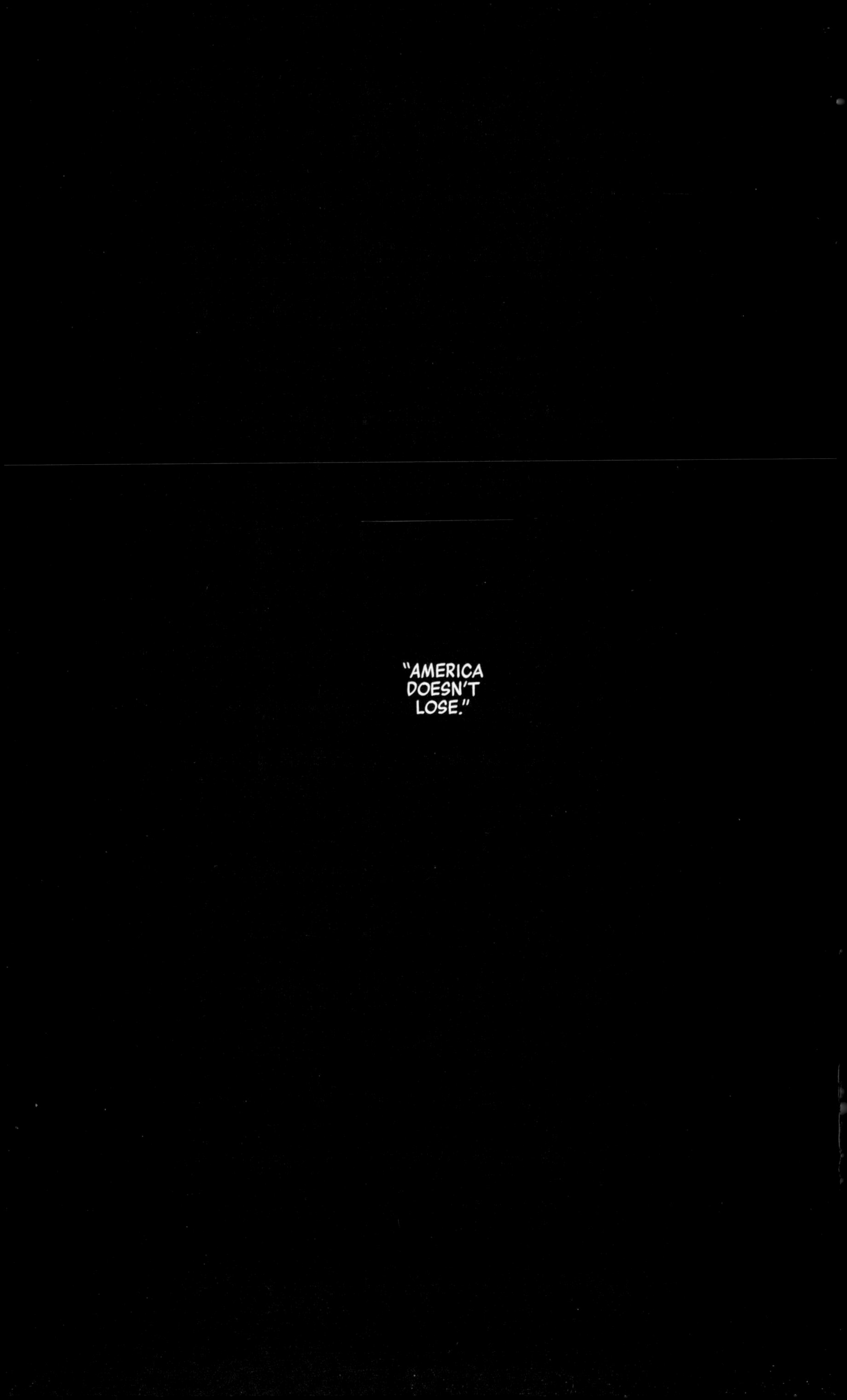
"AMERICA DOESN'T LOSE."

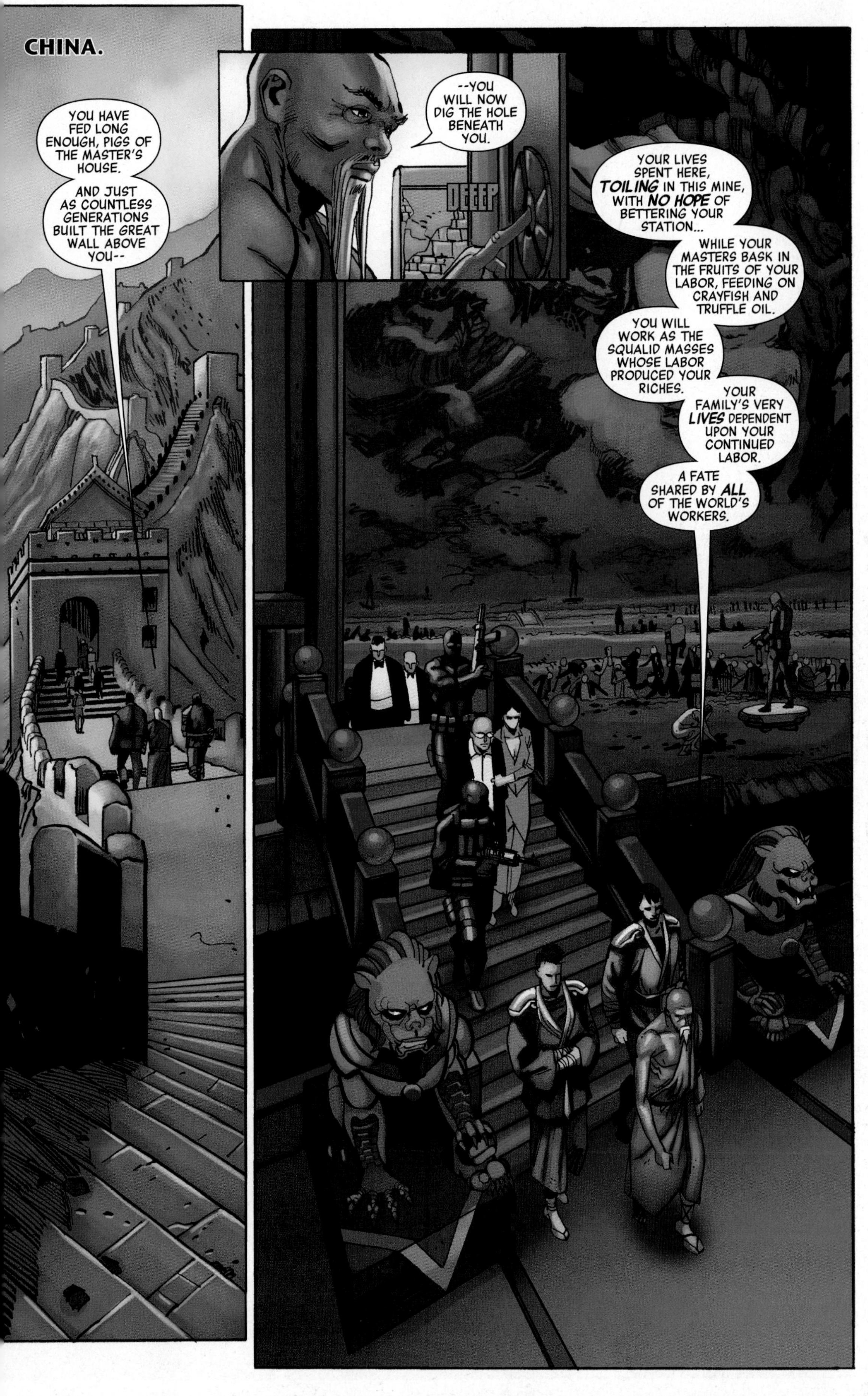
CHINA.
YOU HAVE FED LONG ENOUGH, PIGS OF THE MASTER'S HOUSE.
AND JUST AS COUNTLESS GENERATIONS BUILT THE GREAT WALL ABOVE YOU--
--YOU WILL NOW DIG THE HOLE BENEATH YOU.
DEEEP
YOUR LIVES SPENT HERE, TOILING IN THIS MINE, WITH NO HOPE OF BETTERING YOUR STATION...
WHILE YOUR MASTERS BASK IN THE FRUITS OF YOUR LABOR, FEEDING ON CRAYFISH AND TRUFFLE OIL.
YOU WILL WORK AS THE SQUALID MASSES WHOSE LABOR PRODUCED YOUR RICHES.
YOUR FAMILY'S VERY LIVES DEPENDENT UPON YOUR CONTINUED LABOR.
A FATE SHARED BY ALL OF THE WORLD'S WORKERS.

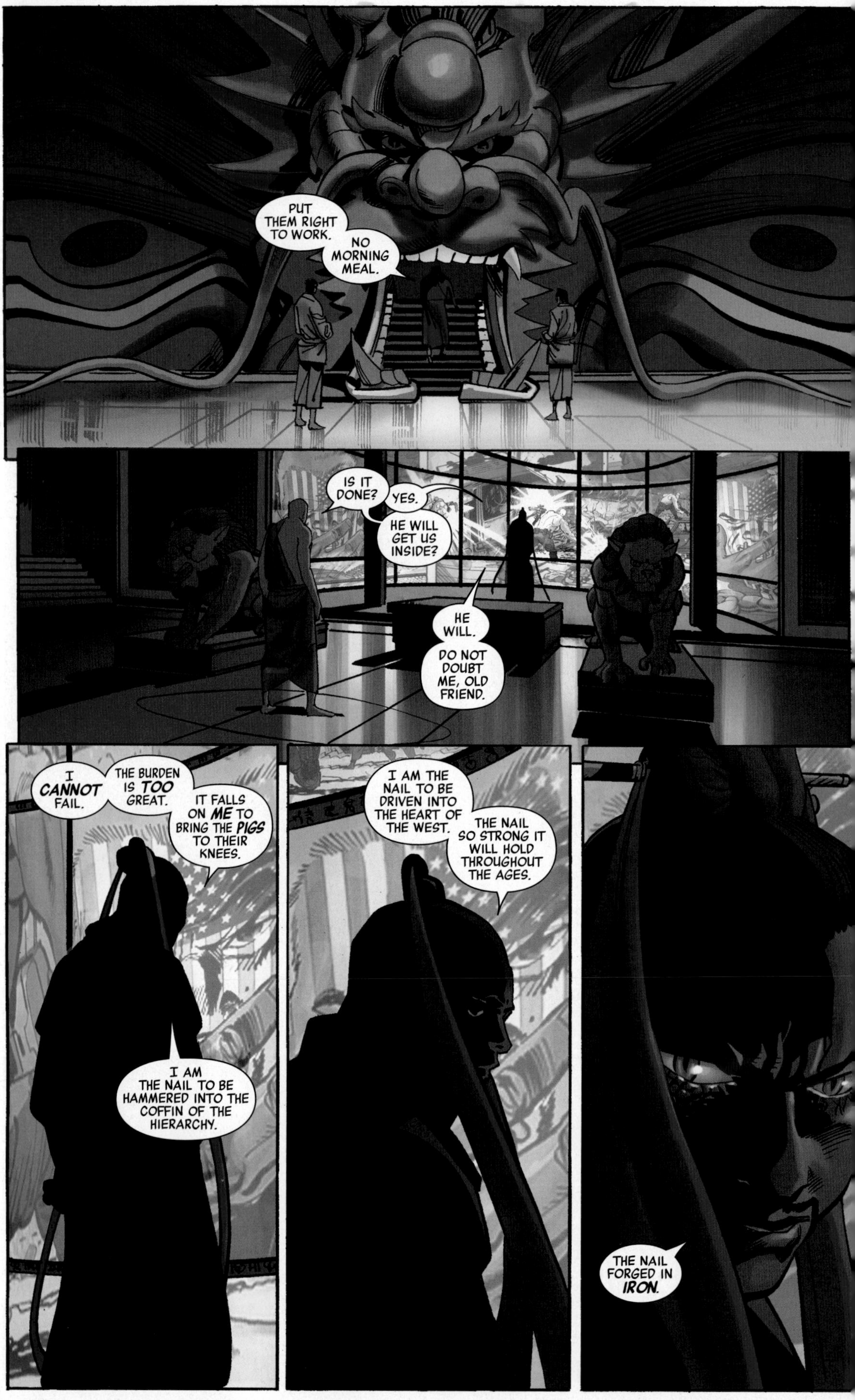
PUT THEM RIGHT TO WORK.
NO MORNING MEAL.
IS IT DONE?
YES.
HE WILL GET US INSIDE?
HE WILL.
DO NOT DOUBT ME, OLD FRIEND.
I CANNOT FAIL.
THE BURDEN IS TOO GREAT.
IT FALLS ON ME TO BRING THE PIGS TO THEIR KNEES.
I AM THE NAIL TO BE HAMMERED INTO THE COFFIN OF THE HIERARCHY.
I AM THE NAIL TO BE DRIVEN INTO THE HEART OF THE WEST.
THE NAIL SO STRONG IT WILL HOLD THROUGHOUT THE AGES.
THE NAIL FORGED IN IRON.

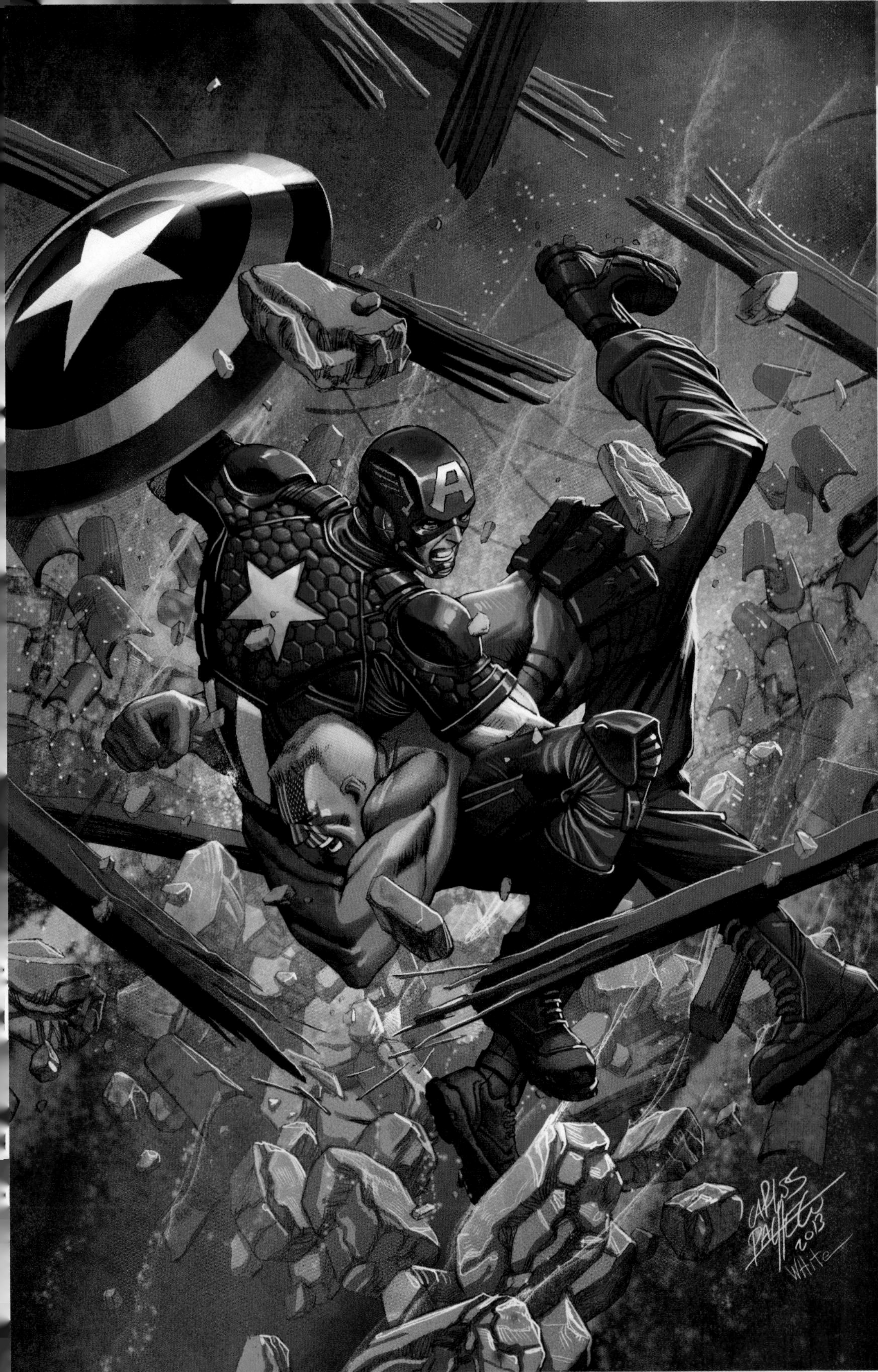

THIRTEEN

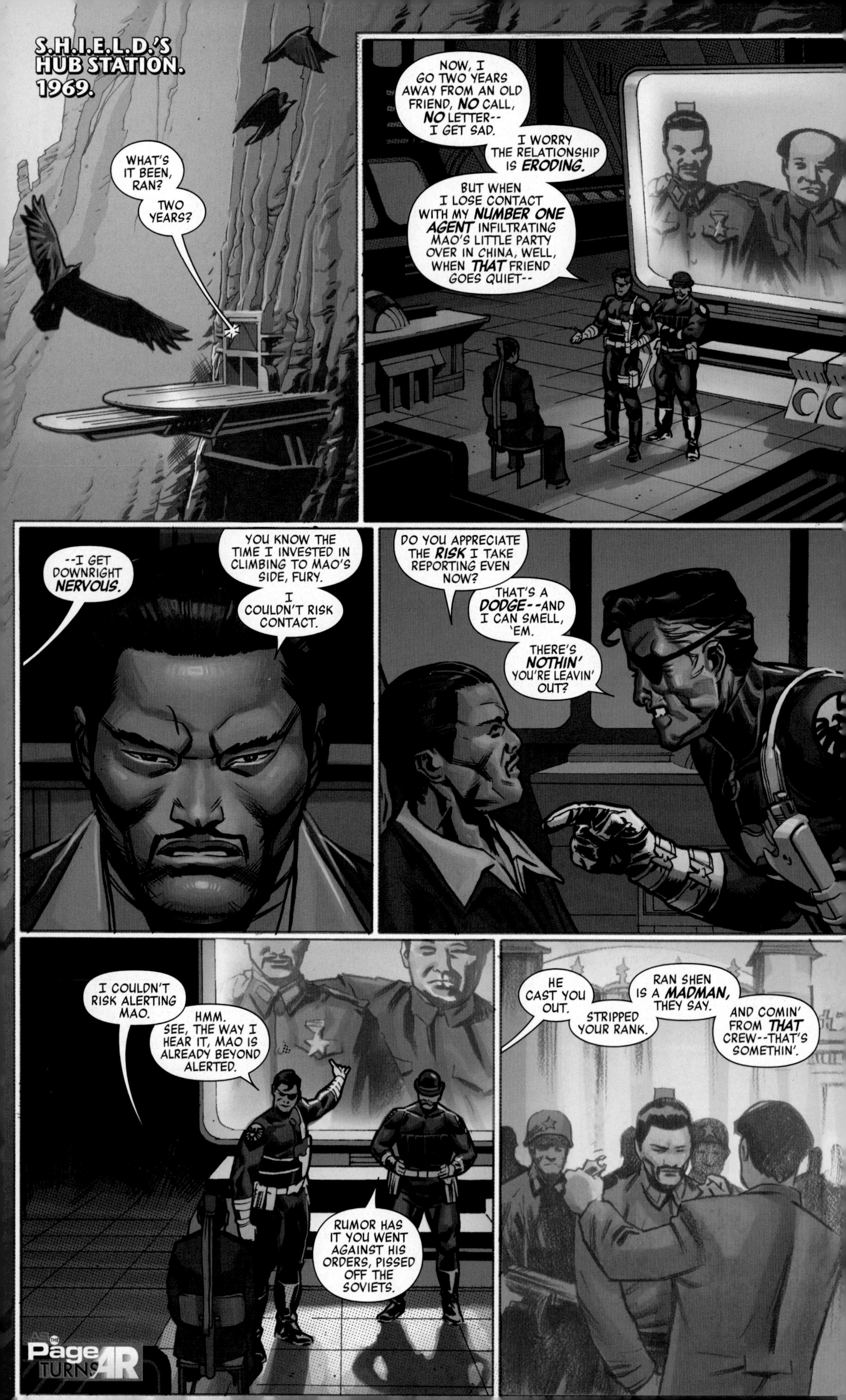
S.H.I.E.L.D.'S HUB STATION. 1969.
WHAT'S IT BEEN, RAN?
TWO YEARS?
NOW, I GO TWO YEARS AWAY FROM AN OLD FRIEND, NO CALL, NO LETTER-- I GET SAD.
I WORRY THE RELATIONSHIP IS ERODING.
BUT WHEN I LOSE CONTACT WITH MY NUMBER ONE AGENT INFILTRATING MAO'S LITTLE PARTY OVER IN CHINA, WELL, WHEN THAT FRIEND GOES QUIET--
--I GET DOWNRIGHT NERVOUS.
YOU KNOW THE TIME I INVESTED IN CLIMBING TO MAO'S SIDE, FURY.
I COULDN'T RISK CONTACT.
DO YOU APPRECIATE THE RISK I TAKE REPORTING EVEN NOW?
THAT'S A DODGE--AND I CAN SMELL, 'EM.
THERE'S NOTHIN' YOU'RE LEAVIN' OUT?
I COULDN'T RISK ALERTING MAO.
HMM. SEE, THE WAY I HEAR IT, MAO IS ALREADY BEYOND ALERTED.
RUMOR HAS IT YOU WENT AGAINST HIS ORDERS, PISSED OFF THE SOVIETS.
HE CAST YOU OUT.
STRIPPED YOUR RANK.
RAN SHEN IS A MADMAN, THEY SAY.
AND COMIN' FROM THAT CREW--THAT'S SOMETHIN'.

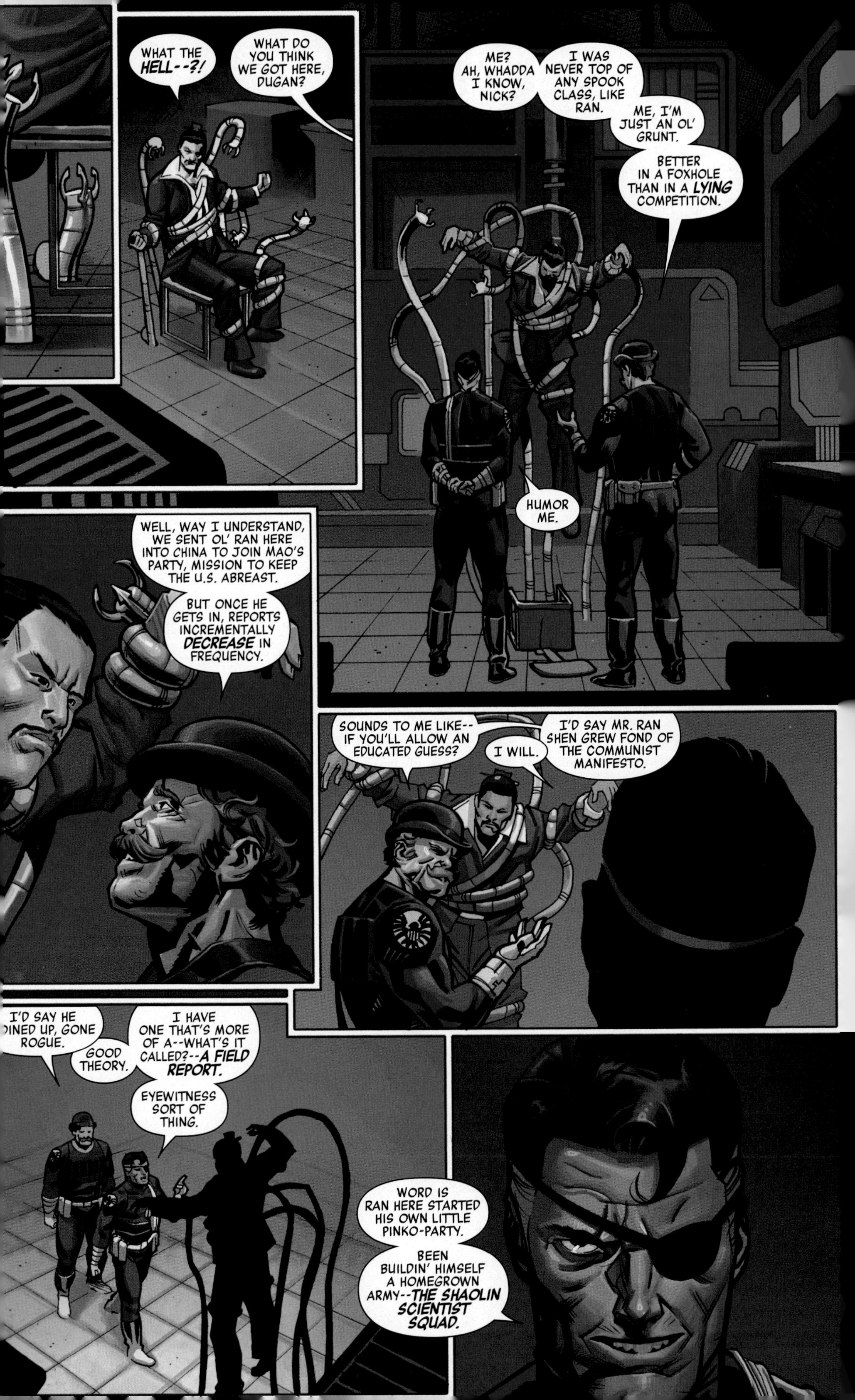

WHAT THE HELL--?!
WHAT DO YOU THINK WE GOT HERE, DUGAN?
ME? AH, WHADDA I KNOW, NICK?
I WAS NEVER TOP OF ANY SPOOK CLASS, LIKE RAN.
ME, I'M JUST AN OL' GRUNT.
BETTER IN A FOXHOLE THAN IN A LYING COMPETITION.
HUMOR ME.
WELL, WAY I UNDERSTAND, WE SENT OL' RAN HERE INTO CHINA TO JOIN MAO'S PARTY, MISSION TO KEEP THE U.S. ABREAST.
BUT ONCE HE GETS IN, REPORTS INCREMENTALLY DECREASE IN FREQUENCY.
SOUNDS TO ME LIKE-- IF YOU'LL ALLOW AN EDUCATED GUESS?
I WILL.
I'D SAY MR. RAN SHEN GREW FOND OF THE COMMUNIST MANIFESTO.
I'D SAY HE DINED UP, GONE ROGUE.
GOOD THEORY.
I HAVE ONE THAT'S MORE OF A--WHAT'S IT CALLED?--A FIELD REPORT.
EYEWITNESS SORT OF THING.
WORD IS RAN HERE STARTED HIS OWN LITTLE PINKO-PARTY.
BEEN BUILDIN' HIMSELF A HOMEGROWN ARMY--THE SHAOLIN SCIENTIST SQUAD.

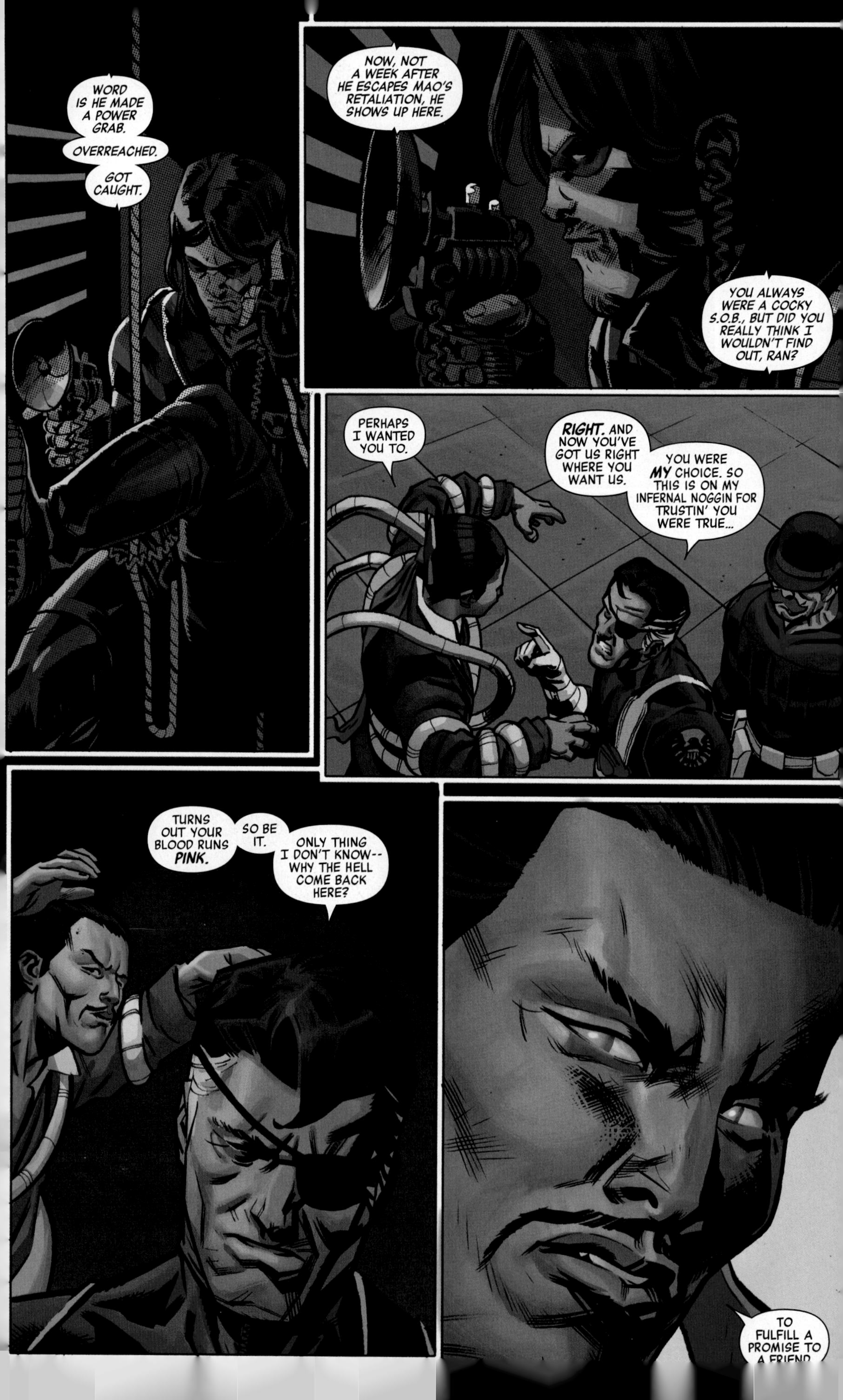
WORD IS HE MADE A POWER GRAB.
OVERREACHED.
GOT CAUGHT.
NOW, NOT A WEEK AFTER HE ESCAPES MAO'S RETALIATION, HE SHOWS UP HERE.
YOU ALWAYS WERE A COCKY S.O.B., BUT DID YOU REALLY THINK I WOULDN'T FIND OUT, RAN?
PERHAPS I WANTED YOU TO.
RIGHT. AND NOW YOU'VE GOT US RIGHT WHERE YOU WANT US.
YOU WERE MY CHOICE. SO THIS IS ON MY INFERNAL NOGGIN FOR TRUSTIN' YOU WERE TRUE...
TURNS OUT YOUR BLOOD RUNS PINK.
SO BE IT.
ONLY THING I DON'T KNOW-- WHY THE HELL COME BACK HERE?
TO FULFILL A PROMISE TO A FRIEND

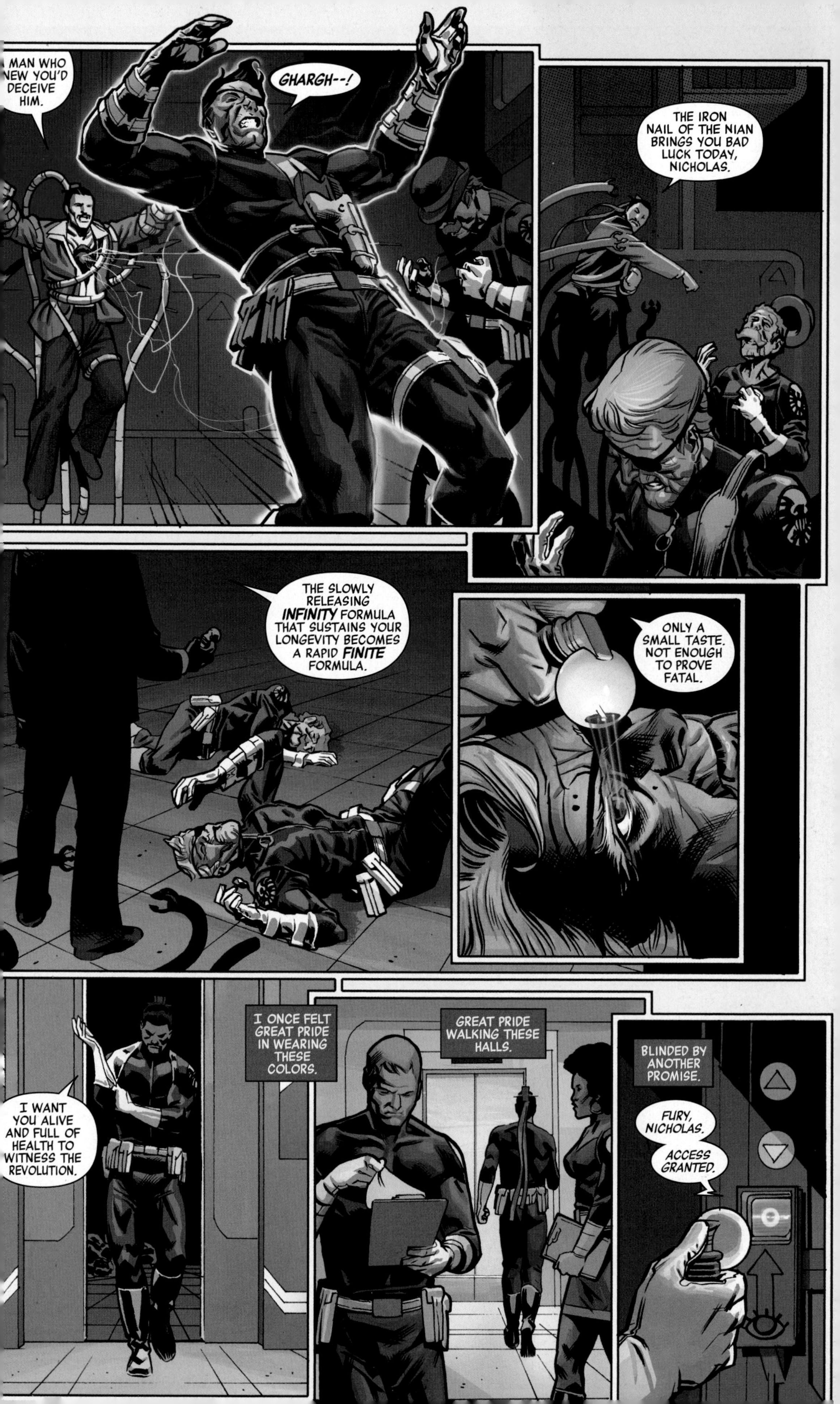

A MAN WHO NEW YOU'D DECEIVE HIM.
GHARGH--!
THE IRON NAIL OF THE NIAN BRINGS YOU BAD LUCK TODAY, NICHOLAS.
THE SLOWLY RELEASING INFINITY FORMULA THAT SUSTAINS YOUR LONGEVITY BECOMES A RAPID FINITE FORMULA.
ONLY A SMALL TASTE. NOT ENOUGH TO PROVE FATAL.
I WANT YOU ALIVE AND FULL OF HEALTH TO WITNESS THE REVOLUTION.
I ONCE FELT GREAT PRIDE IN WEARING THESE COLORS.
GREAT PRIDE WALKING THESE HALLS.
BLINDED BY ANOTHER PROMISE.
FURY, NICHOLAS.
ACCESS GRANTED.

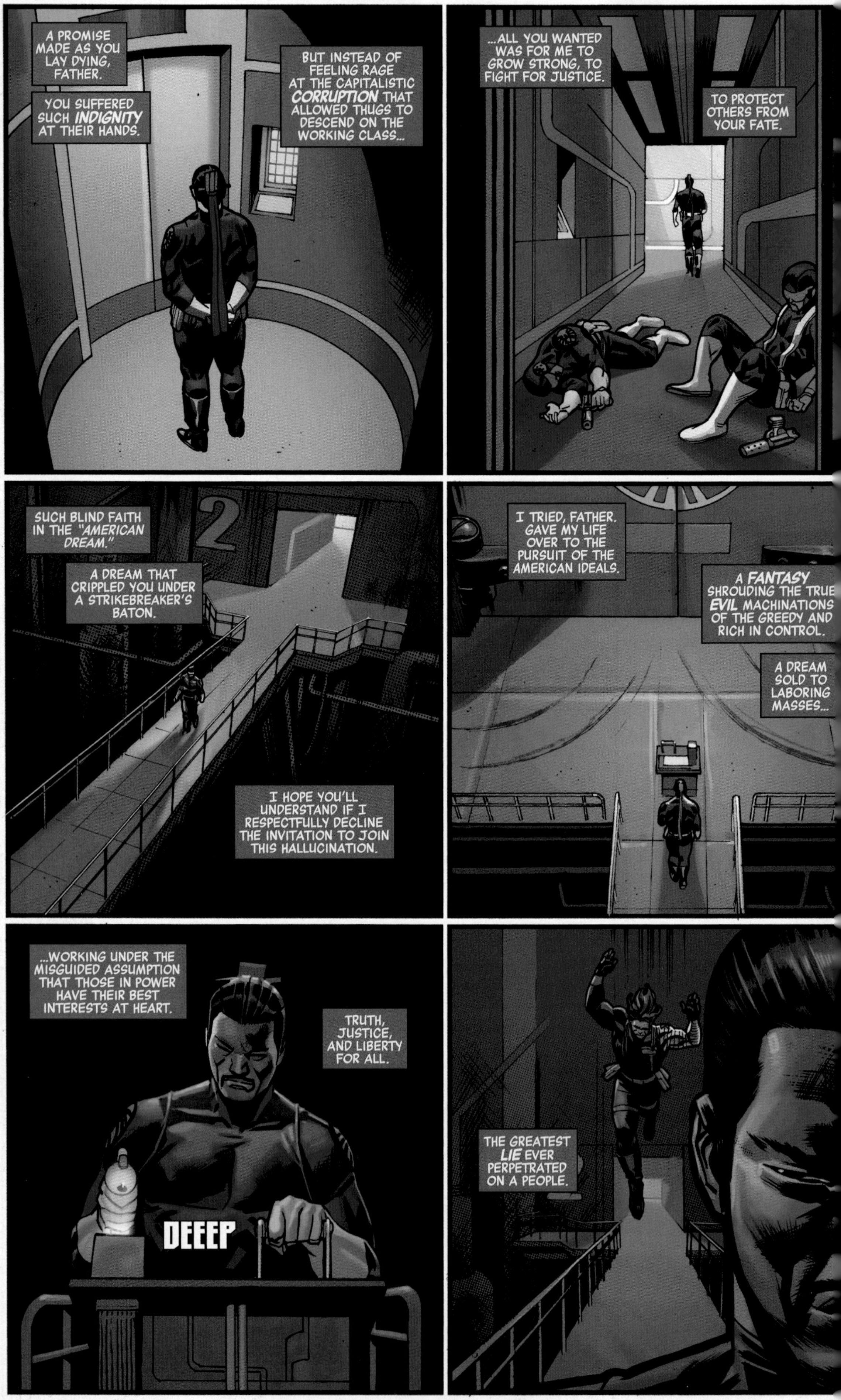
A PROMISE MADE AS YOU LAY DYING, FATHER.
YOU SUFFERED SUCH INDIGNITY AT THEIR HANDS.
BUT INSTEAD OF FEELING RAGE AT THE CAPITALISTIC CORRUPTION THAT ALLOWED THUGS TO DESCEND ON THE WORKING CLASS...
...ALL YOU WANTED WAS FOR ME TO GROW STRONG, TO FIGHT FOR JUSTICE.
TO PROTECT OTHERS FROM YOUR FATE.
SUCH BLIND FAITH IN THE "AMERICAN DREAM."
A DREAM THAT CRIPPLED YOU UNDER A STRIKEBREAKER'S BATON.
2
I HOPE YOU'LL UNDERSTAND IF I RESPECTFULLY DECLINE THE INVITATION TO JOIN THIS HALLUCINATION.
I TRIED, FATHER. GAVE MY LIFE OVER TO THE PURSUIT OF THE AMERICAN IDEALS.
A FANTASY SHROUDING THE TRUE EVIL MACHINATIONS OF THE GREEDY AND RICH IN CONTROL.
A DREAM SOLD TO LABORING MASSES...
...WORKING UNDER THE MISGUIDED ASSUMPTION THAT THOSE IN POWER HAVE THEIR BEST INTERESTS AT HEART.
TRUTH, JUSTICE, AND LIBERTY FOR ALL.
DEEEP
THE GREATEST LIE EVER PERPETRATED ON A PEOPLE.

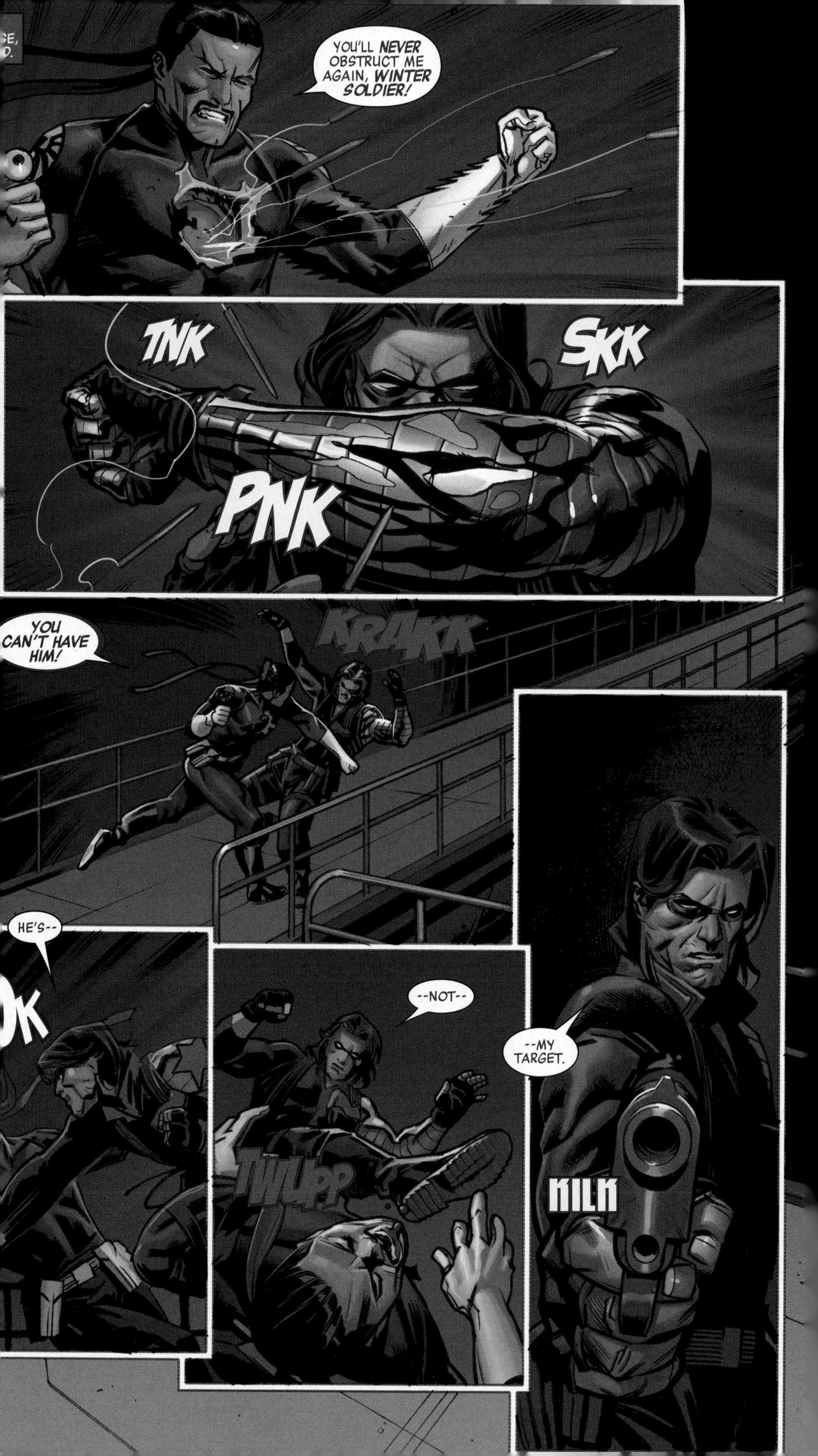
YOU'LL NEVER OBSTRUCT ME AGAIN, WINTER SOLDIER!
TNK
SKK
PNK
KRAKK
YOU CAN'T HAVE HIM!
HE'S--
--NOT--
TWUPP
--MY TARGET.
KILK

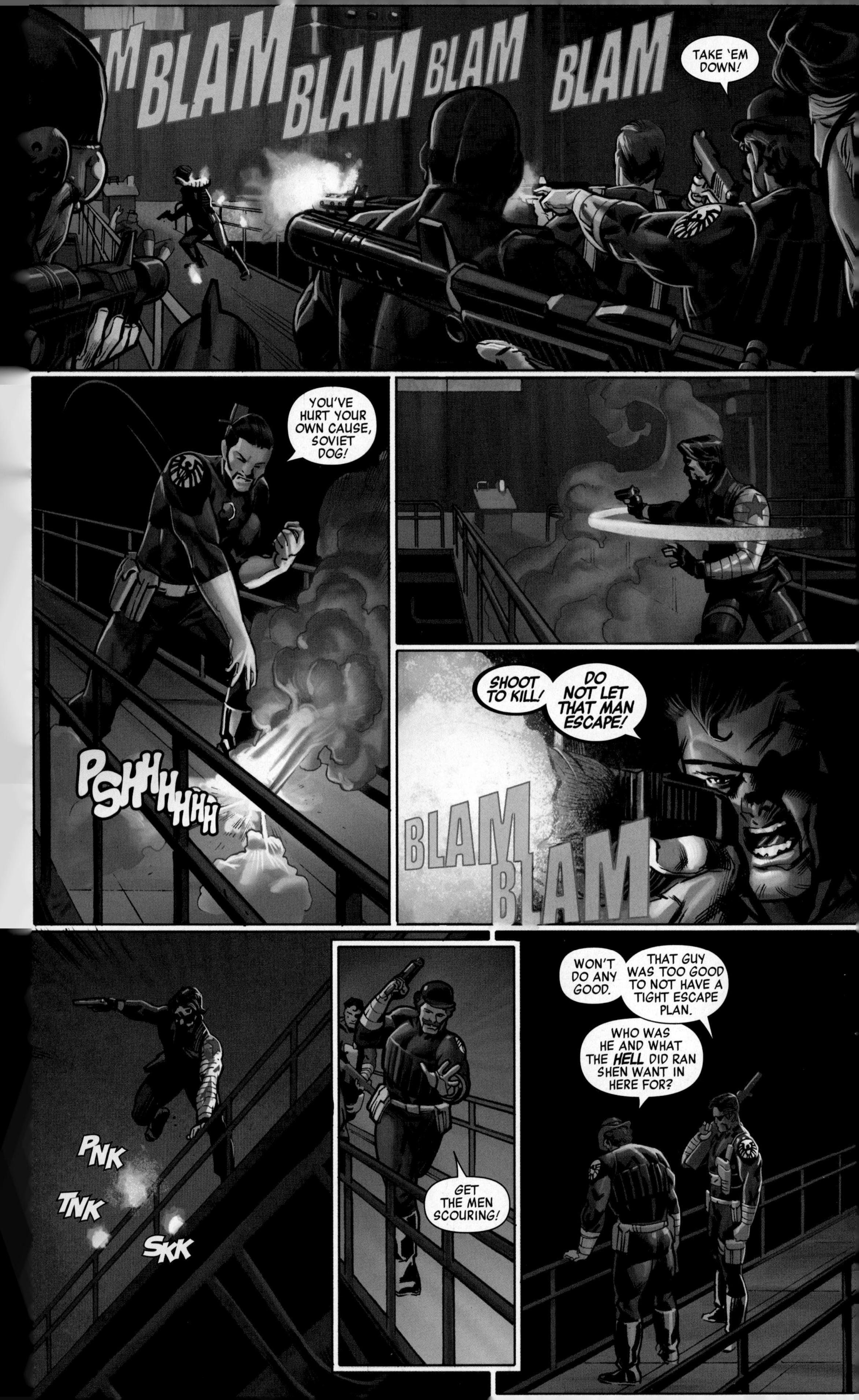
BLAM BLAM BLAM BLAM BLAM
TAKE 'EM DOWN!
YOU'VE HURT YOUR OWN CAUSE, SOVIET DOG!
PSHHHHHH
SHOOT TO KILL!
DO NOT LET THAT MAN ESCAPE!
BLAM BLAM
PNK
TNK
SKK
GET THE MEN SCOURING!
WON'T DO ANY GOOD.
THAT GUY WAS TOO GOOD TO NOT HAVE A TIGHT ESCAPE PLAN.
WHO WAS HE AND WHAT THE HELL DID RAN SHEN WANT IN HERE FOR?

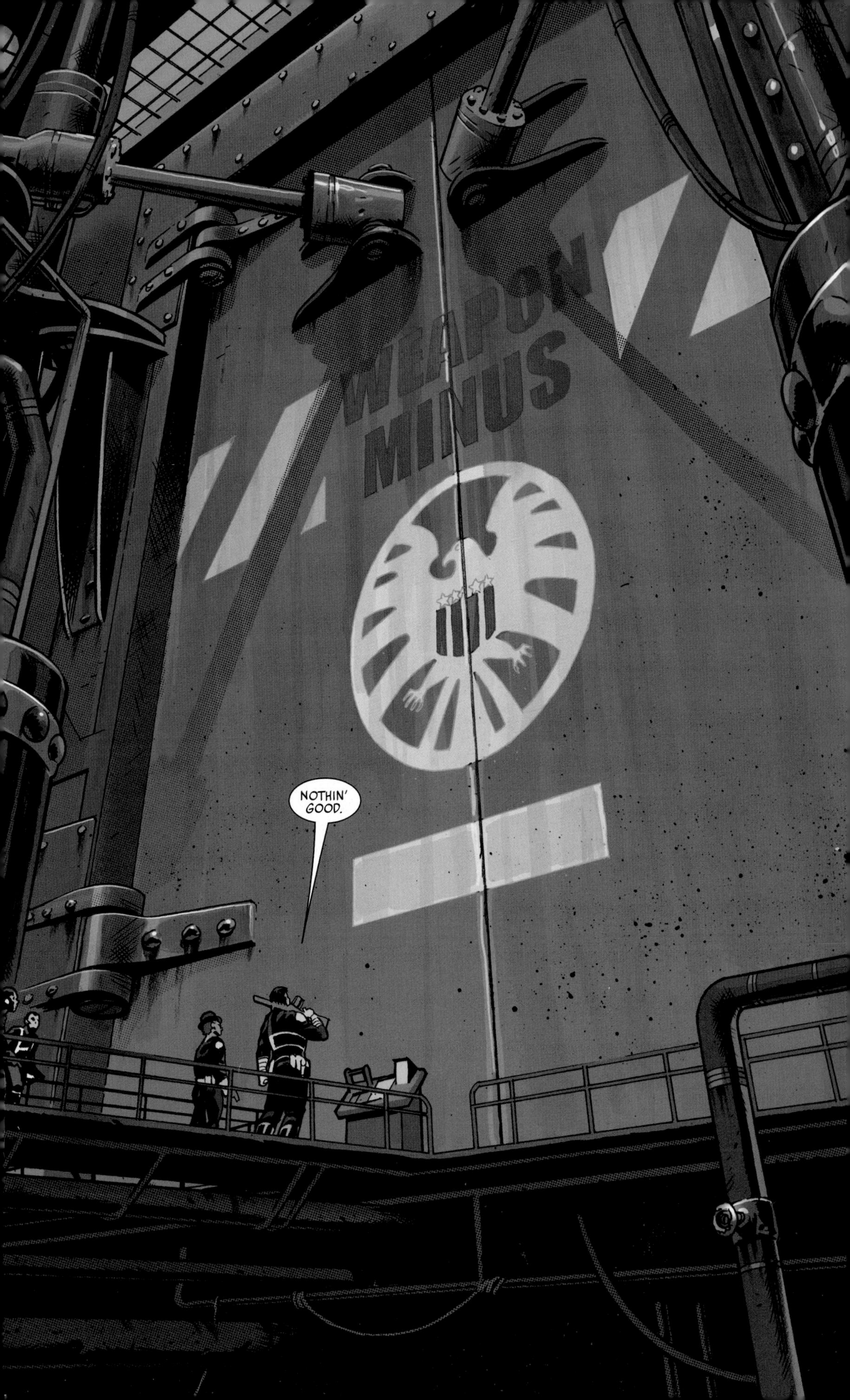
WEAPON MINUS
NOTHIN' GOOD.

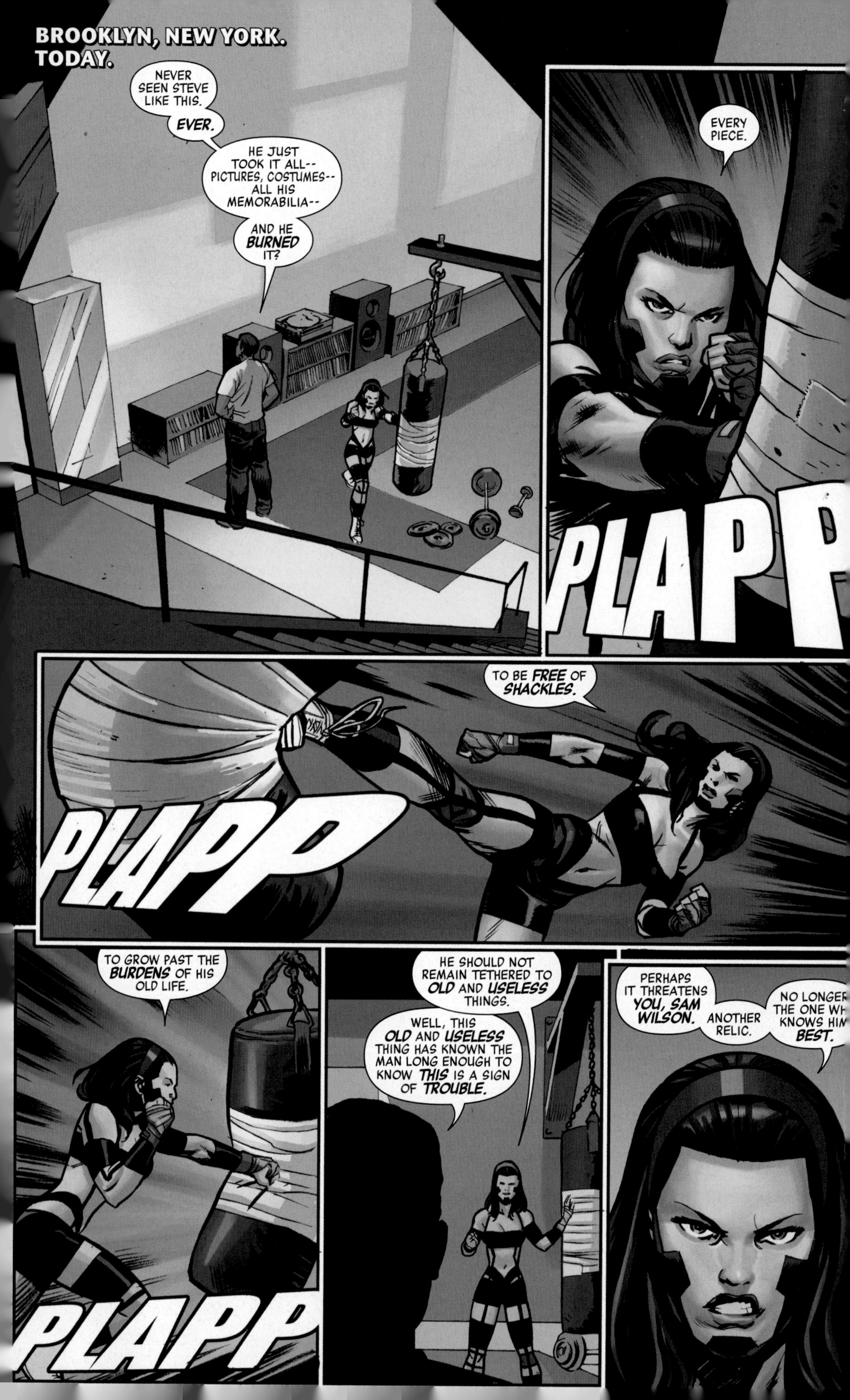

BROOKLYN, NEW YORK. TODAY.
NEVER SEEN STEVE LIKE THIS.
EVER.
HE JUST TOOK IT ALL-- PICTURES, COSTUMES-- ALL HIS MEMORABILIA--
AND HE BURNED IT?
EVERY PIECE.
PLAPP
TO BE FREE OF SHACKLES.
PLAPP
TO GROW PAST THE BURDENS OF HIS OLD LIFE.
PLAPP
HE SHOULD NOT REMAIN TETHERED TO OLD AND USELESS THINGS.
WELL, THIS OLD AND USELESS THING HAS KNOWN THE MAN LONG ENOUGH TO KNOW THIS IS A SIGN OF TROUBLE.
PERHAPS IT THREATENS YOU, SAM WILSON.
ANOTHER RELIC.
NO LONGER THE ONE WH KNOWS HIM BEST.

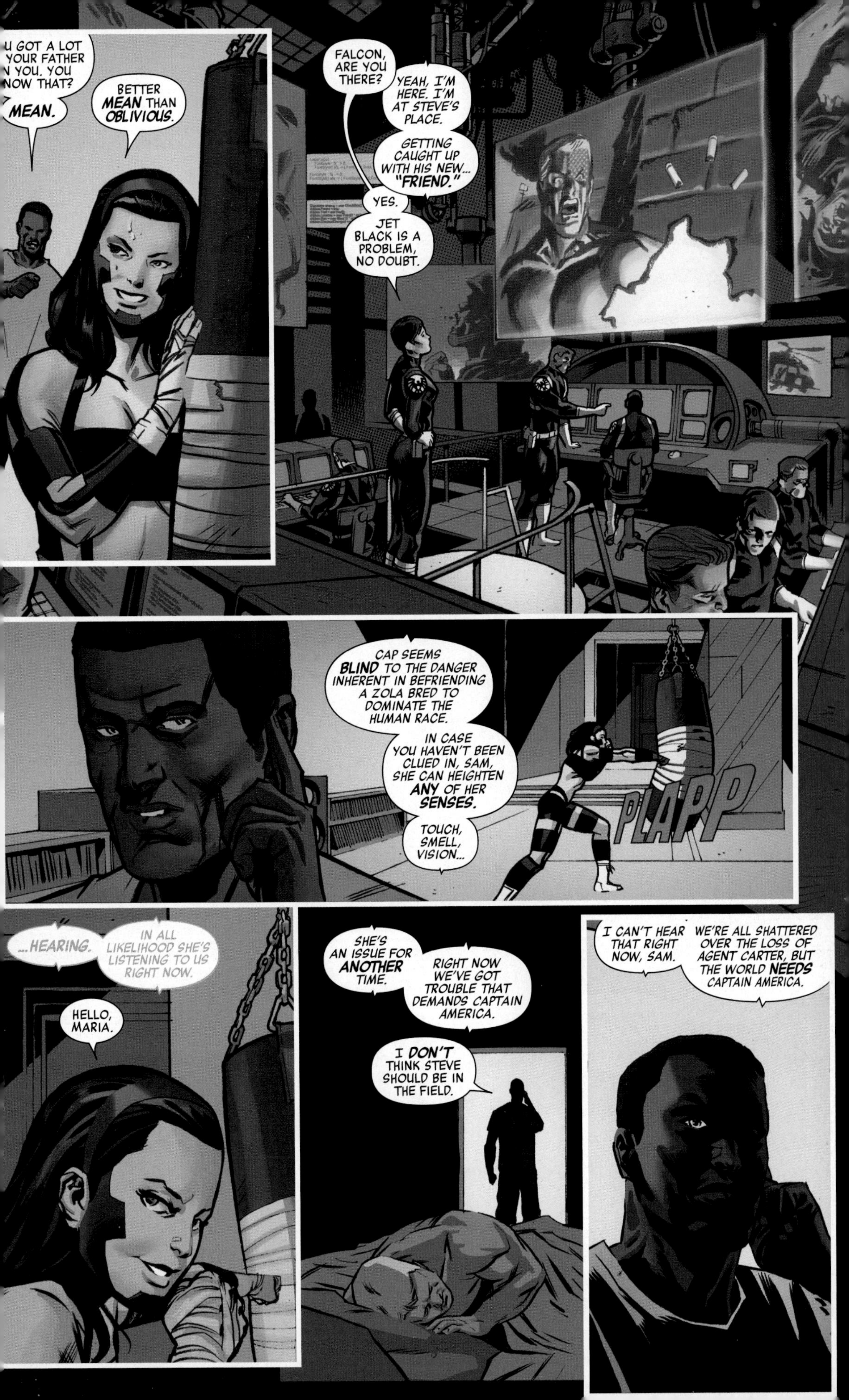

U GOT A LOT YOUR FATHER N YOU. YOU NOW THAT?
MEAN.
BETTER MEAN THAN OBLIVIOUS.
FALCON, ARE YOU THERE?
YEAH, I'M HERE. I'M AT STEVE'S PLACE.
GETTING CAUGHT UP WITH HIS NEW... "FRIEND."
YES.
JET BLACK IS A PROBLEM, NO DOUBT.
CAP SEEMS BLIND TO THE DANGER INHERENT IN BEFRIENDING A ZOLA BRED TO DOMINATE THE HUMAN RACE.
IN CASE YOU HAVEN'T BEEN CLUED IN, SAM, SHE CAN HEIGHTEN ANY OF HER SENSES.
TOUCH, SMELL, VISION...
PLAPP
...HEARING.
IN ALL LIKELIHOOD SHE'S LISTENING TO US RIGHT NOW.
HELLO, MARIA.
SHE'S AN ISSUE FOR ANOTHER TIME.
RIGHT NOW WE'VE GOT TROUBLE THAT DEMANDS CAPTAIN AMERICA.
I DON'T THINK STEVE SHOULD BE IN THE FIELD.
I CAN'T HEAR THAT RIGHT NOW, SAM.
WE'RE ALL SHATTERED OVER THE LOSS OF AGENT CARTER, BUT THE WORLD NEEDS CAPTAIN AMERICA.

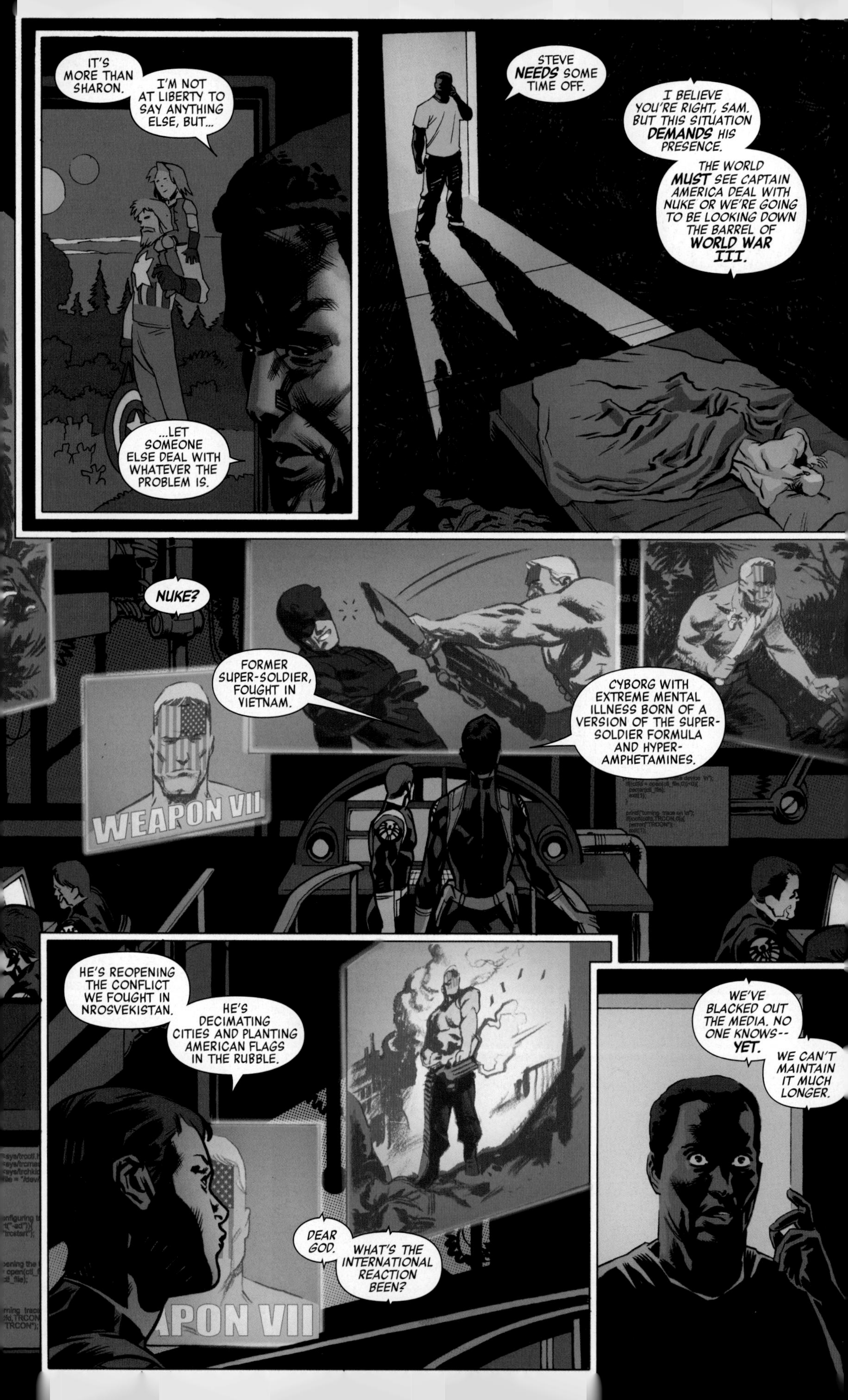
IT'S MORE THAN SHARON.
I'M NOT AT LIBERTY TO SAY ANYTHING ELSE, BUT...
...LET SOMEONE ELSE DEAL WITH WHATEVER THE PROBLEM IS.
STEVE NEEDS SOME TIME OFF.
I BELIEVE YOU'RE RIGHT, SAM. BUT THIS SITUATION DEMANDS HIS PRESENCE.
THE WORLD MUST SEE CAPTAIN AMERICA DEAL WITH NUKE OR WE'RE GOING TO BE LOOKING DOWN THE BARREL OF WORLD WAR III.
NUKE?
FORMER SUPER-SOLDIER, FOUGHT IN VIETNAM.
CYBORG WITH EXTREME MENTAL ILLNESS BORN OF A VERSION OF THE SUPER-SOLDIER FORMULA AND HYPER-AMPHETAMINES.
WEAPON VII
HE'S REOPENING THE CONFLICT WE FOUGHT IN NROSVEKISTAN.
HE'S DECIMATING CITIES AND PLANTING AMERICAN FLAGS IN THE RUBBLE.
APON VII
DEAR GOD.
WHAT'S THE INTERNATIONAL REACTION BEEN?
WE'VE BLACKED OUT THE MEDIA. NO ONE KNOWS-- YET.
WE CAN'T MAINTAIN IT MUCH LONGER.

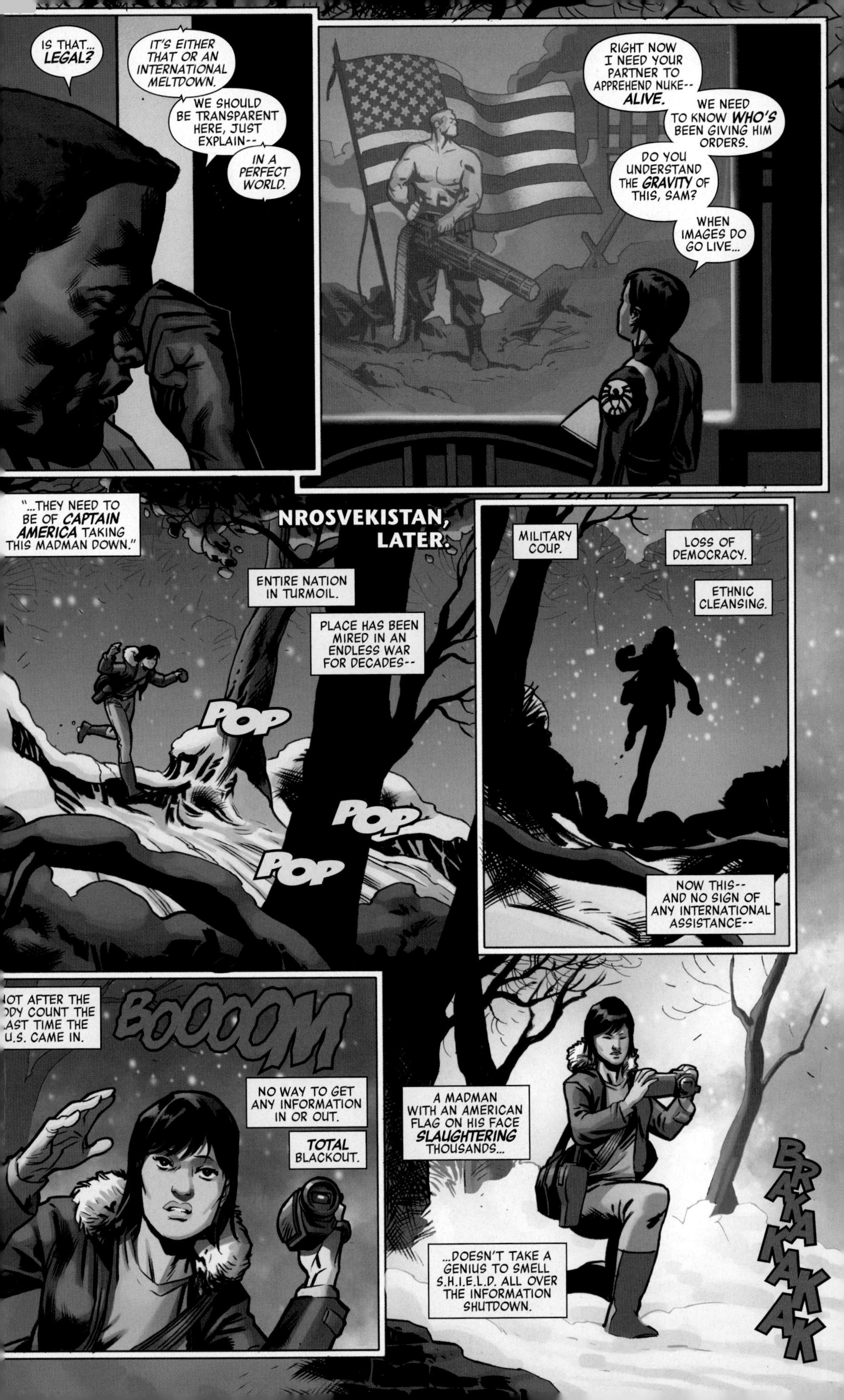
IS THAT... LEGAL?
IT'S EITHER THAT OR AN INTERNATIONAL MELTDOWN.
WE SHOULD BE TRANSPARENT HERE, JUST EXPLAIN--
IN A PERFECT WORLD.
RIGHT NOW I NEED YOUR PARTNER TO APPREHEND NUKE-- ALIVE.
WE NEED TO KNOW WHO'S BEEN GIVING HIM ORDERS.
DO YOU UNDERSTAND THE GRAVITY OF THIS, SAM?
WHEN IMAGES DO GO LIVE...
"...THEY NEED TO BE OF CAPTAIN AMERICA TAKING THIS MADMAN DOWN."
NROSVEKISTAN, LATER.
ENTIRE NATION IN TURMOIL.
PLACE HAS BEEN MIRED IN AN ENDLESS WAR FOR DECADES--
POP
POP
POP
MILITARY COUP.
LOSS OF DEMOCRACY.
ETHNIC CLEANSING.
NOW THIS-- AND NO SIGN OF ANY INTERNATIONAL ASSISTANCE--
NOT AFTER THE BODY COUNT THE LAST TIME THE U.S. CAME IN.
BOOOOM
NO WAY TO GET ANY INFORMATION IN OR OUT.
TOTAL BLACKOUT.
A MADMAN WITH AN AMERICAN FLAG ON HIS FACE SLAUGHTERING THOUSANDS...
...DOESN'T TAKE A GENIUS TO SMELL S.H.I.E.L.D. ALL OVER THE INFORMATION SHUTDOWN.
BRAKAKAKAK

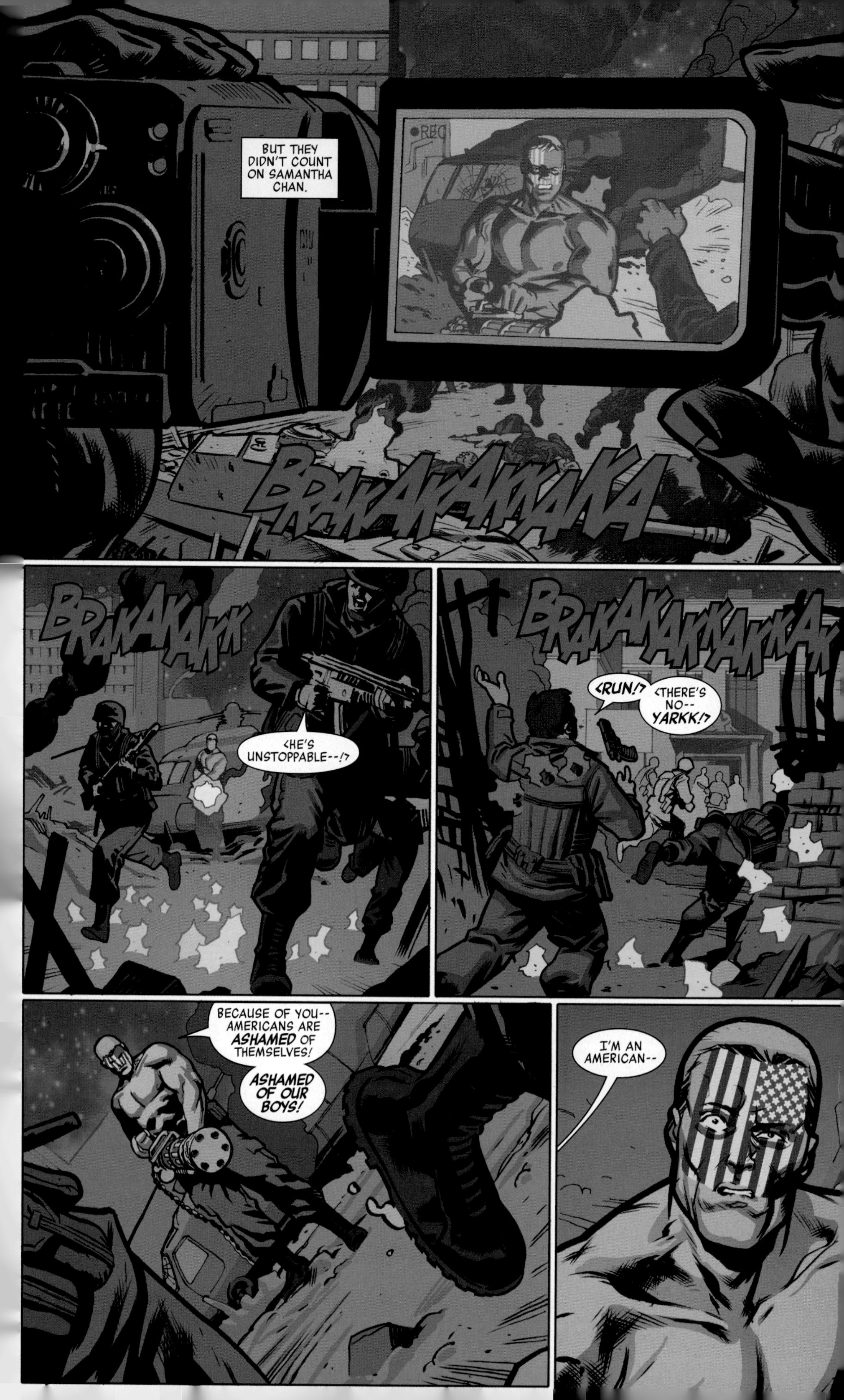

BUT THEY DIDN'T COUNT ON SAMANTHA CHAN.
REC
BRAKAKAKKAKA
BRAKAKAKK
<HE'S UNSTOPPABLE--!>
BRAKAKAKKAKKAK
<RUN!>
<THERE'S NO-- YARKK!>
BECAUSE OF YOU-- AMERICANS ARE ASHAMED OF THEMSELVES!
ASHAMED OF OUR BOYS!
I'M AN AMERICAN--

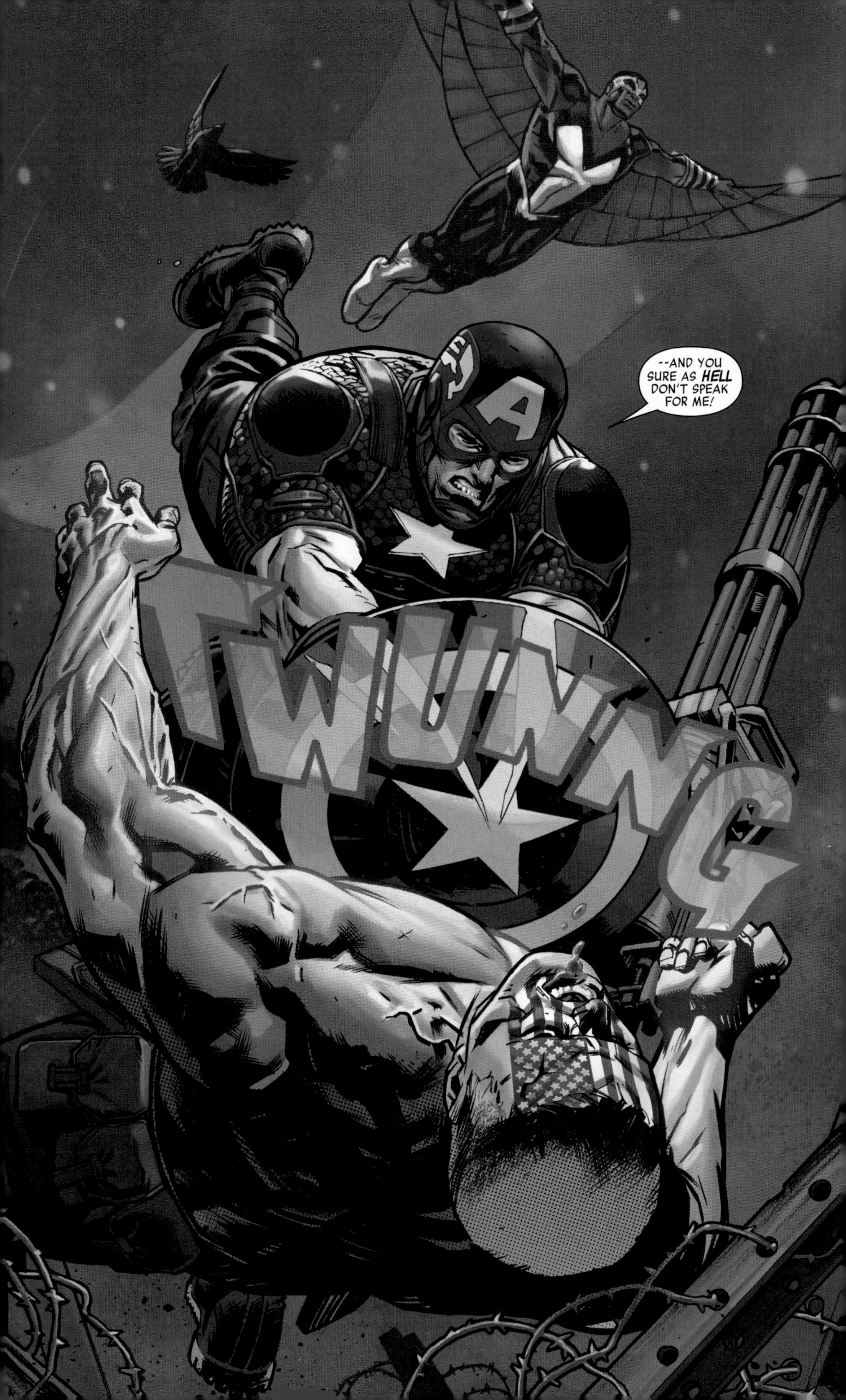
--AND YOU SURE AS HELL DON'T SPEAK FOR ME!
TWUNNG

EVERY GREAT NATION SUFFERS A DECLINE--

--THIS MAN IS A LIVING REMINDER OF OUR DARKEST HOUR--

KWUDD

--A RELIC OF AN AMERICA I WASN'T THERE TO HELP.

ONE CHANCE, SOLDIER. STAND DOWN.

I'M UNDER ORD FROM TH GENERAL

HIS EYES--

--BLANK--

--OUT OF HIS MIND.

NO REASONING WITH HIM--

--TOO POWERFUL TO RISK.

TWUNGG

GIVE IT EVERYTHING I HAVE--

BLOK

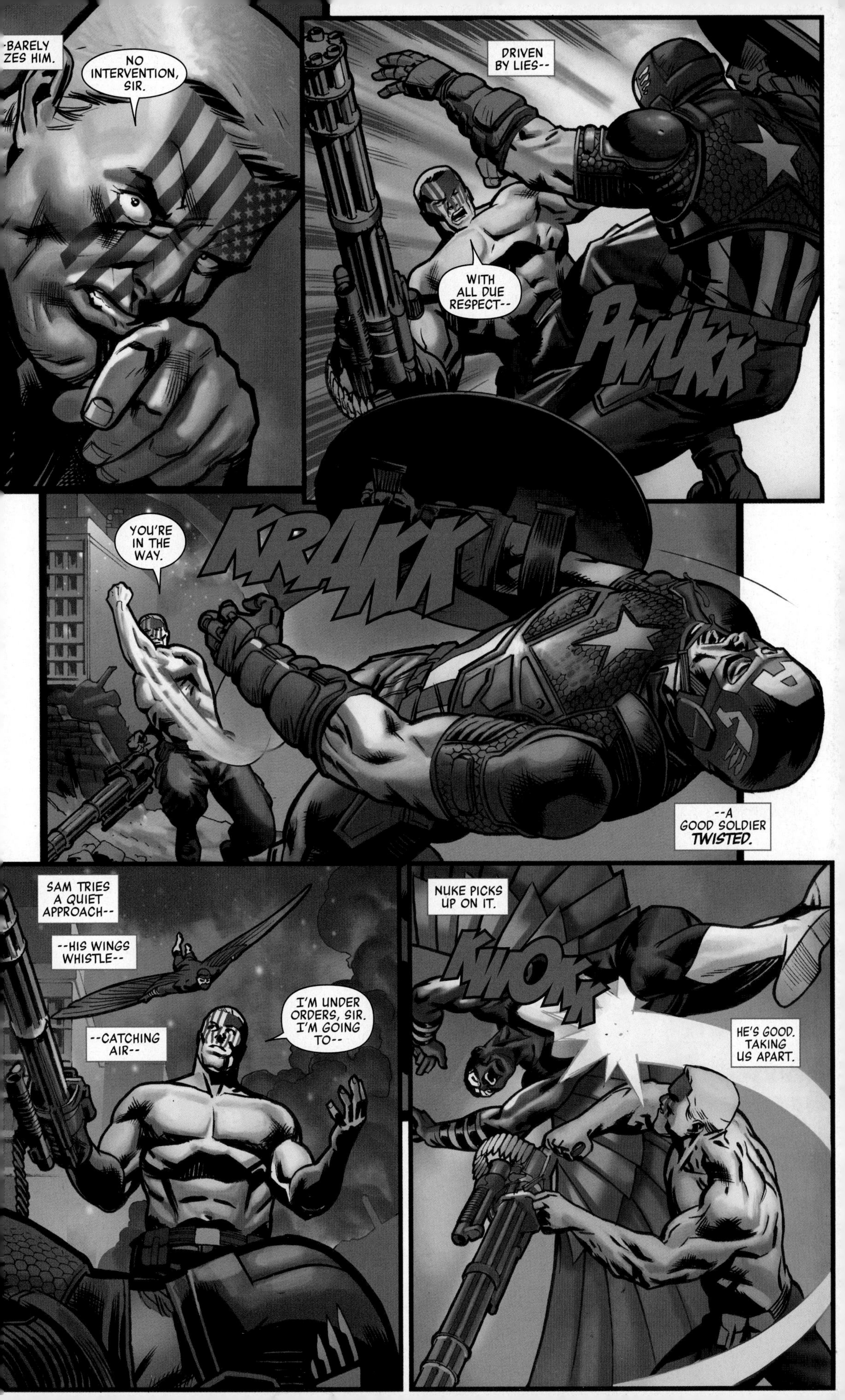
-BARELY
ZES HIM.
NO INTERVENTION, SIR.
DRIVEN BY LIES--
WITH ALL DUE RESPECT--
PWUKK
YOU'RE IN THE WAY.
KRAKK
--A GOOD SOLDIER TWISTED.
SAM TRIES A QUIET APPROACH--
--HIS WINGS WHISTLE--
--CATCHING AIR--
I'M UNDER ORDERS, SIR. I'M GOING TO--
NUKE PICKS UP ON IT.
NWOK
HE'S GOOD. TAKING US APART.

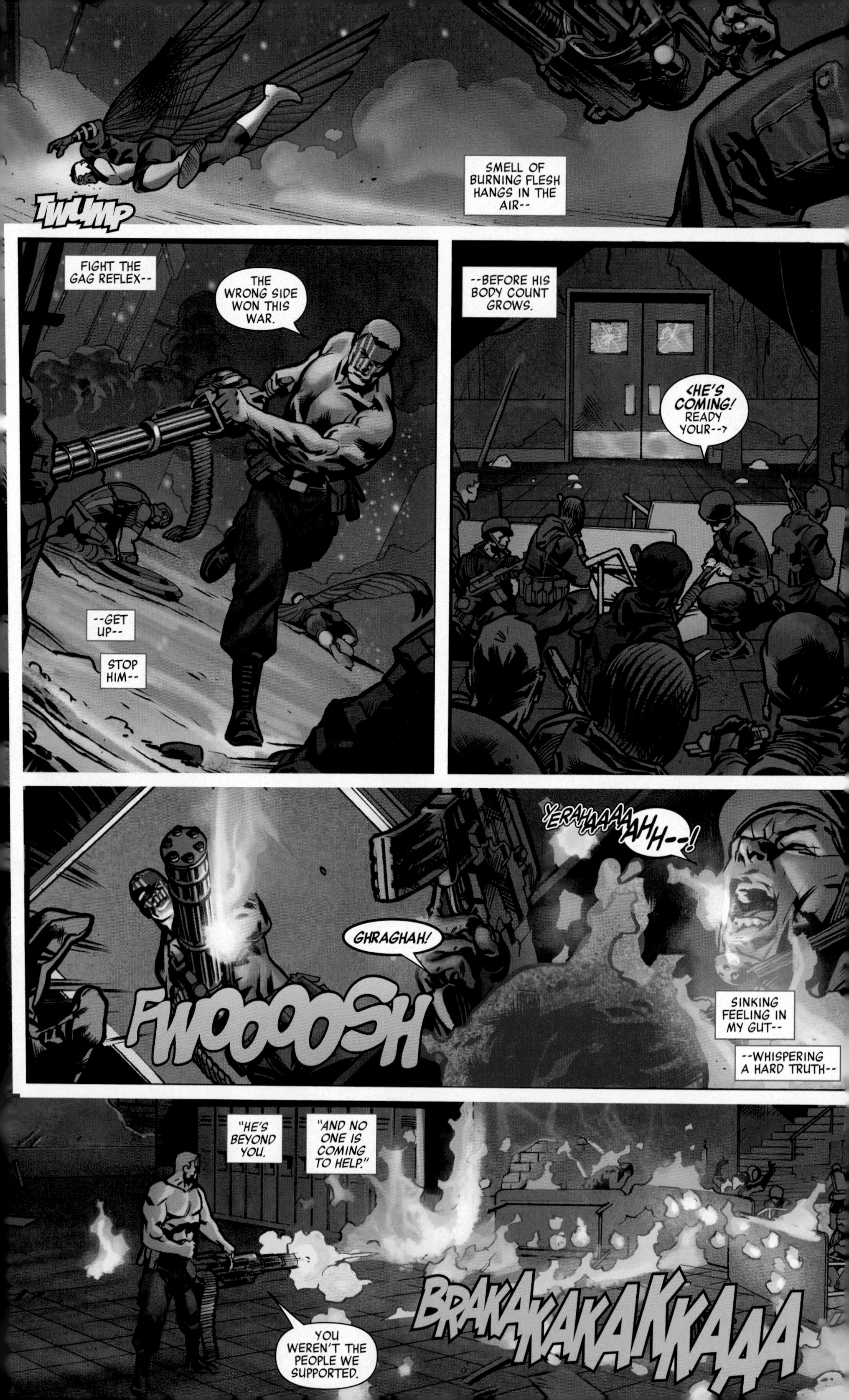
SMELL OF BURNING FLESH HANGS IN THE AIR--
TWUMP
FIGHT THE GAG REFLEX--
THE WRONG SIDE WON THIS WAR.
--GET UP--
STOP HIM--
--BEFORE HIS BODY COUNT GROWS.
<HE'S COMING! READY YOUR-->
GHRAGHAH!
FWOOOOSH
YERAHAAAAAAHH--!
SINKING FEELING IN MY GUT--
--WHISPERING A HARD TRUTH--
"HE'S BEYOND YOU.
"AND NO ONE IS COMING TO HELP."
YOU WEREN'T THE PEOPLE WE SUPPORTED.
BRAKAKAKAKAKKAAA

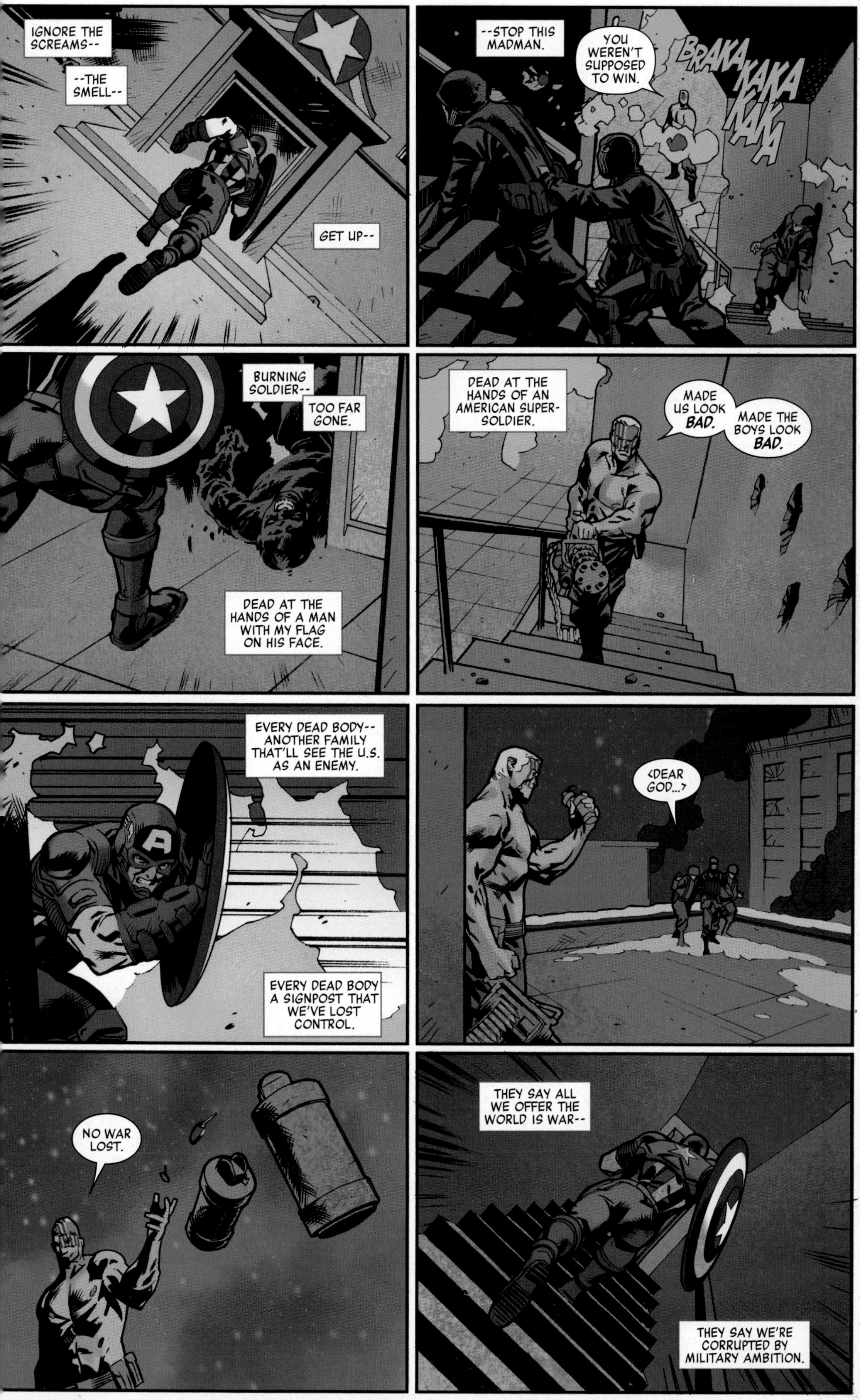
IGNORE THE SCREAMS--
--THE SMELL--
GET UP--
--STOP THIS MADMAN.
YOU WEREN'T SUPPOSED TO WIN.
BRAKAKAKAKAKAKA
BURNING SOLDIER--
TOO FAR GONE.
DEAD AT THE HANDS OF A MAN WITH MY FLAG ON HIS FACE.
DEAD AT THE HANDS OF AN AMERICAN SUPER-SOLDIER.
MADE US LOOK BAD.
MADE THE BOYS LOOK BAD.
EVERY DEAD BODY--ANOTHER FAMILY THAT'LL SEE THE U.S. AS AN ENEMY.
EVERY DEAD BODY A SIGNPOST THAT WE'VE LOST CONTROL.
<DEAR GOD...>
NO WAR LOST.
THEY SAY ALL WE OFFER THE WORLD IS WAR--
THEY SAY WE'RE CORRUPTED BY MILITARY AMBITION.

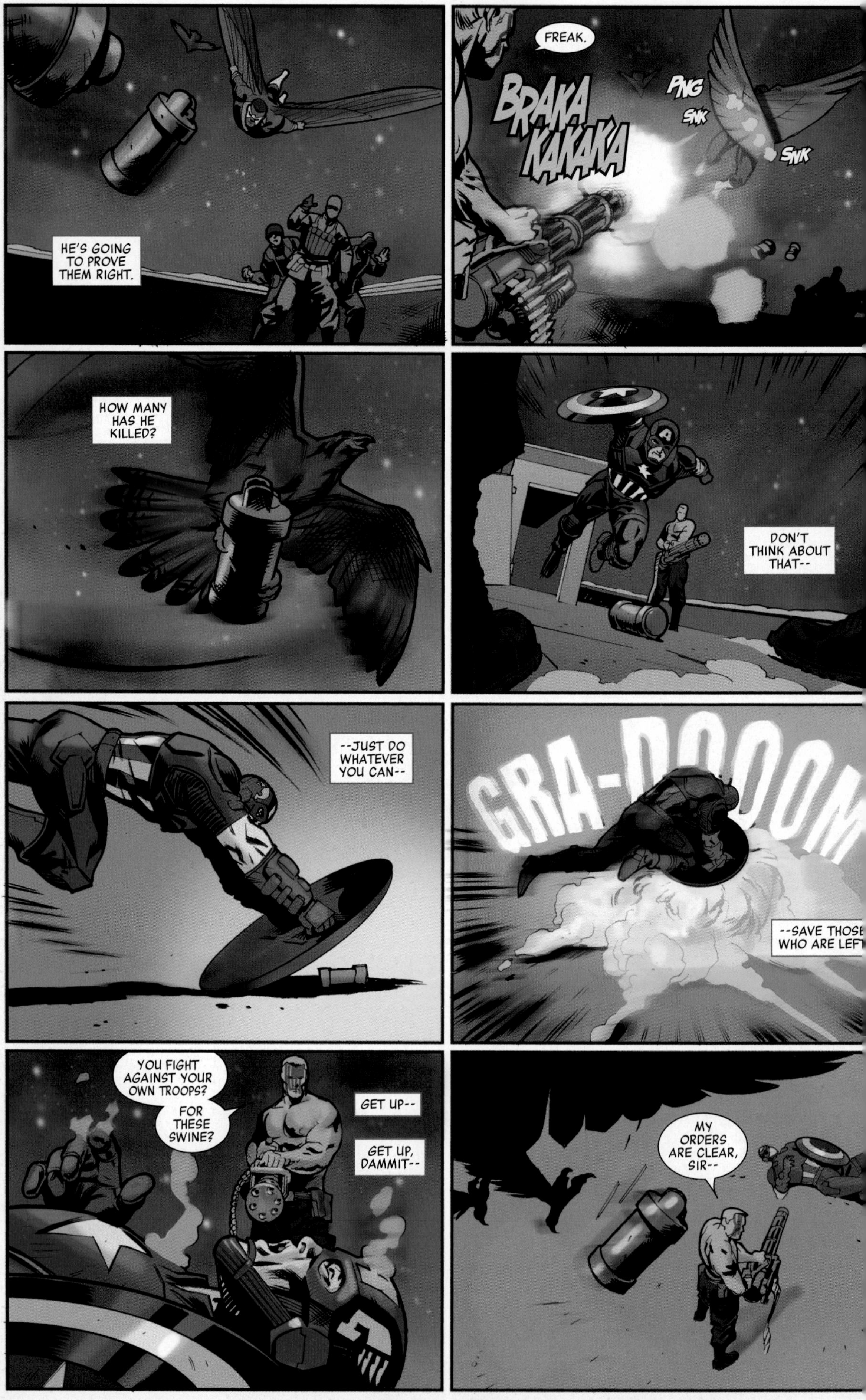
HE'S GOING TO PROVE THEM RIGHT.
FREAK.
BRAKA KAKAKA
PNG
SNK
SNK
HOW MANY HAS HE KILLED?
DON'T THINK ABOUT THAT--
--JUST DO WHATEVER YOU CAN--
GRA-DOOOM
--SAVE THOSE WHO ARE LEFT
YOU FIGHT AGAINST YOUR OWN TROOPS?
FOR THESE SWINE?
GET UP--
GET UP, DAMMIT--
MY ORDERS ARE CLEAR, SIR--

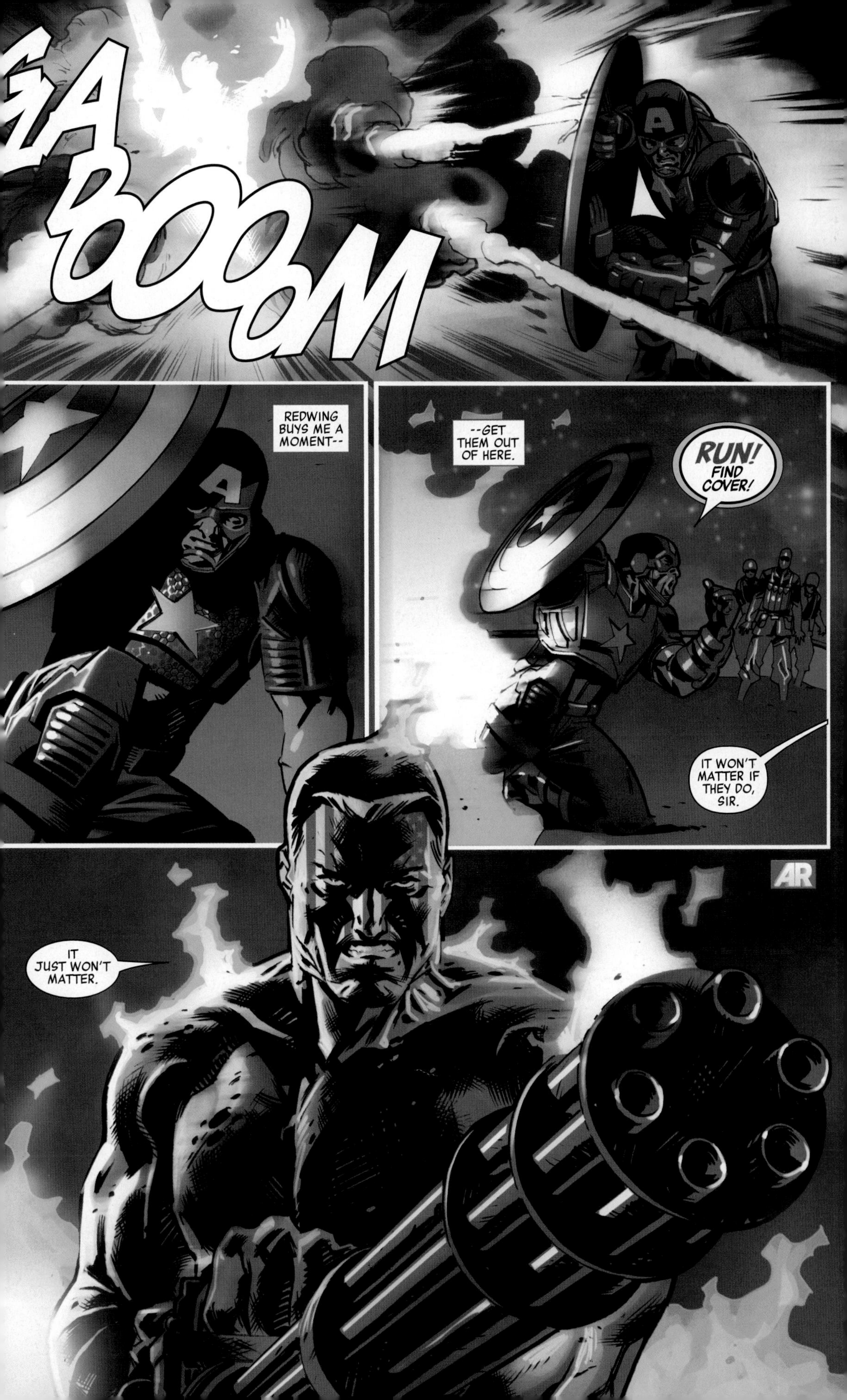

GA BOOOM
REDWING BUYS ME A MOMENT--
--GET THEM OUT OF HERE.
RUN! FIND COVER!
IT WON'T MATTER IF THEY DO, SIR.
IT JUST WON'T MATTER.

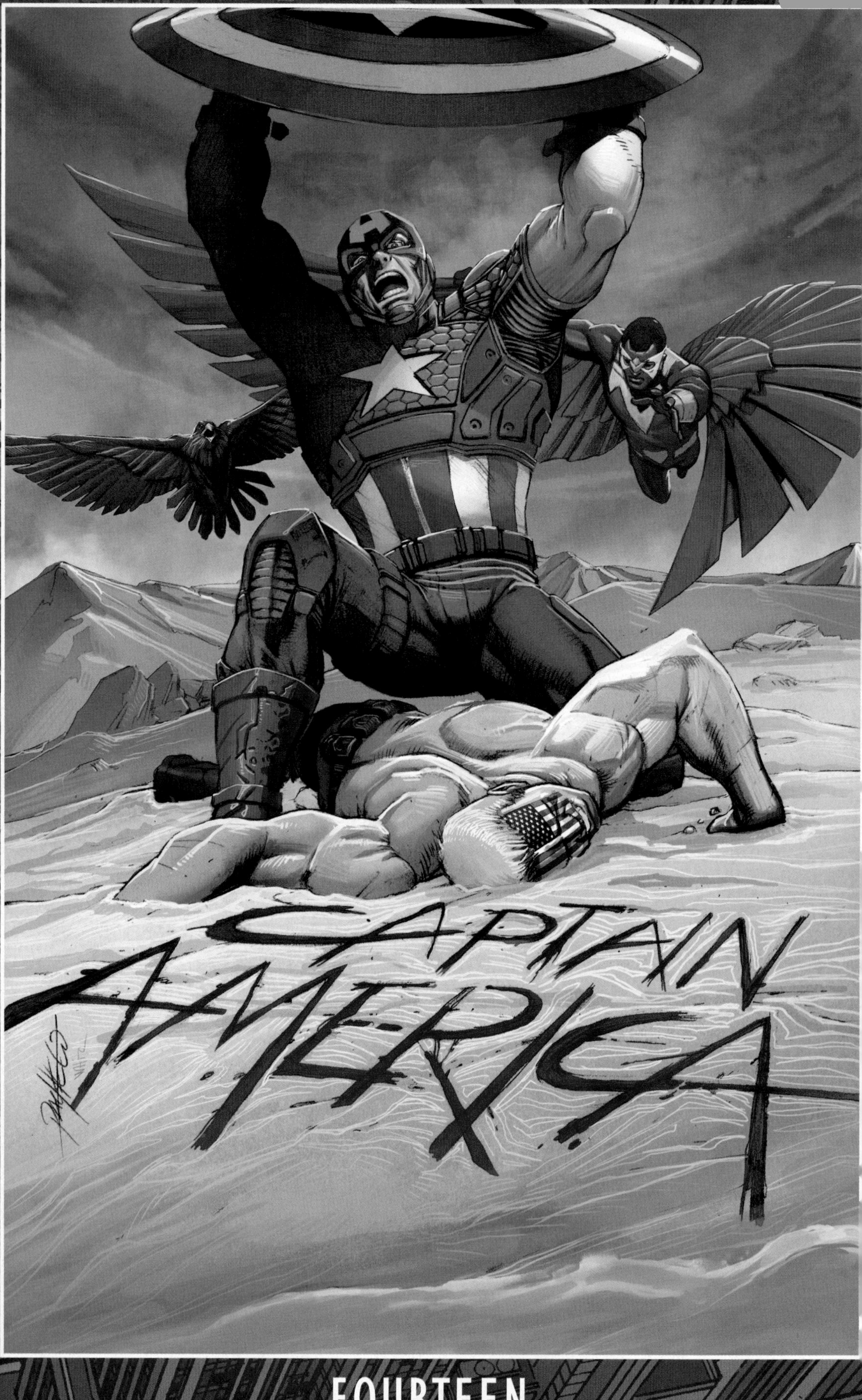
CAPTAIN AMERICA

FOURTEEN

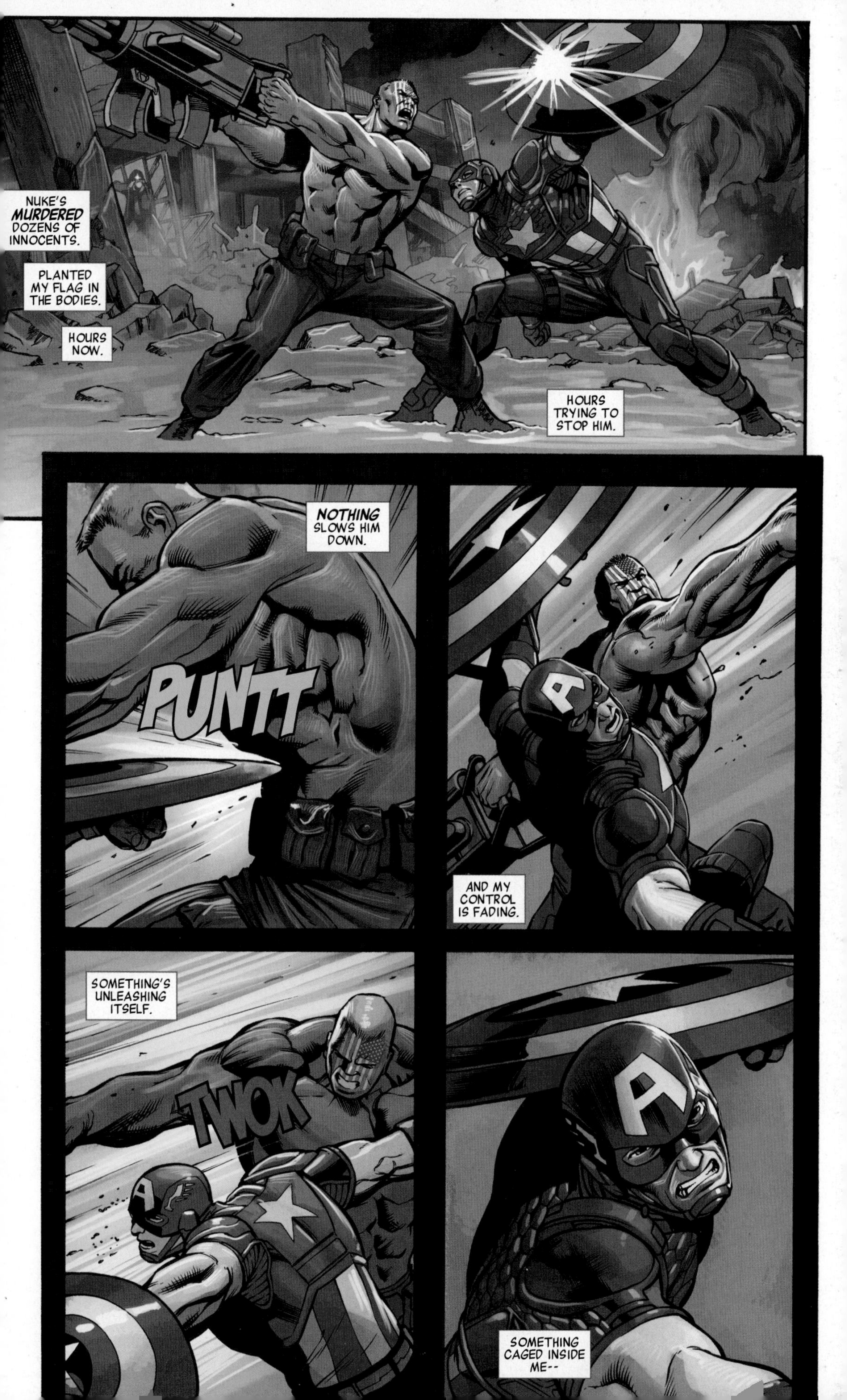
NUKE'S MURDERED DOZENS OF INNOCENTS.
PLANTED MY FLAG IN THE BODIES.
HOURS NOW.
HOURS TRYING TO STOP HIM.
NOTHING SLOWS HIM DOWN.
PUNTT
AND MY CONTROL IS FADING.
SOMETHING'S UNLEASHING ITSELF.
TWOK
SOMETHING CAGED INSIDE ME--

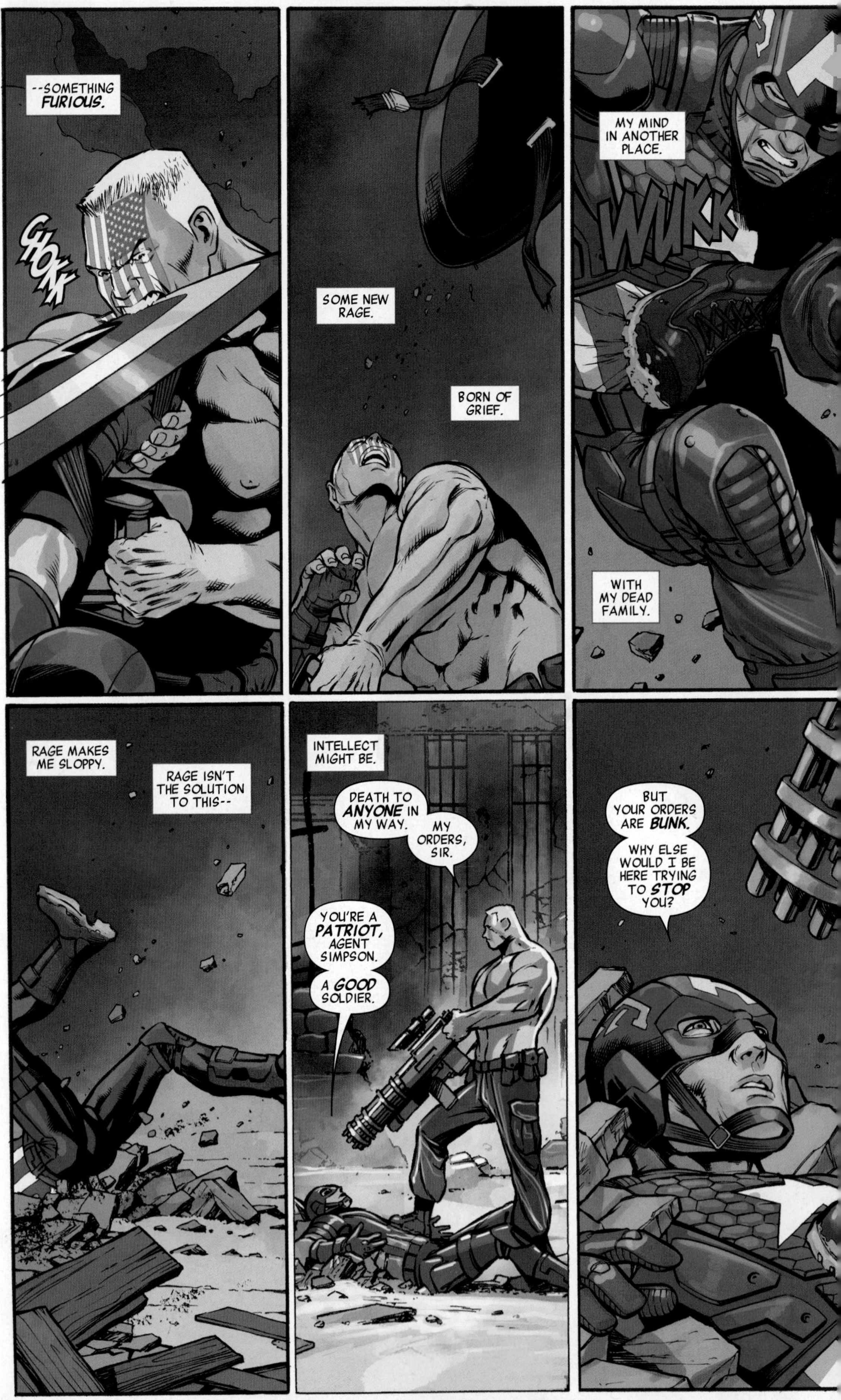
--SOMETHING FURIOUS.
CHOKK
SOME NEW RAGE.
BORN OF GRIEF.
MY MIND IN ANOTHER PLACE.
WUKK
WITH MY DEAD FAMILY.
RAGE MAKES ME SLOPPY.
RAGE ISN'T THE SOLUTION TO THIS--
INTELLECT MIGHT BE.
DEATH TO ANYONE IN MY WAY.
MY ORDERS, SIR.
YOU'RE A PATRIOT, AGENT SIMPSON.
A GOOD SOLDIER.
BUT YOUR ORDERS ARE BUNK.
WHY ELSE WOULD I BE HERE TRYING TO STOP YOU?

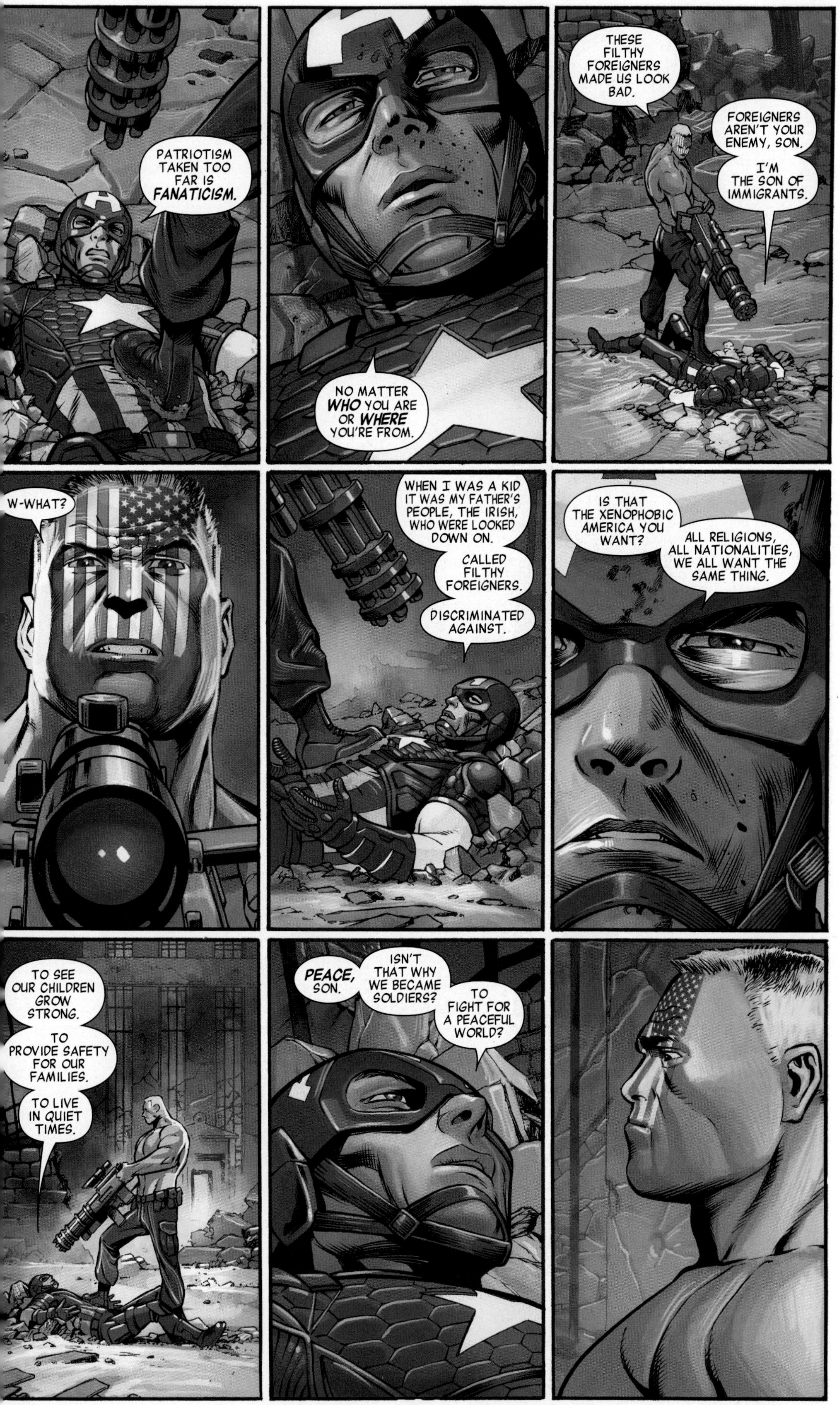
PATRIOTISM TAKEN TOO FAR IS FANATICISM.
NO MATTER WHO YOU ARE OR WHERE YOU'RE FROM.
THESE FILTHY FOREIGNERS MADE US LOOK BAD.
FOREIGNERS AREN'T YOUR ENEMY, SON.
I'M THE SON OF IMMIGRANTS.
W-WHAT?
WHEN I WAS A KID IT WAS MY FATHER'S PEOPLE, THE IRISH, WHO WERE LOOKED DOWN ON.
CALLED FILTHY FOREIGNERS.
DISCRIMINATED AGAINST.
IS THAT THE XENOPHOBIC AMERICA YOU WANT?
ALL RELIGIONS, ALL NATIONALITIES, WE ALL WANT THE SAME THING.
TO SEE OUR CHILDREN GROW STRONG.
TO PROVIDE SAFETY FOR OUR FAMILIES.
TO LIVE IN QUIET TIMES.
PEACE, SON.
ISN'T THAT WHY WE BECAME SOLDIERS?
TO FIGHT FOR A PEACEFUL WORLD?

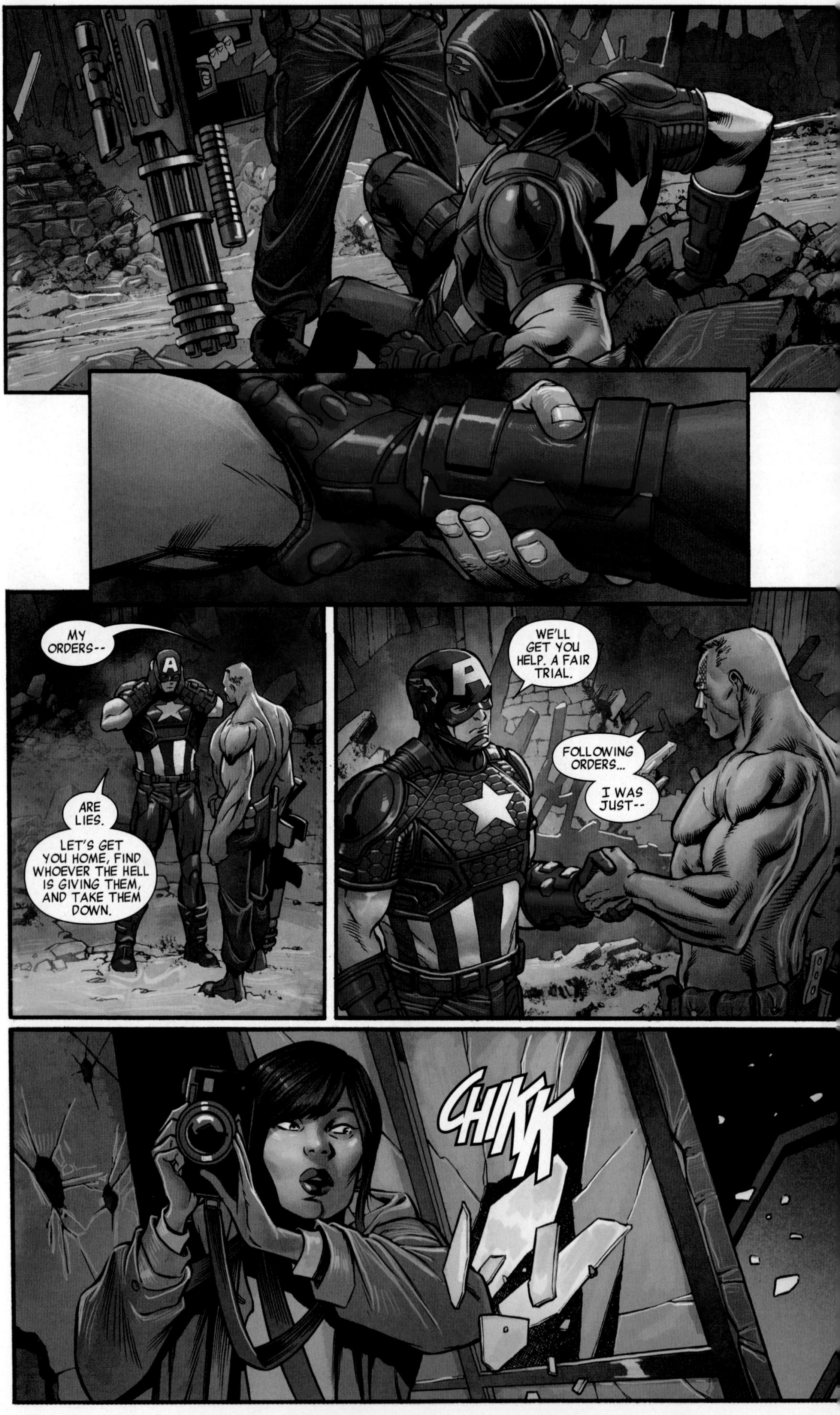
MY ORDERS--
ARE LIES.
LET'S GET YOU HOME, FIND WHOEVER THE HELL IS GIVING THEM, AND TAKE THEM DOWN.
WE'LL GET YOU HELP. A FAIR TRIAL.
FOLLOWING ORDERS...
I WAS JUST--
CHIKK

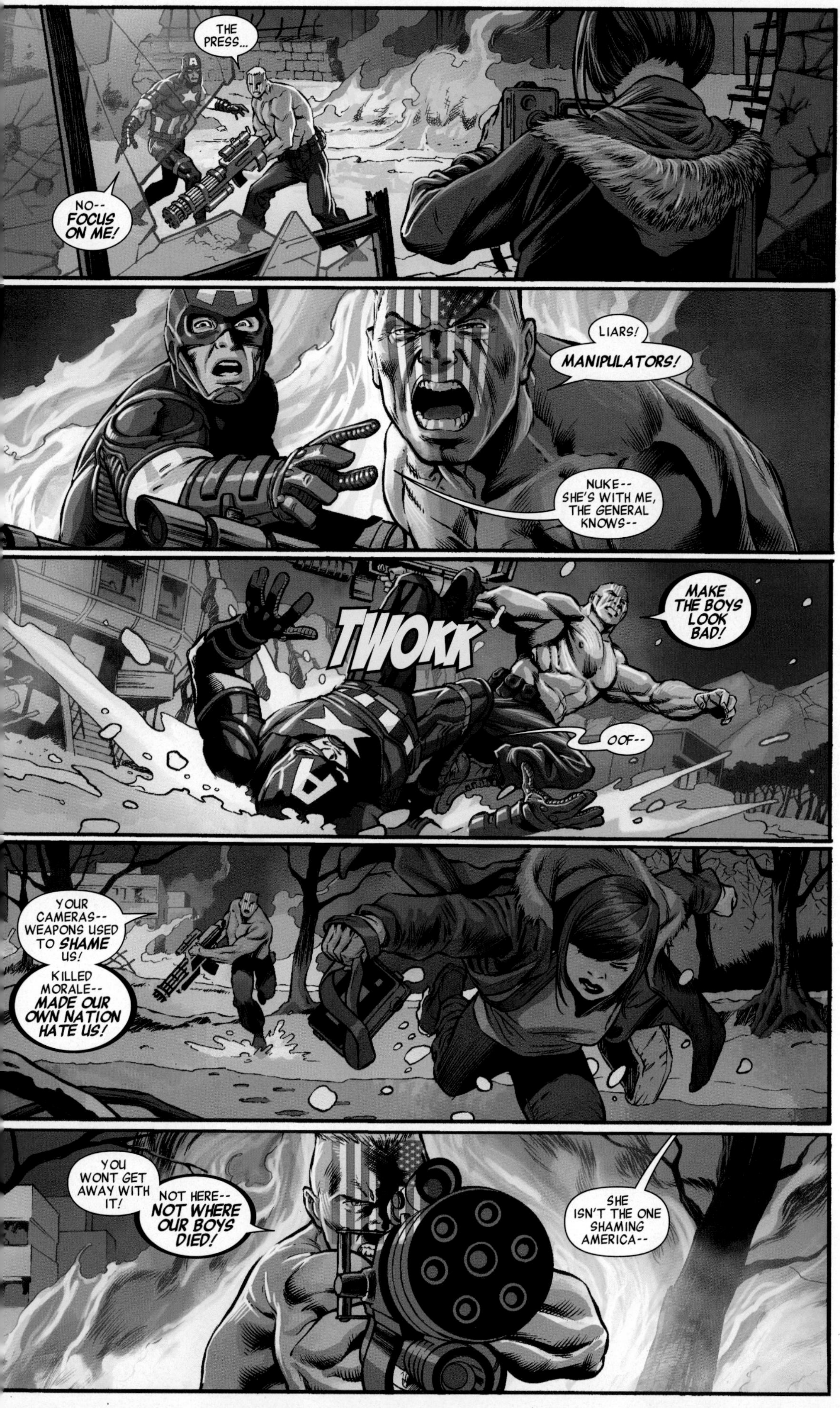
THE PRESS...
NO-- FOCUS ON ME!
LIARS!
MANIPULATORS!
NUKE-- SHE'S WITH ME, THE GENERAL KNOWS--
TWOKK
MAKE THE BOYS LOOK BAD!
OOF--
YOUR CAMERAS-- WEAPONS USED TO SHAME US!
KILLED MORALE-- MADE OUR OWN NATION HATE US!
YOU WONT GET AWAY WITH IT!
NOT HERE-- NOT WHERE OUR BOYS DIED!
SHE ISN'T THE ONE SHAMING AMERICA--

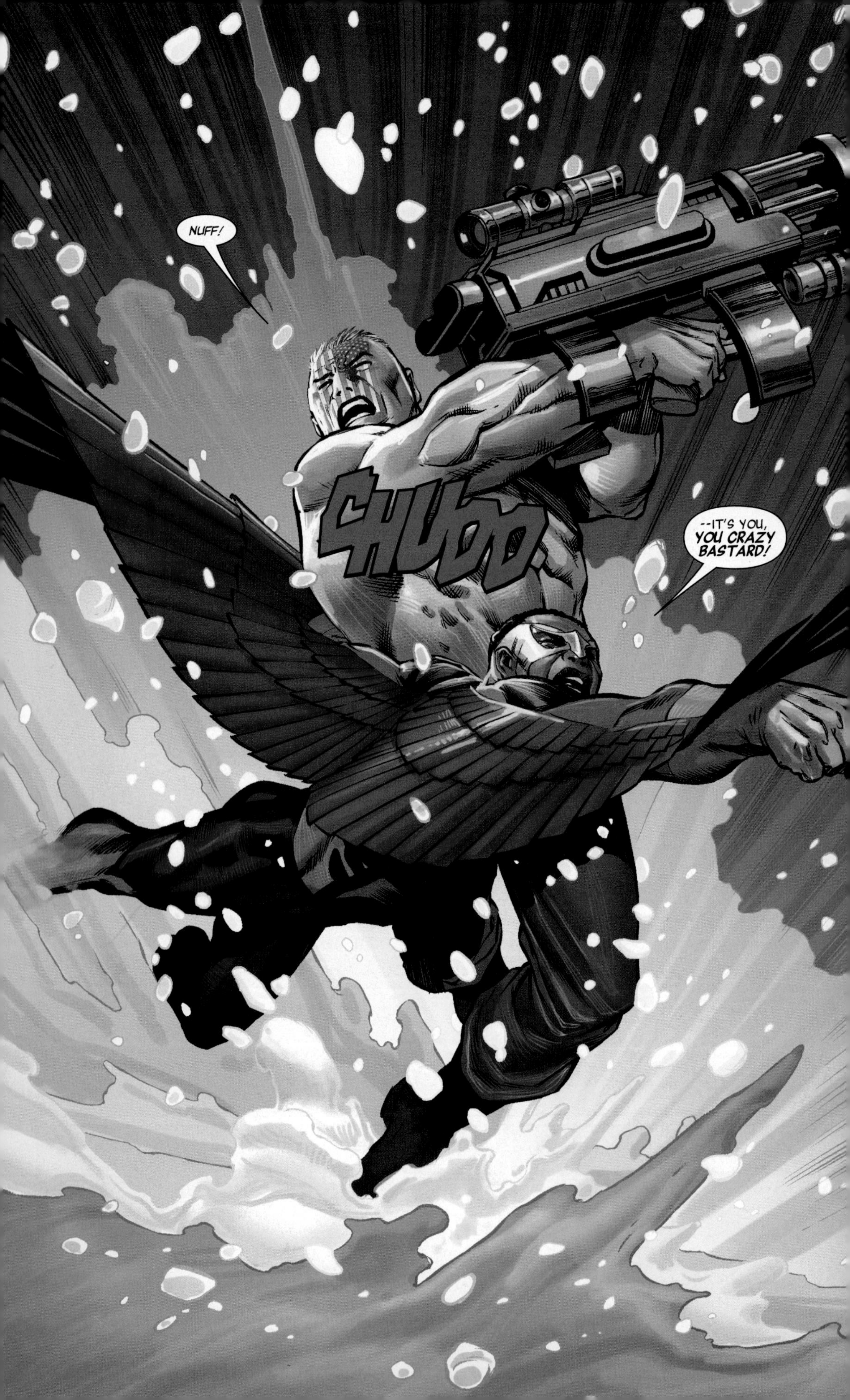
NUFF!
CHUDD
--IT'S YOU, YOU CRAZY BASTARD!

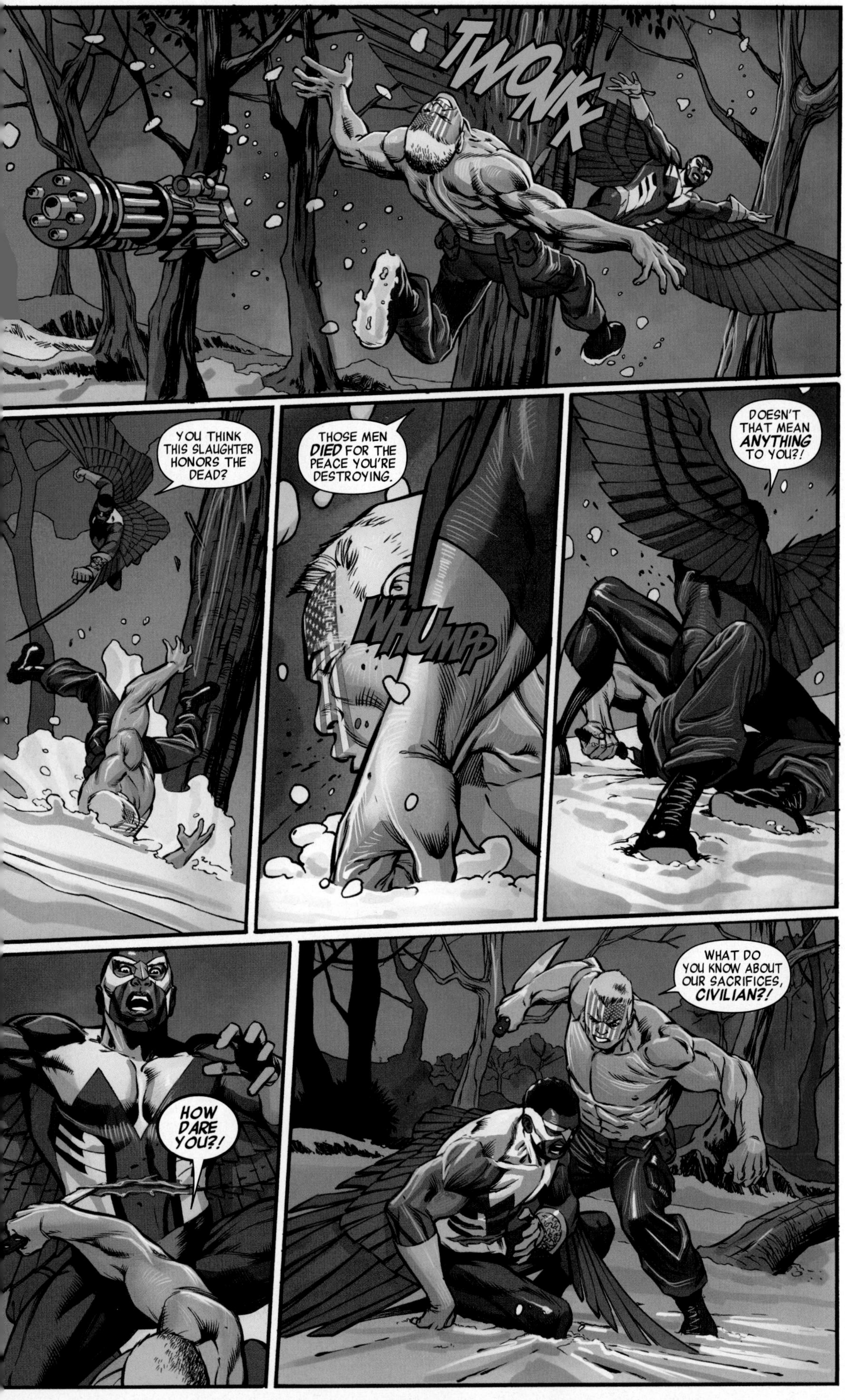
TWONK
YOU THINK THIS SLAUGHTER HONORS THE DEAD?
THOSE MEN **DIED** FOR THE PEACE YOU'RE DESTROYING.
WHUMPP
DOESN'T THAT MEAN **ANYTHING** TO YOU?!
HOW DARE YOU?!
WHAT DO YOU KNOW ABOUT OUR SACRIFICES, **CIVILIAN?!**

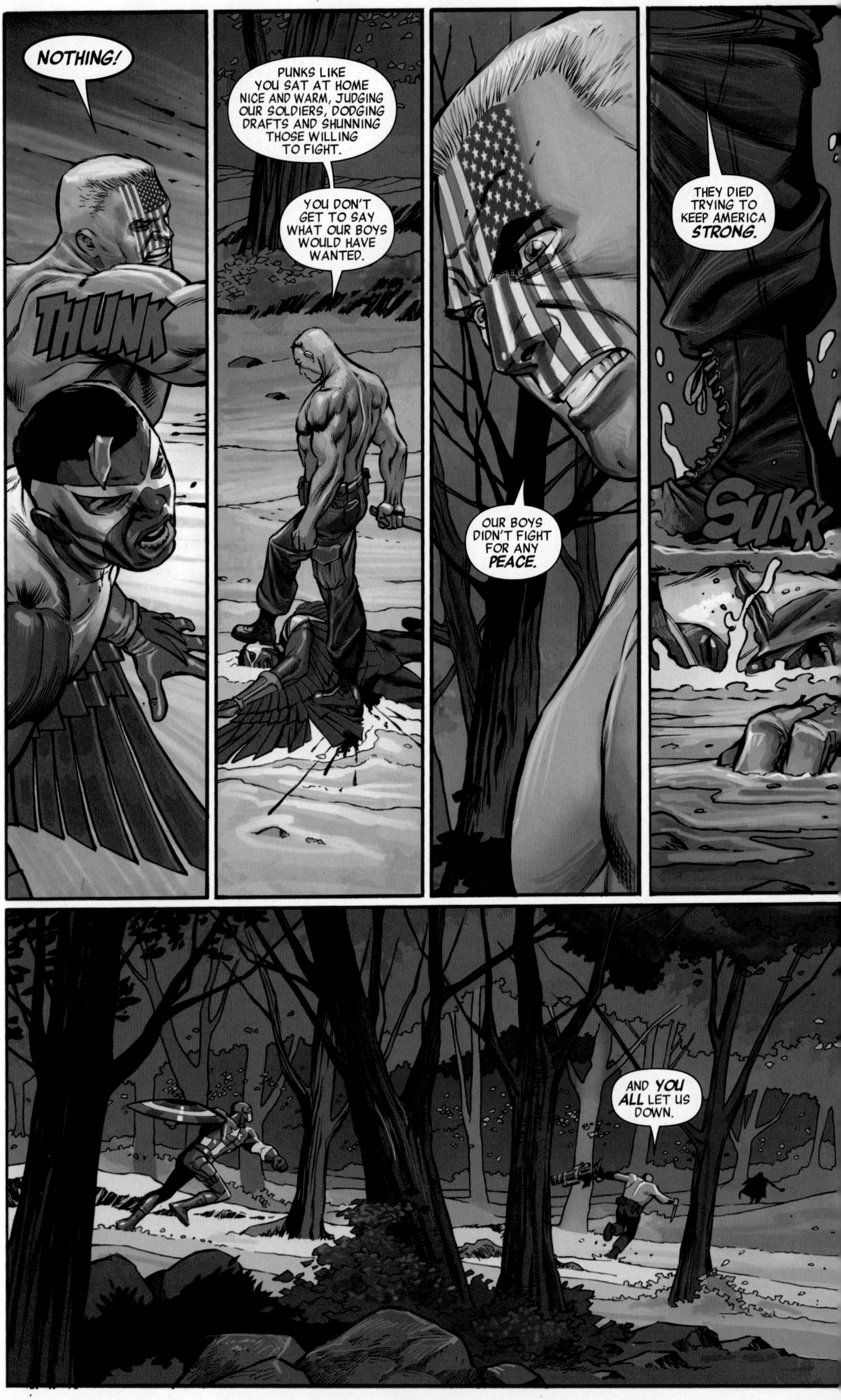
NOTHING!
THUNK
PUNKS LIKE YOU SAT AT HOME NICE AND WARM, JUDGING OUR SOLDIERS, DODGING DRAFTS AND SHUNNING THOSE WILLING TO FIGHT.
YOU DON'T GET TO SAY WHAT OUR BOYS WOULD HAVE WANTED.
OUR BOYS DIDN'T FIGHT FOR ANY PEACE.
THEY DIED TRYING TO KEEP AMERICA STRONG.
SUKK
AND YOU ALL LET US DOWN.

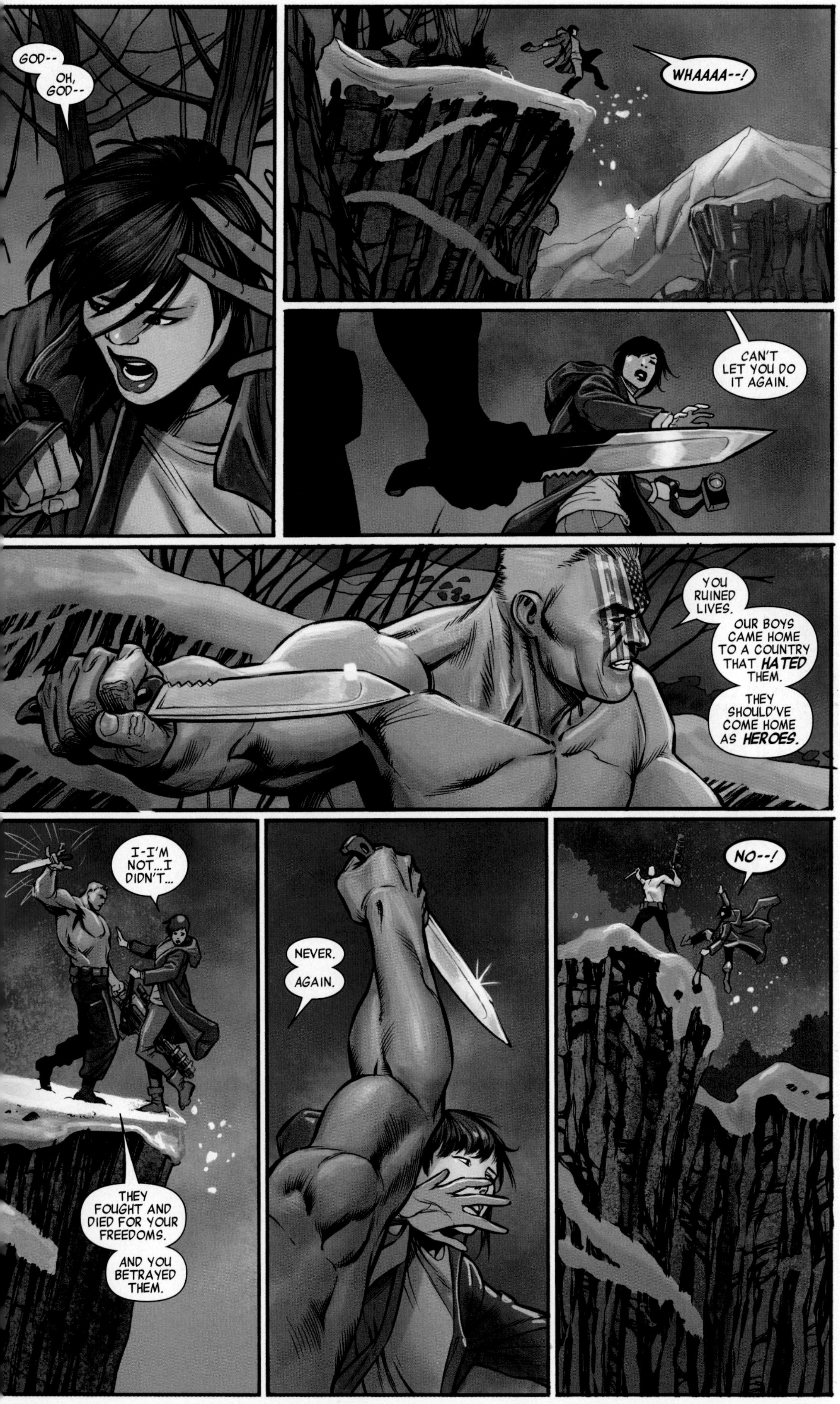
GOD--
OH, GOD--
WHAAAA--!
CAN'T LET YOU DO IT AGAIN.
YOU RUINED LIVES.
OUR BOYS CAME HOME TO A COUNTRY THAT HATED THEM.
THEY SHOULD'VE COME HOME AS HEROES.
I-I'M NOT...I DIDN'T...
THEY FOUGHT AND DIED FOR YOUR FREEDOMS.
AND YOU BETRAYED THEM.
NEVER.
AGAIN.
NO--!

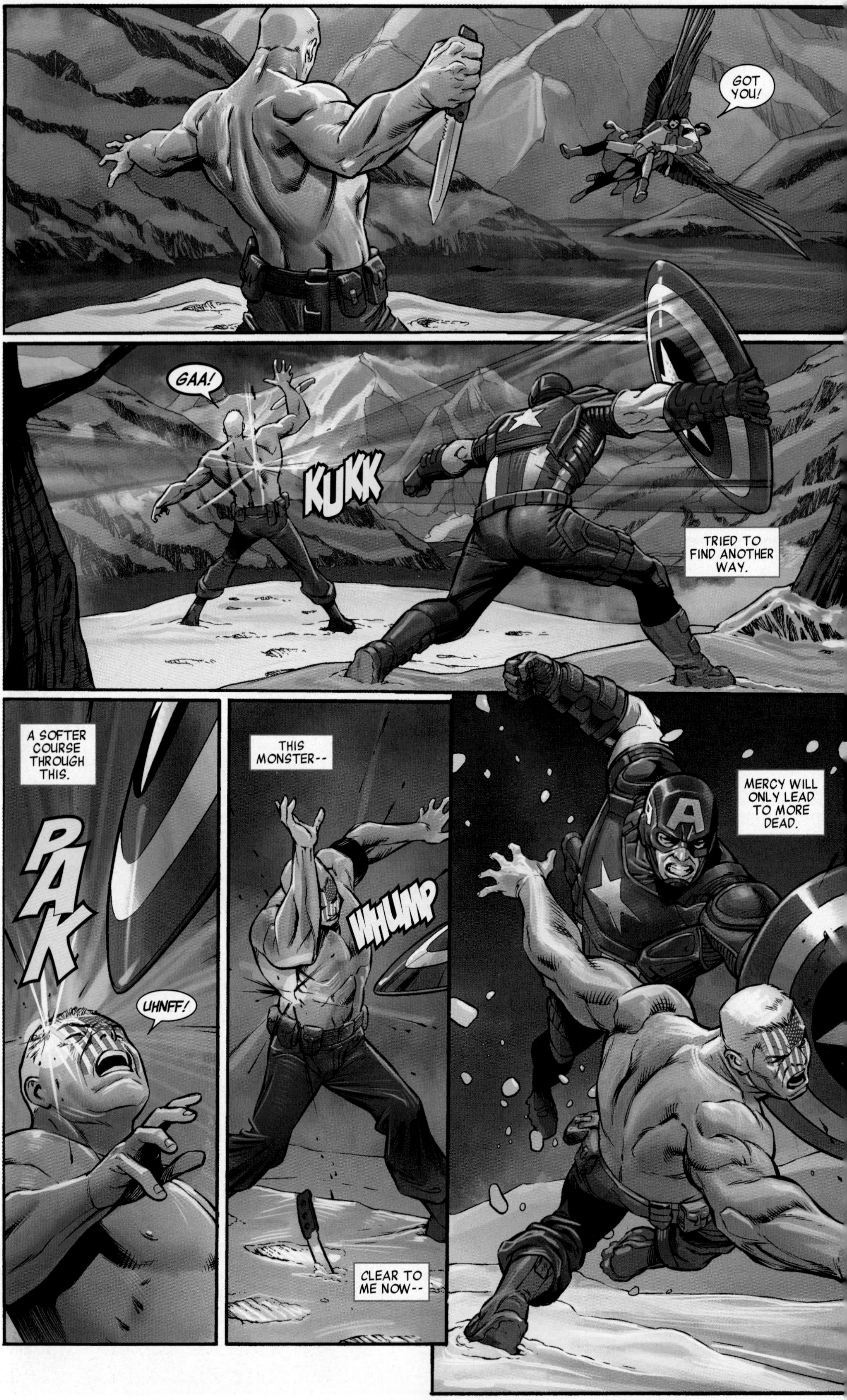
GOT YOU!
GAA!
KUKK
TRIED TO FIND ANOTHER WAY.
A SOFTER COURSE THROUGH THIS.
PAK
UHNFF!
THIS MONSTER--
WHUMP
CLEAR TO ME NOW--
MERCY WILL ONLY LEAD TO MORE DEAD.

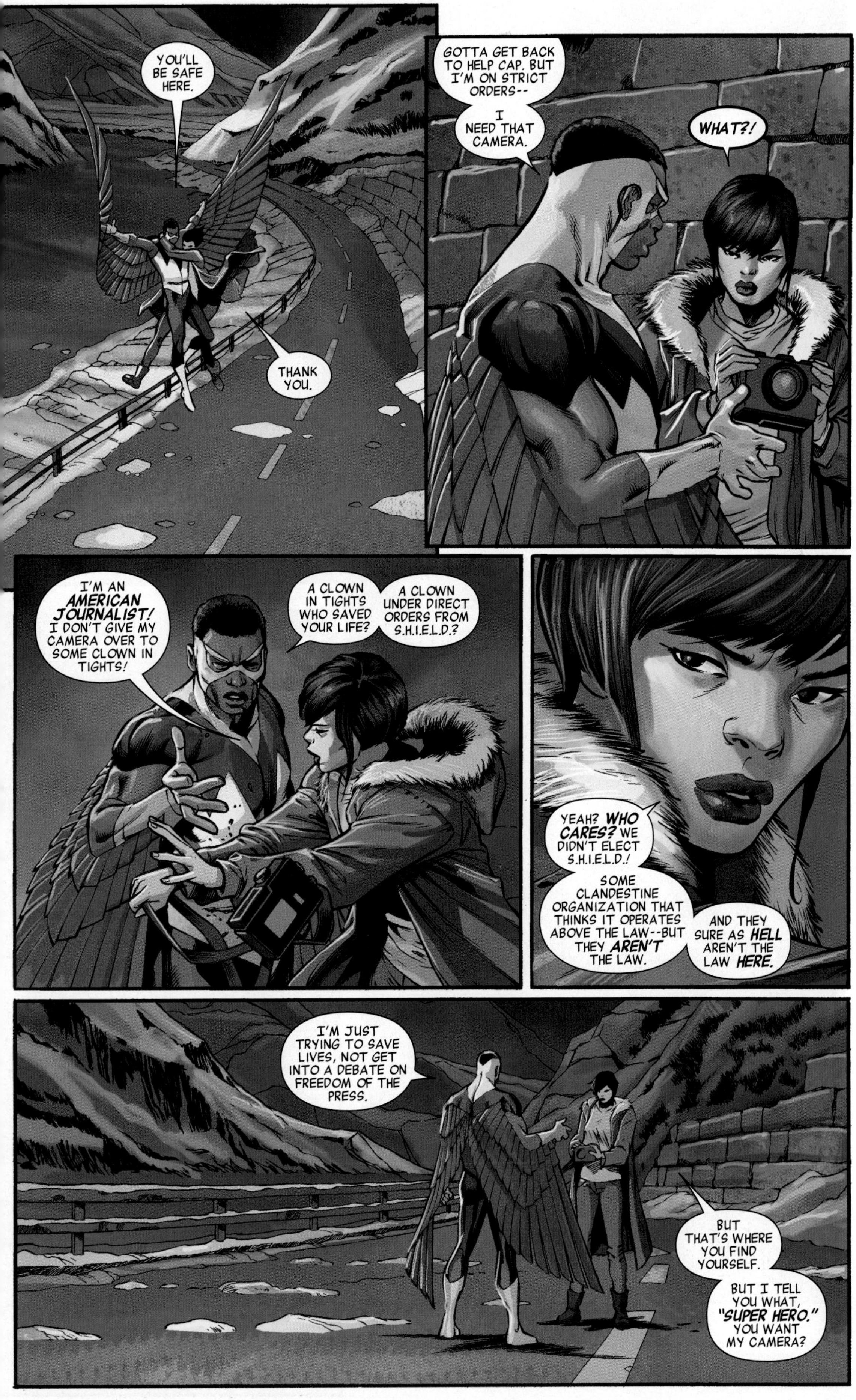

YOU'LL BE SAFE HERE.
THANK YOU.
GOTTA GET BACK TO HELP CAP. BUT I'M ON STRICT ORDERS--
I NEED THAT CAMERA.
WHAT?!
I'M AN AMERICAN JOURNALIST! I DON'T GIVE MY CAMERA OVER TO SOME CLOWN IN TIGHTS!
A CLOWN IN TIGHTS WHO SAVED YOUR LIFE?
A CLOWN UNDER DIRECT ORDERS FROM S.H.I.E.L.D.?
YEAH? WHO CARES? WE DIDN'T ELECT S.H.I.E.L.D.!
SOME CLANDESTINE ORGANIZATION THAT THINKS IT OPERATES ABOVE THE LAW--BUT THEY AREN'T THE LAW.
AND THEY SURE AS HELL AREN'T THE LAW HERE.
I'M JUST TRYING TO SAVE LIVES, NOT GET INTO A DEBATE ON FREEDOM OF THE PRESS.
BUT THAT'S WHERE YOU FIND YOURSELF.
BUT I TELL YOU WHAT, "SUPER HERO." YOU WANT MY CAMERA?

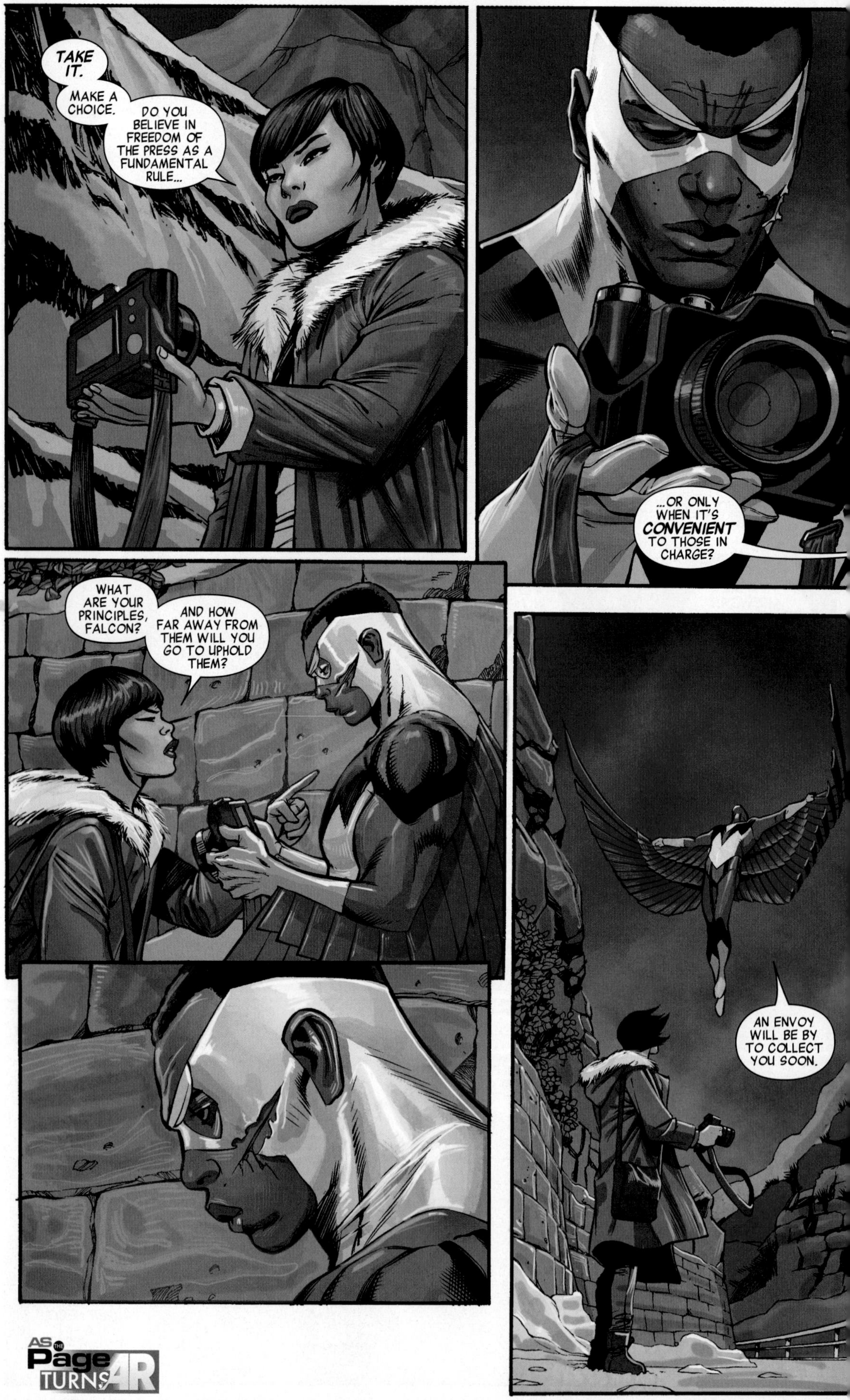
TAKE IT.
MAKE A CHOICE.
DO YOU BELIEVE IN FREEDOM OF THE PRESS AS A FUNDAMENTAL RULE...
...OR ONLY WHEN IT'S CONVENIENT TO THOSE IN CHARGE?
WHAT ARE YOUR PRINCIPLES, FALCON?
AND HOW FAR AWAY FROM THEM WILL YOU GO TO UPHOLD THEM?
AN ENVOY WILL BE BY TO COLLECT YOU SOON.

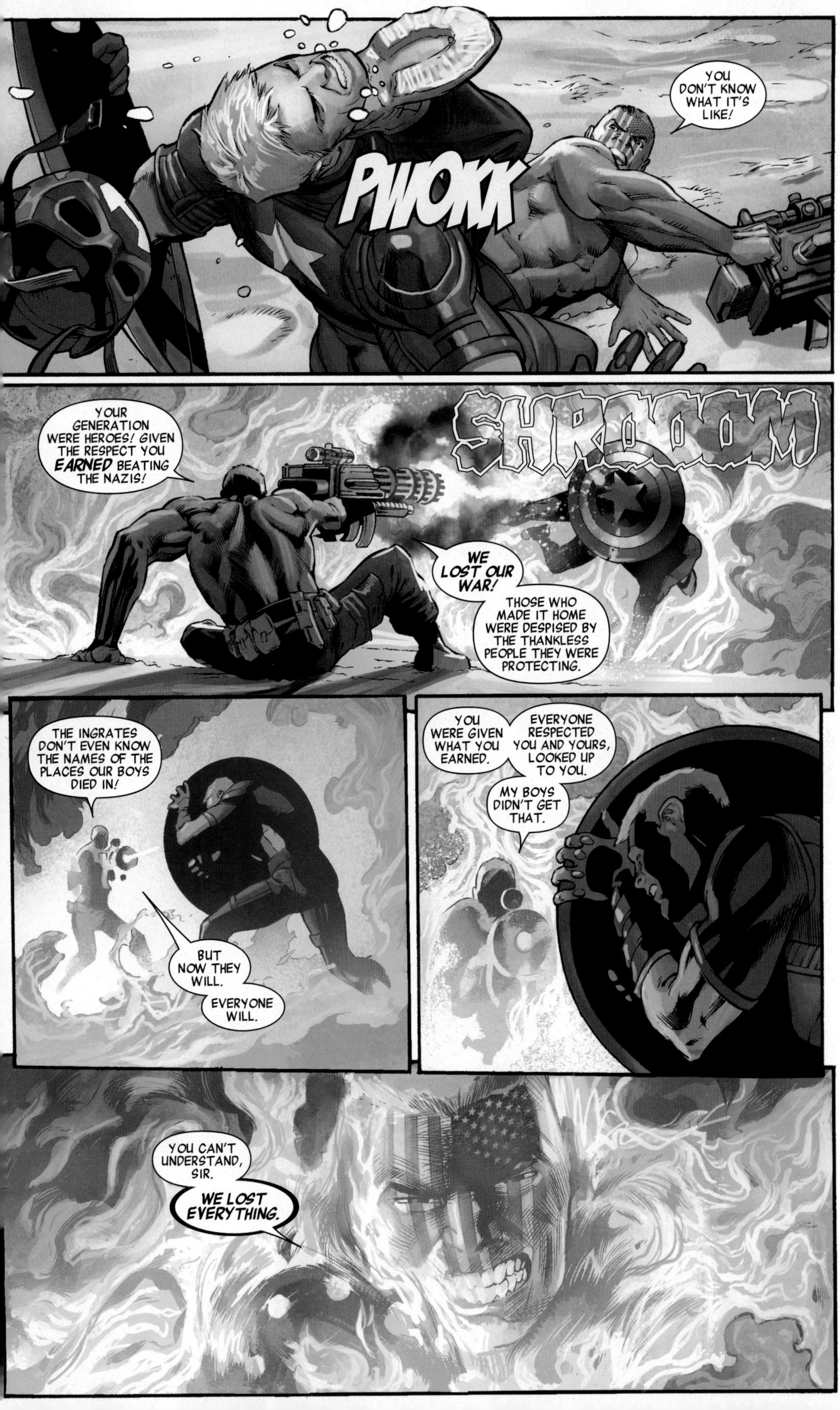
PWOKK
YOU DON'T KNOW WHAT IT'S LIKE!
SHROOOM
YOUR GENERATION WERE HEROES! GIVEN THE RESPECT YOU EARNED BEATING THE NAZIS!
WE LOST OUR WAR!
THOSE WHO MADE IT HOME WERE DESPISED BY THE THANKLESS PEOPLE THEY WERE PROTECTING.
THE INGRATES DON'T EVEN KNOW THE NAMES OF THE PLACES OUR BOYS DIED IN!
BUT NOW THEY WILL.
EVERYONE WILL.
YOU WERE GIVEN WHAT YOU EARNED.
EVERYONE RESPECTED YOU AND YOURS, LOOKED UP TO YOU.
MY BOYS DIDN'T GET THAT.
YOU CAN'T UNDERSTAND, SIR.
WE LOST EVERYTHING.

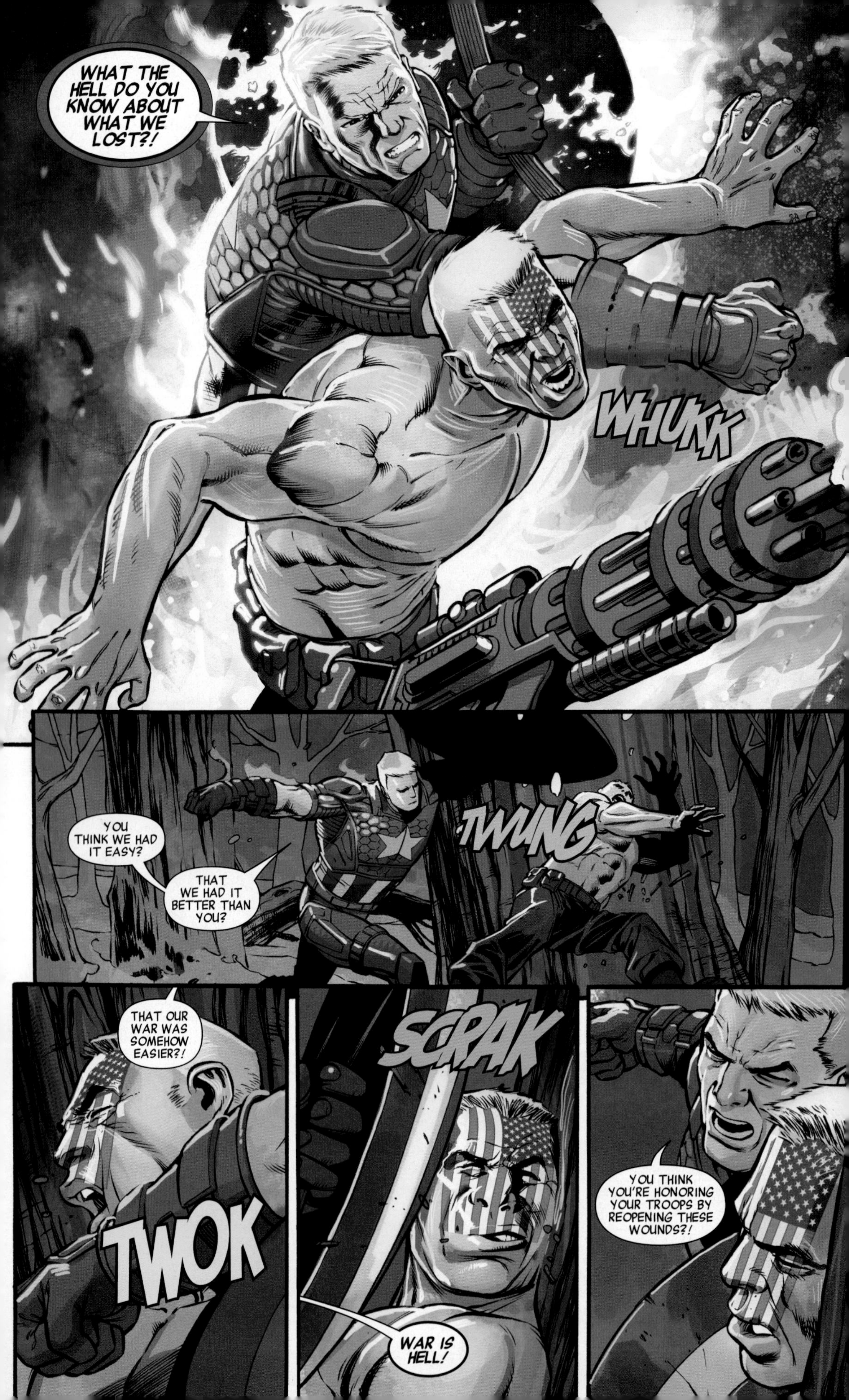
WHAT THE HELL DO YOU KNOW ABOUT WHAT WE LOST?!
WHUKK
YOU THINK WE HAD IT EASY?
THAT WE HAD IT BETTER THAN YOU?
TWUNG
THAT OUR WAR WAS SOMEHOW EASIER?!
TWOK
SCRAK
WAR IS HELL!
YOU THINK YOU'RE HONORING YOUR TROOPS BY REOPENING THESE WOUNDS?!

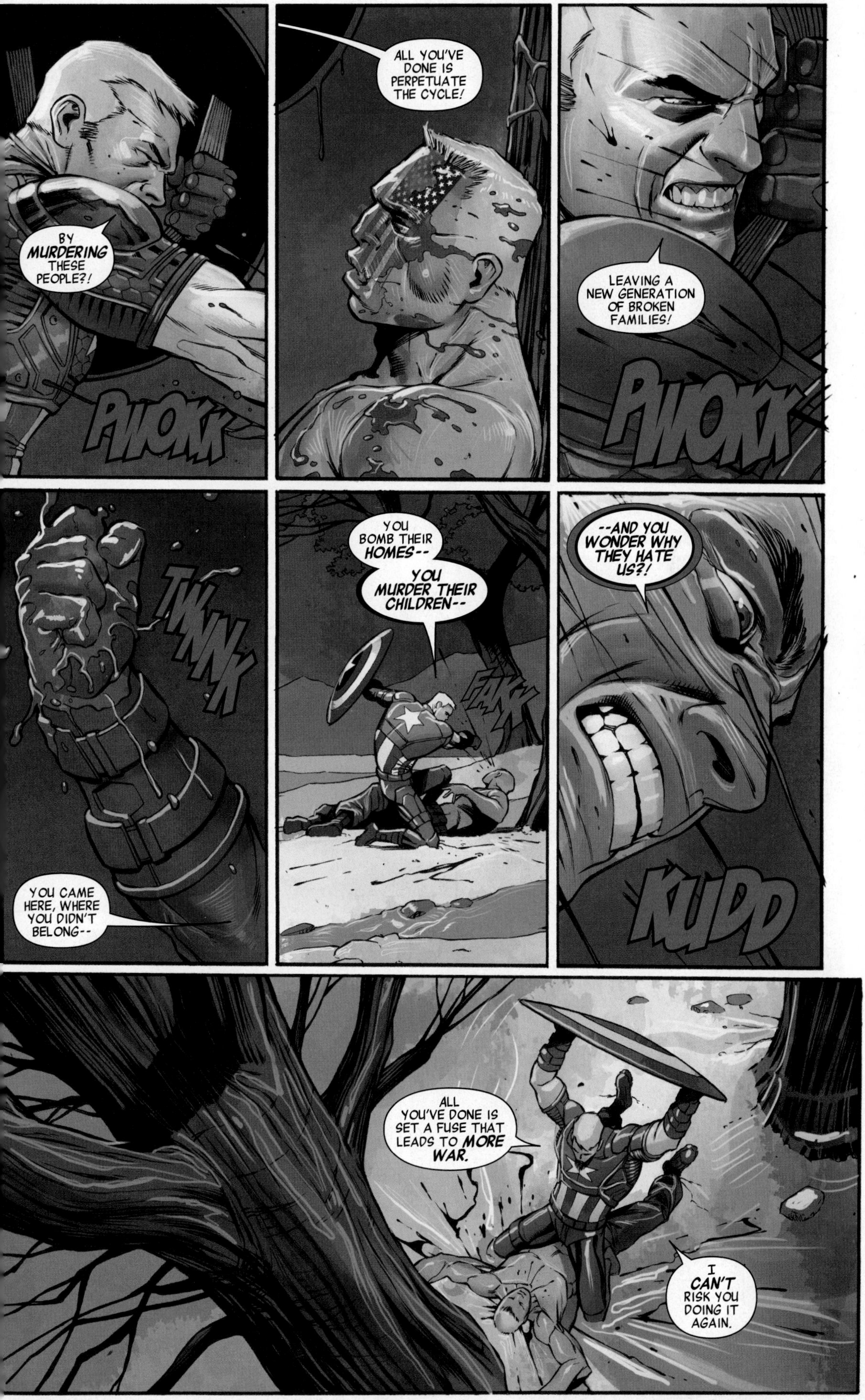

BY MURDERING THESE PEOPLE?!
PWOKK
ALL YOU'VE DONE IS PERPETUATE THE CYCLE!
LEAVING A NEW GENERATION OF BROKEN FAMILIES!
PWOKK
TWNNK
YOU CAME HERE, WHERE YOU DIDN'T BELONG--
YOU BOMB THEIR HOMES--
YOU MURDER THEIR CHILDREN--
FAKK
--AND YOU WONDER WHY THEY HATE US?!
KUDD
ALL YOU'VE DONE IS SET A FUSE THAT LEADS TO MORE WAR.
I CAN'T RISK YOU DOING IT AGAIN.

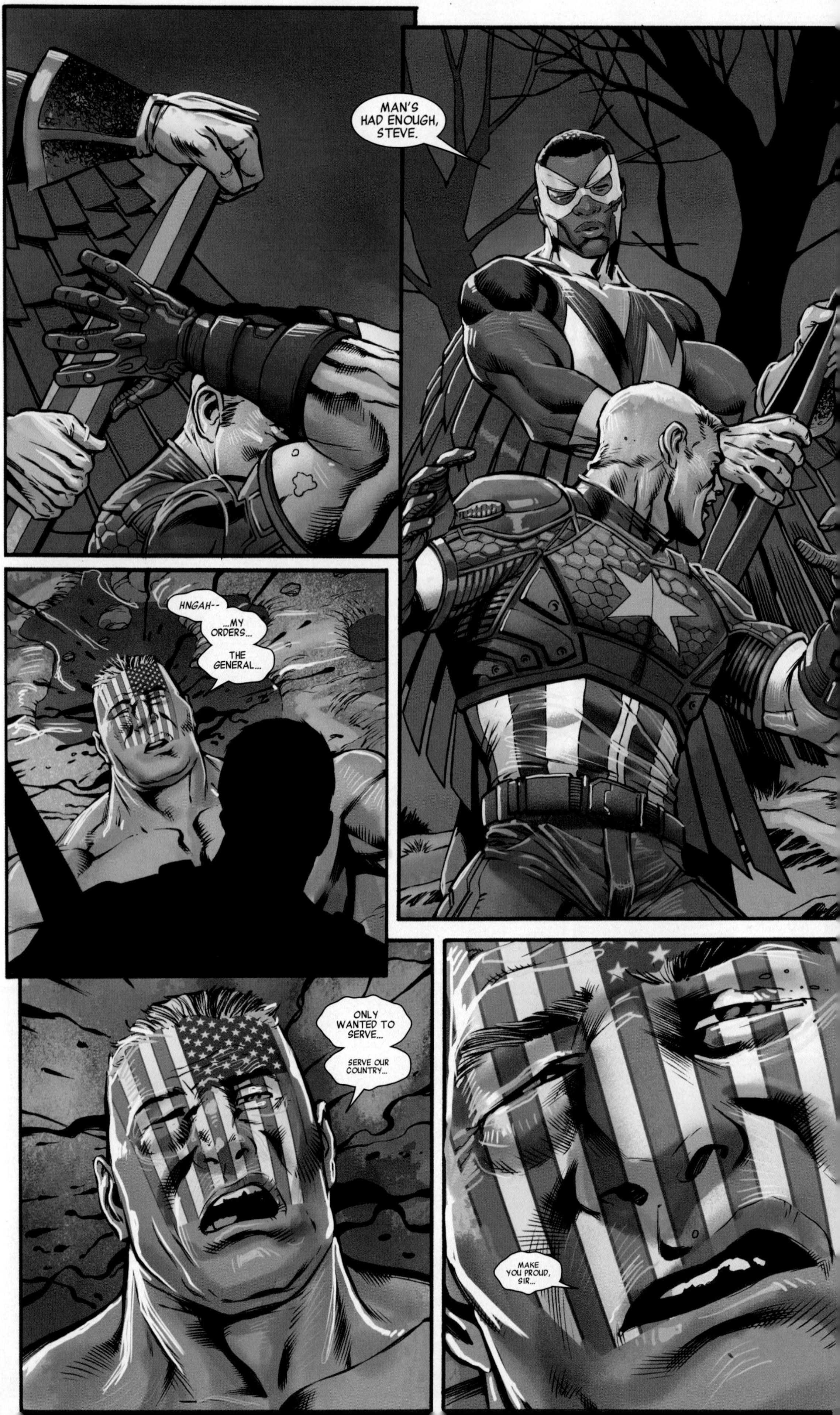
MAN'S HAD ENOUGH, STEVE.
HNGAH--
...MY ORDERS...
THE GENERAL...
ONLY WANTED TO SERVE...
SERVE OUR COUNTRY...
MAKE YOU PROUD, SIR...

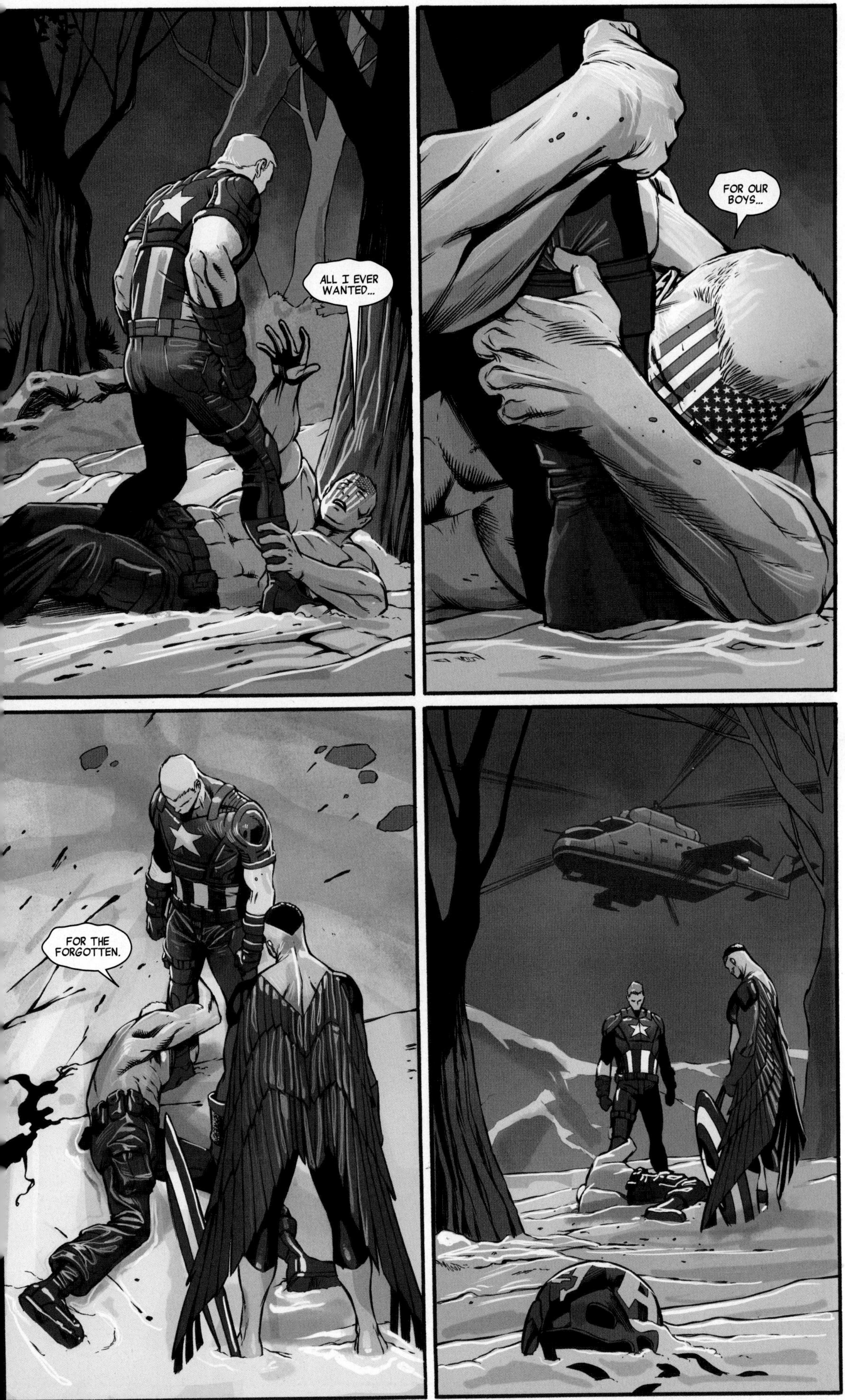
ALL I EVER WANTED...
FOR OUR BOYS...
FOR THE FORGOTTEN.

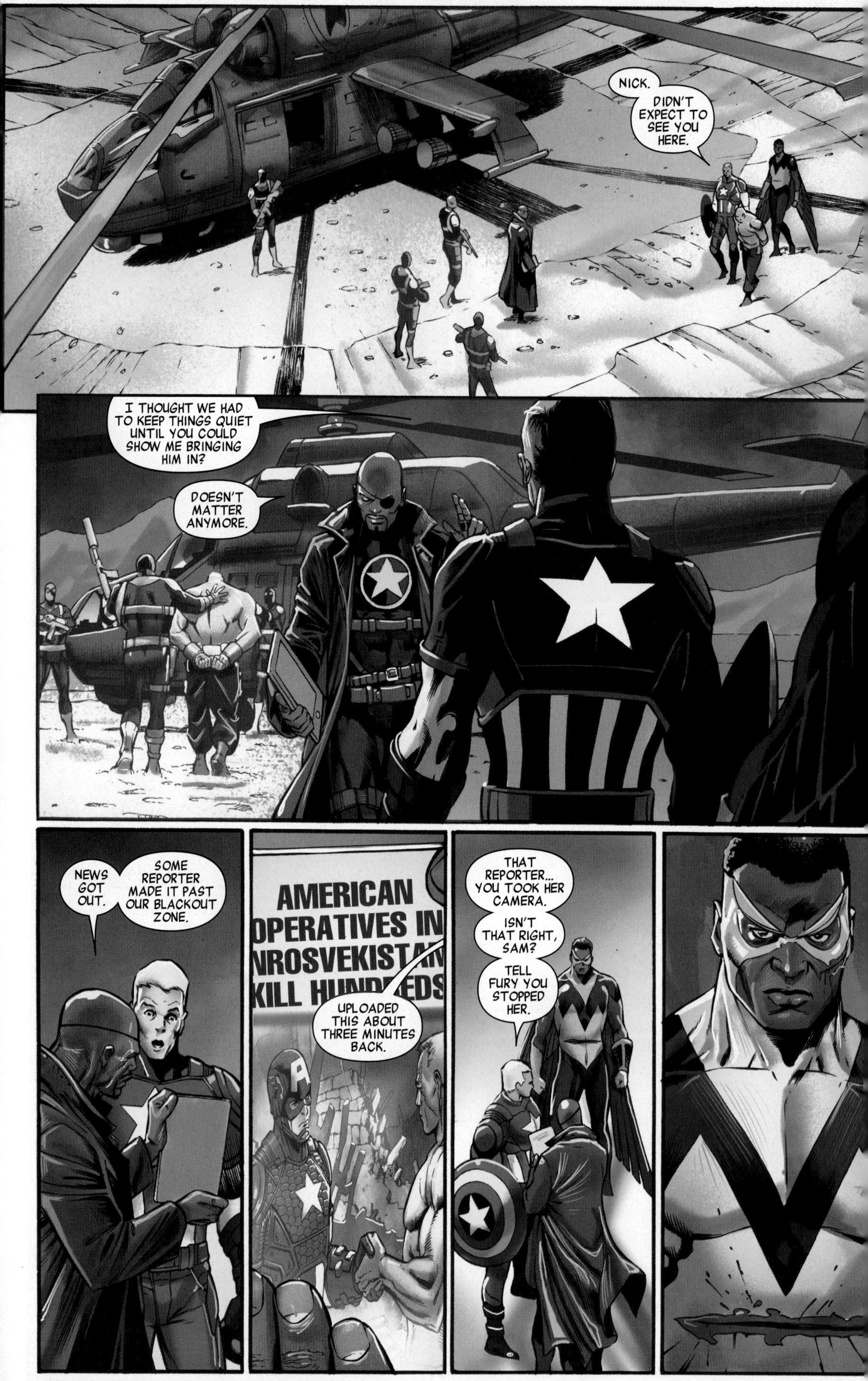
NICK.
DIDN'T EXPECT TO SEE YOU HERE.
I THOUGHT WE HAD TO KEEP THINGS QUIET UNTIL YOU COULD SHOW ME BRINGING HIM IN?
DOESN'T MATTER ANYMORE.
NEWS GOT OUT.
SOME REPORTER MADE IT PAST OUR BLACKOUT ZONE.
AMERICAN OPERATIVES IN NROSVEKISTAN KILL HUNDREDS
UPLOADED THIS ABOUT THREE MINUTES BACK.
THAT REPORTER... YOU TOOK HER CAMERA.
ISN'T THAT RIGHT, SAM?
TELL FURY YOU STOPPED HER.

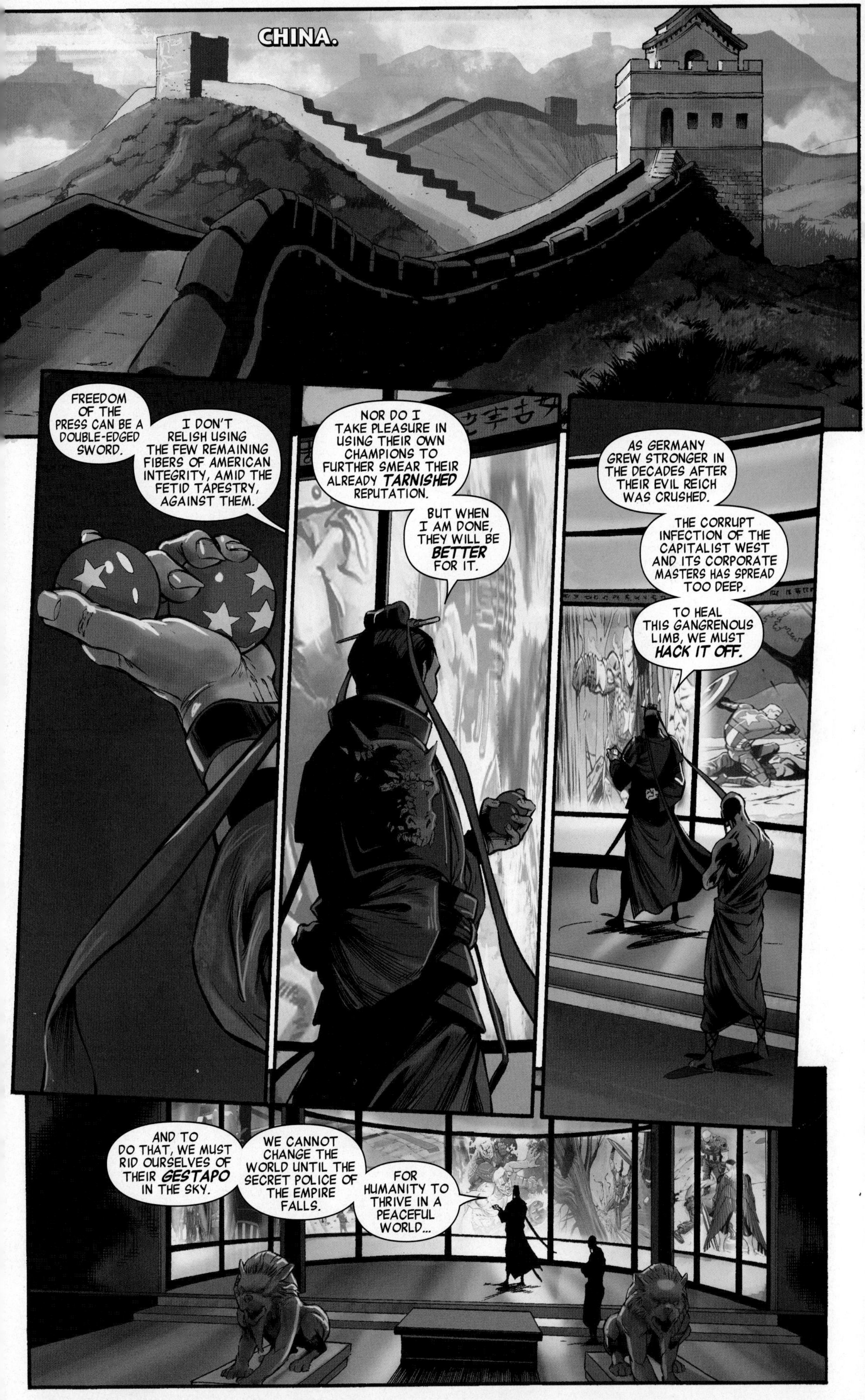
CHINA.
FREEDOM OF THE PRESS CAN BE A DOUBLE-EDGED SWORD.
I DON'T RELISH USING THE FEW REMAINING FIBERS OF AMERICAN INTEGRITY, AMID THE FETID TAPESTRY, AGAINST THEM.
NOR DO I TAKE PLEASURE IN USING THEIR OWN CHAMPIONS TO FURTHER SMEAR THEIR ALREADY TARNISHED REPUTATION.
BUT WHEN I AM DONE, THEY WILL BE BETTER FOR IT.
AS GERMANY GREW STRONGER IN THE DECADES AFTER THEIR EVIL REICH WAS CRUSHED.
THE CORRUPT INFECTION OF THE CAPITALIST WEST AND ITS CORPORATE MASTERS HAS SPREAD TOO DEEP.
TO HEAL THIS GANGRENOUS LIMB, WE MUST HACK IT OFF.
AND TO DO THAT, WE MUST RID OURSELVES OF THEIR GESTAPO IN THE SKY.
WE CANNOT CHANGE THE WORLD UNTIL THE SECRET POLICE OF THE EMPIRE FALLS.
FOR HUMANITY TO THRIVE IN A PEACEFUL WORLD...

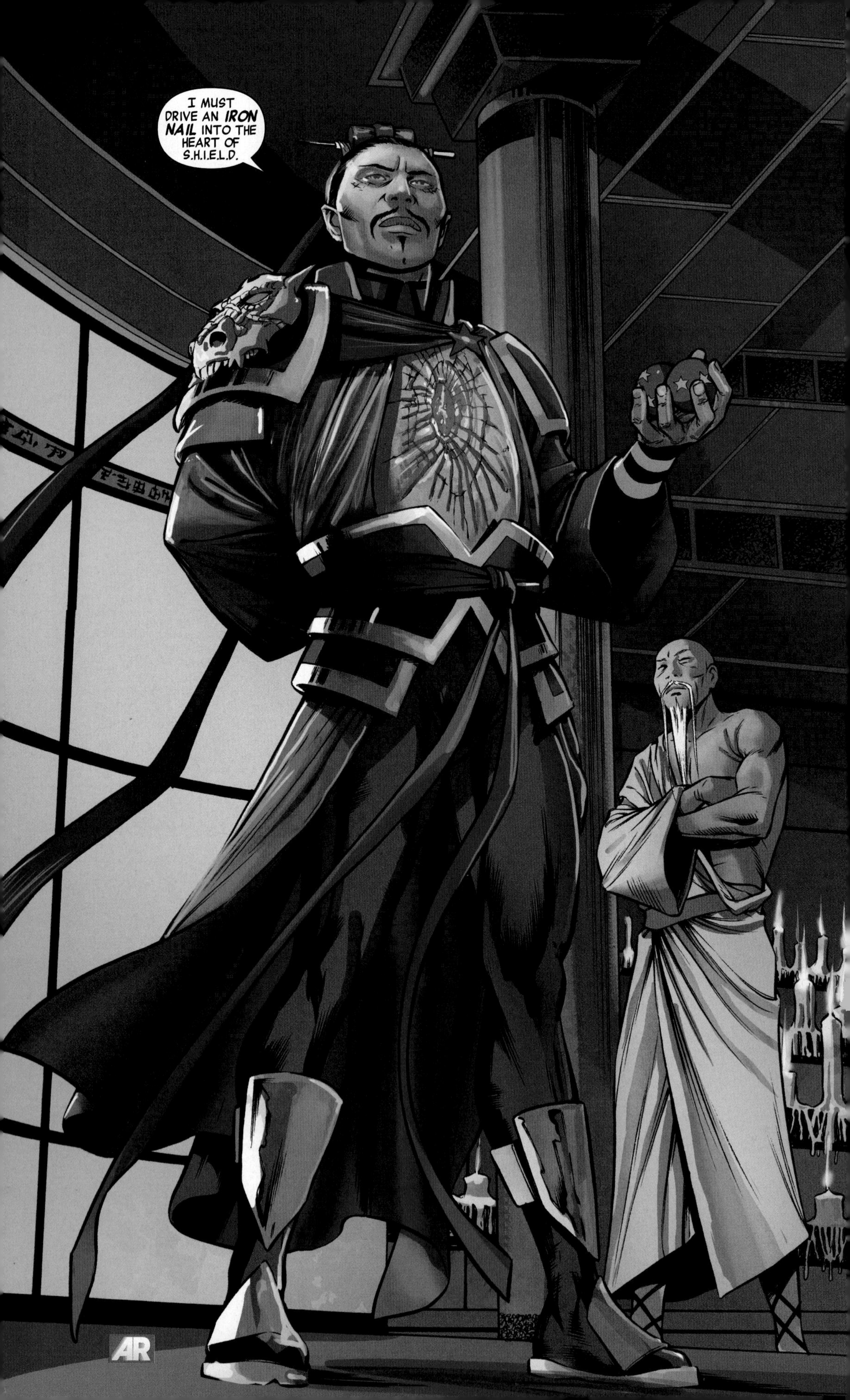
I MUST DRIVE AN IRON NAIL INTO THE HEART OF S.H.I.E.L.D.

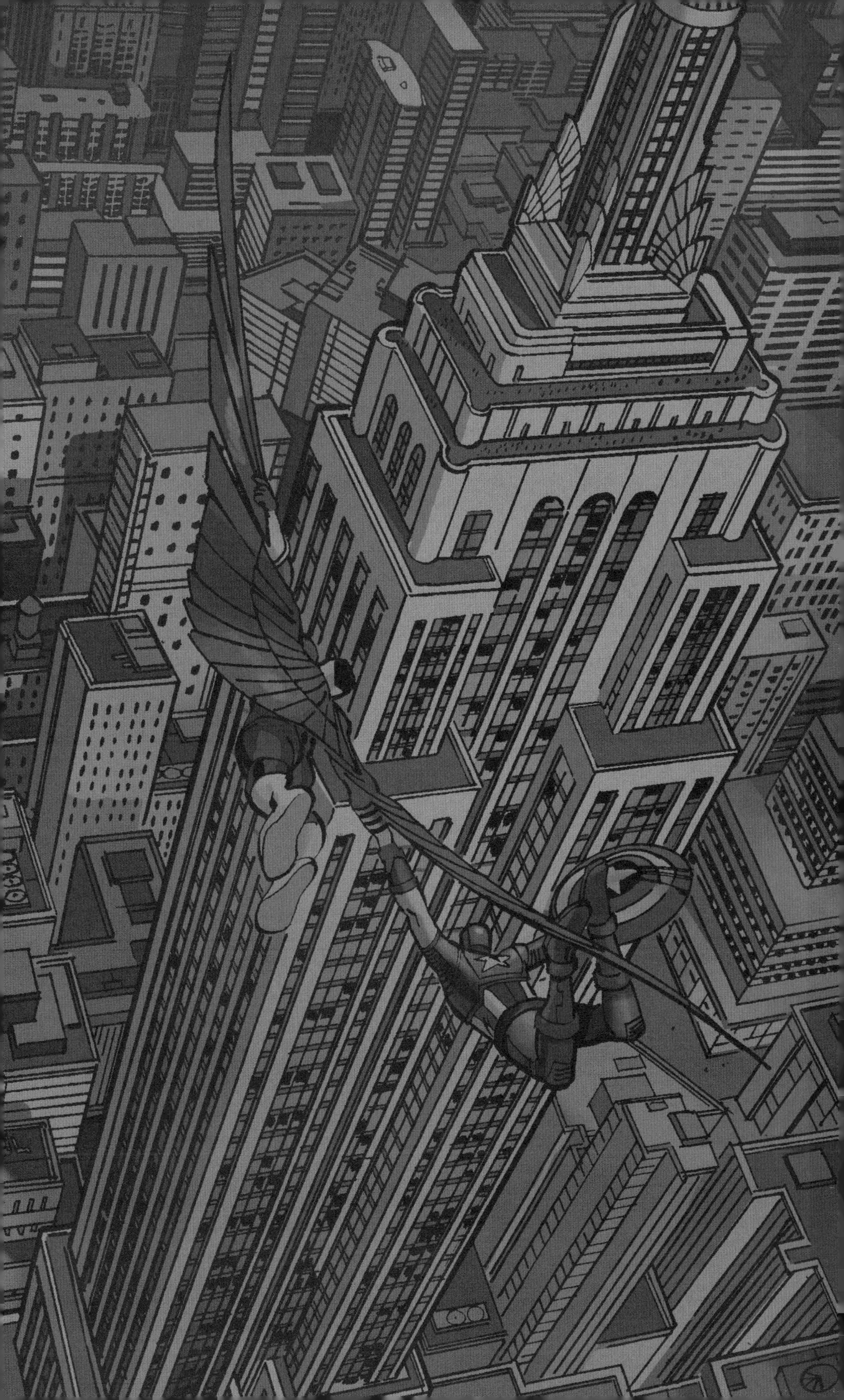

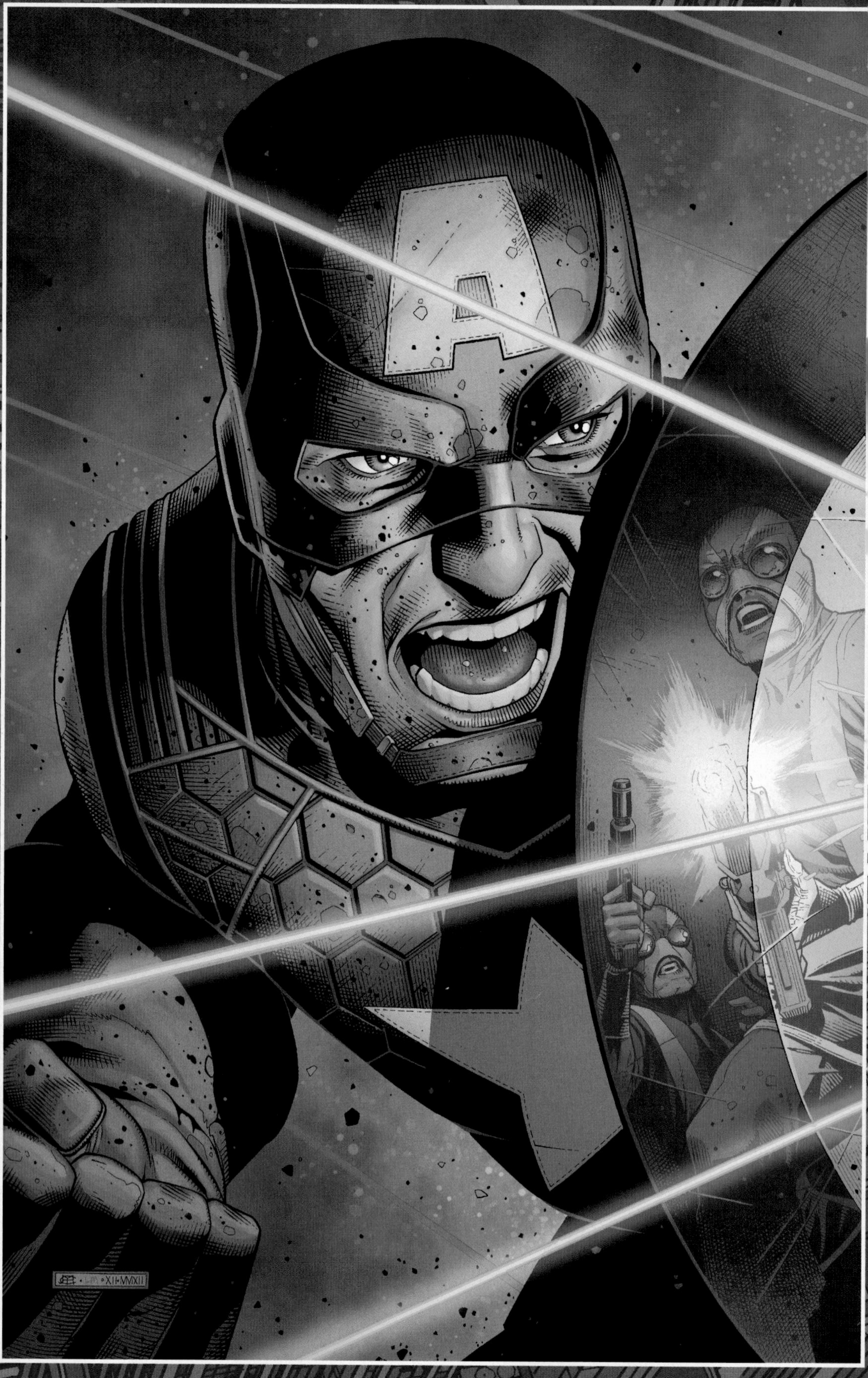

FIFTEEN

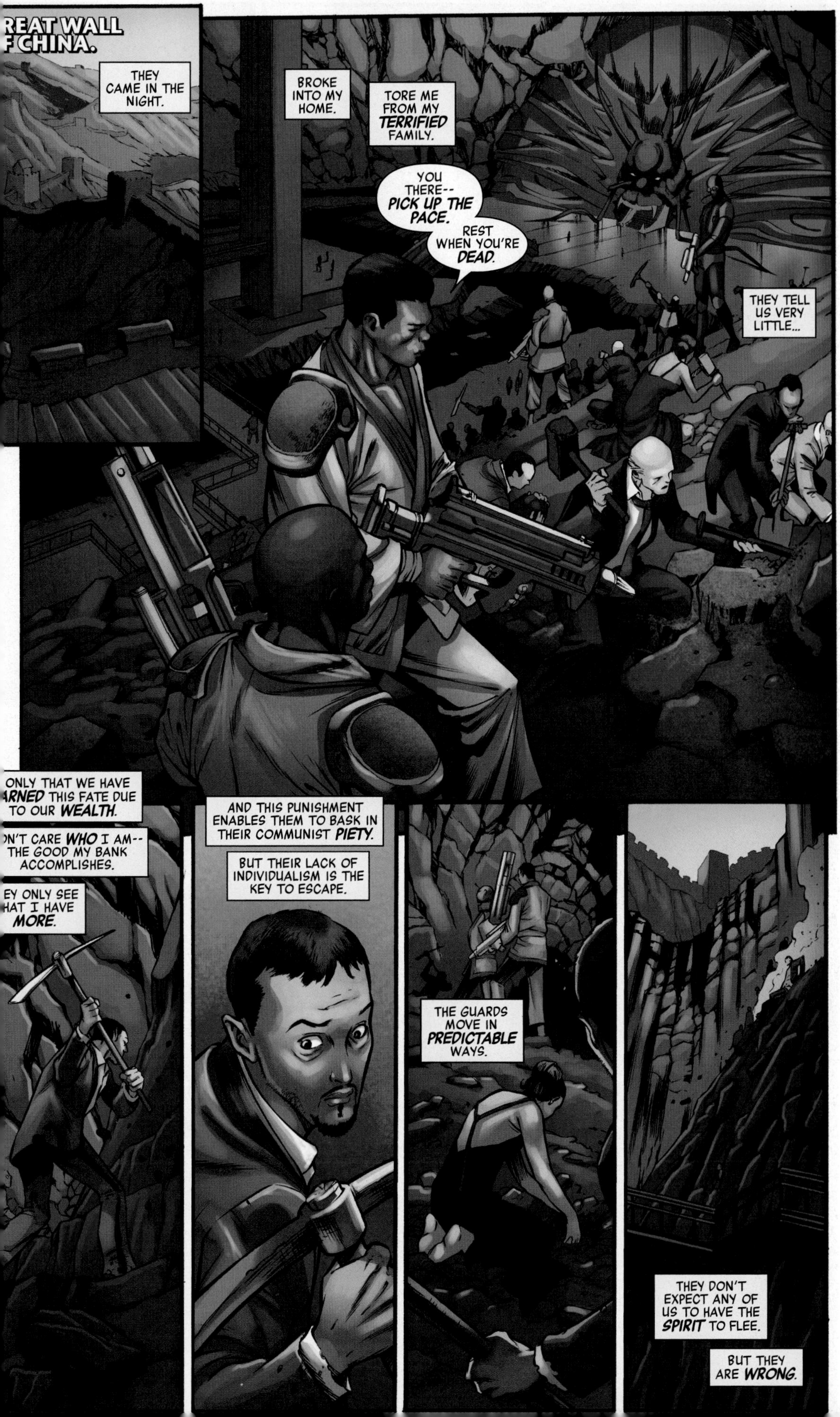
REAT WALL
F CHINA.
THEY CAME IN THE NIGHT.
BROKE INTO MY HOME.
TORE ME FROM MY TERRIFIED FAMILY.
YOU THERE-- PICK UP THE PACE.
REST WHEN YOU'RE DEAD.
THEY TELL US VERY LITTLE...
ONLY THAT WE HAVE
ARNED THIS FATE DUE TO OUR WEALTH.
N'T CARE WHO I AM-- THE GOOD MY BANK ACCOMPLISHES.
EY ONLY SEE
HAT I HAVE MORE.
AND THIS PUNISHMENT ENABLES THEM TO BASK IN THEIR COMMUNIST PIETY.
BUT THEIR LACK OF INDIVIDUALISM IS THE KEY TO ESCAPE.
THE GUARDS MOVE IN PREDICTABLE WAYS.
THEY DON'T EXPECT ANY OF US TO HAVE THE SPIRIT TO FLEE.
BUT THEY ARE WRONG.

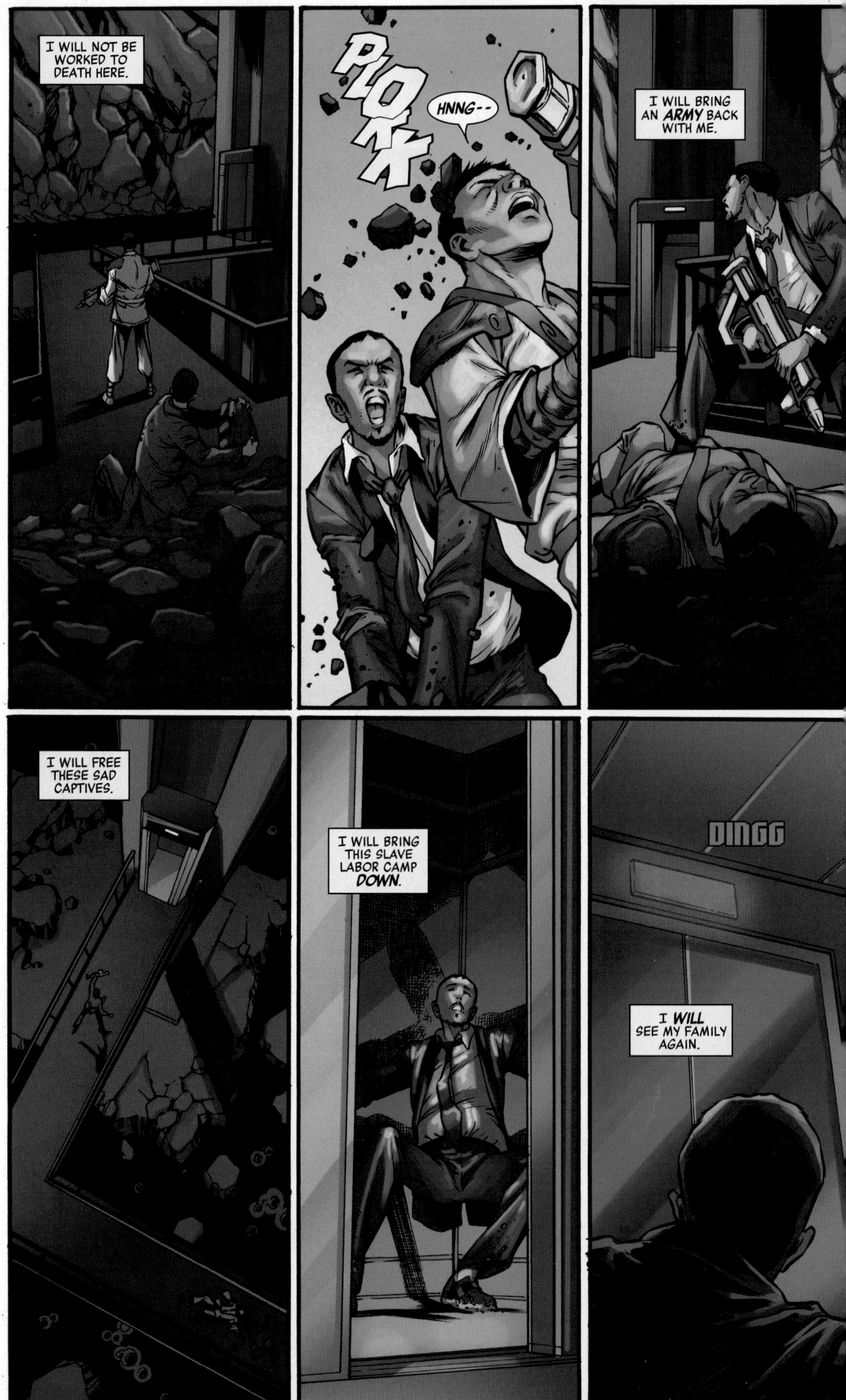
I WILL NOT BE WORKED TO DEATH HERE.
PLOKK
HNNG--
I WILL BRING AN ARMY BACK WITH ME.
I WILL FREE THESE SAD CAPTIVES.
I WILL BRING THIS SLAVE LABOR CAMP DOWN.
DINGG
I WILL SEE MY FAMILY AGAIN.

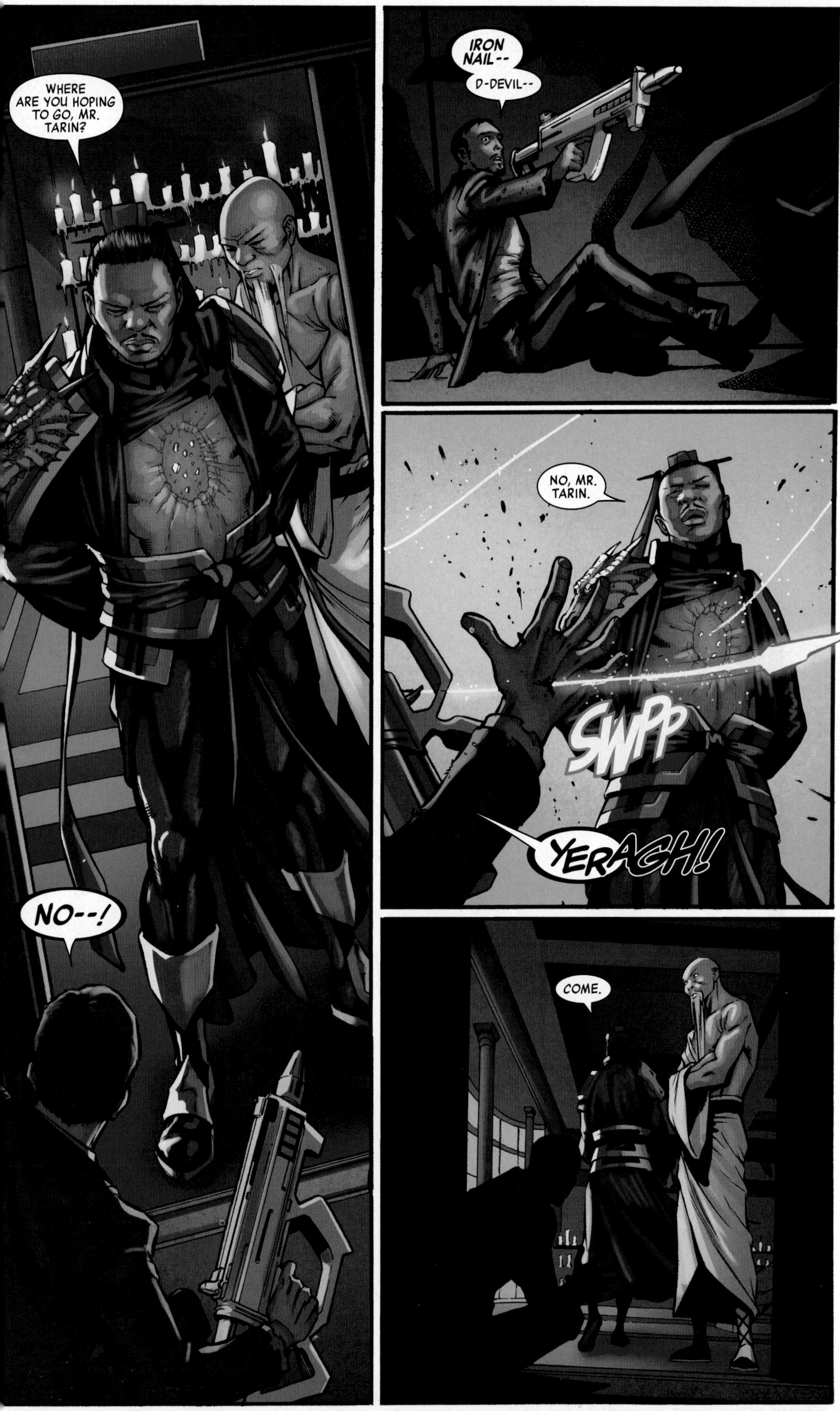
WHERE ARE YOU HOPING TO GO, MR. TARIN?
NO--!
IRON NAIL--
D-DEVIL--
NO, MR. TARIN.
SWPP
YERAGH!
COME.

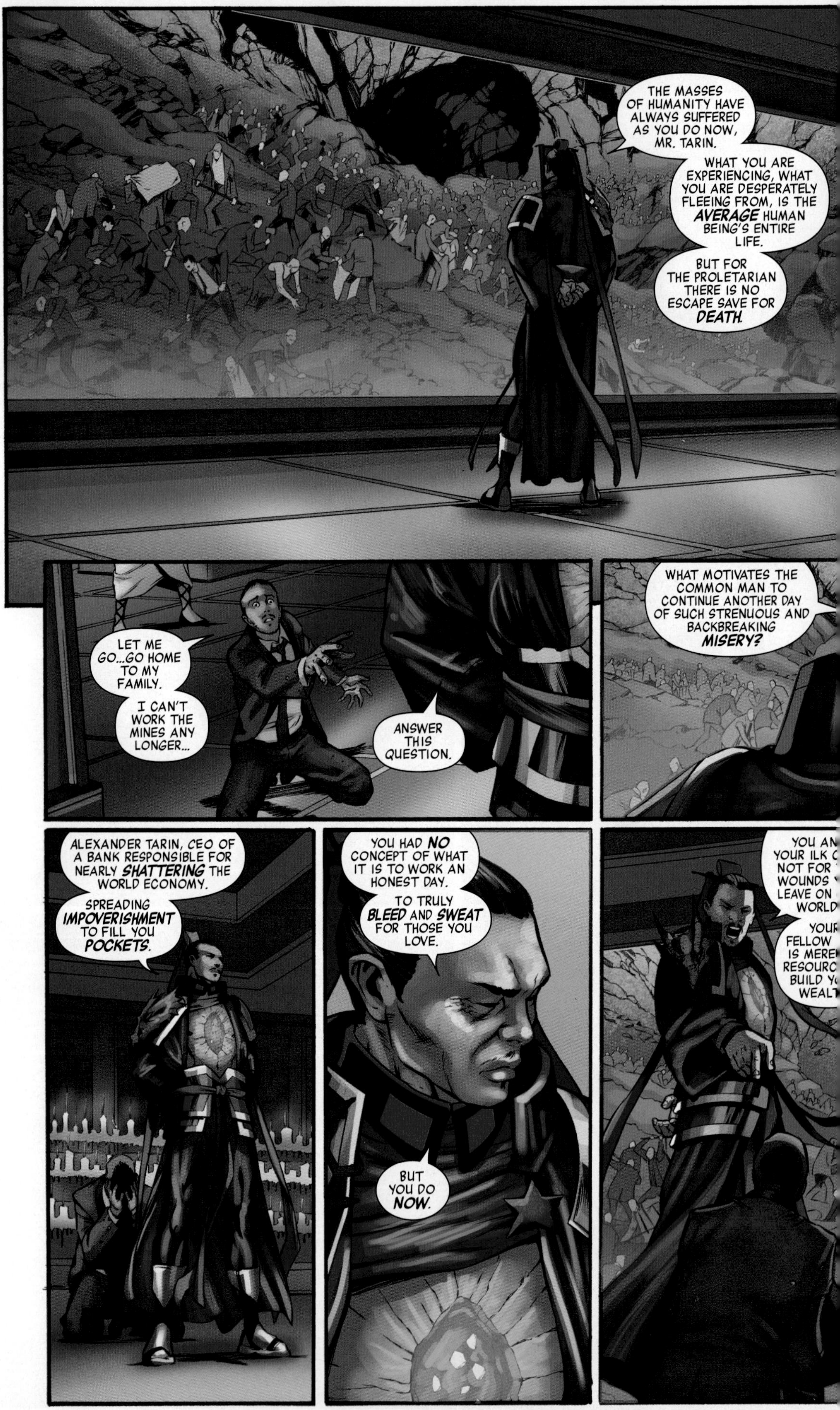

THE MASSES OF HUMANITY HAVE ALWAYS SUFFERED AS YOU DO NOW, MR. TARIN.
WHAT YOU ARE EXPERIENCING, WHAT YOU ARE DESPERATELY FLEEING FROM, IS THE AVERAGE HUMAN BEING'S ENTIRE LIFE.
BUT FOR THE PROLETARIAN THERE IS NO ESCAPE SAVE FOR DEATH.
LET ME GO...GO HOME TO MY FAMILY.
I CAN'T WORK THE MINES ANY LONGER...
ANSWER THIS QUESTION.
WHAT MOTIVATES THE COMMON MAN TO CONTINUE ANOTHER DAY OF SUCH STRENUOUS AND BACKBREAKING MISERY?
ALEXANDER TARIN, CEO OF A BANK RESPONSIBLE FOR NEARLY SHATTERING THE WORLD ECONOMY.
SPREADING IMPOVERISHMENT TO FILL YOU POCKETS.
YOU HAD NO CONCEPT OF WHAT IT IS TO WORK AN HONEST DAY.
TO TRULY BLEED AND SWEAT FOR THOSE YOU LOVE.
BUT YOU DO NOW.

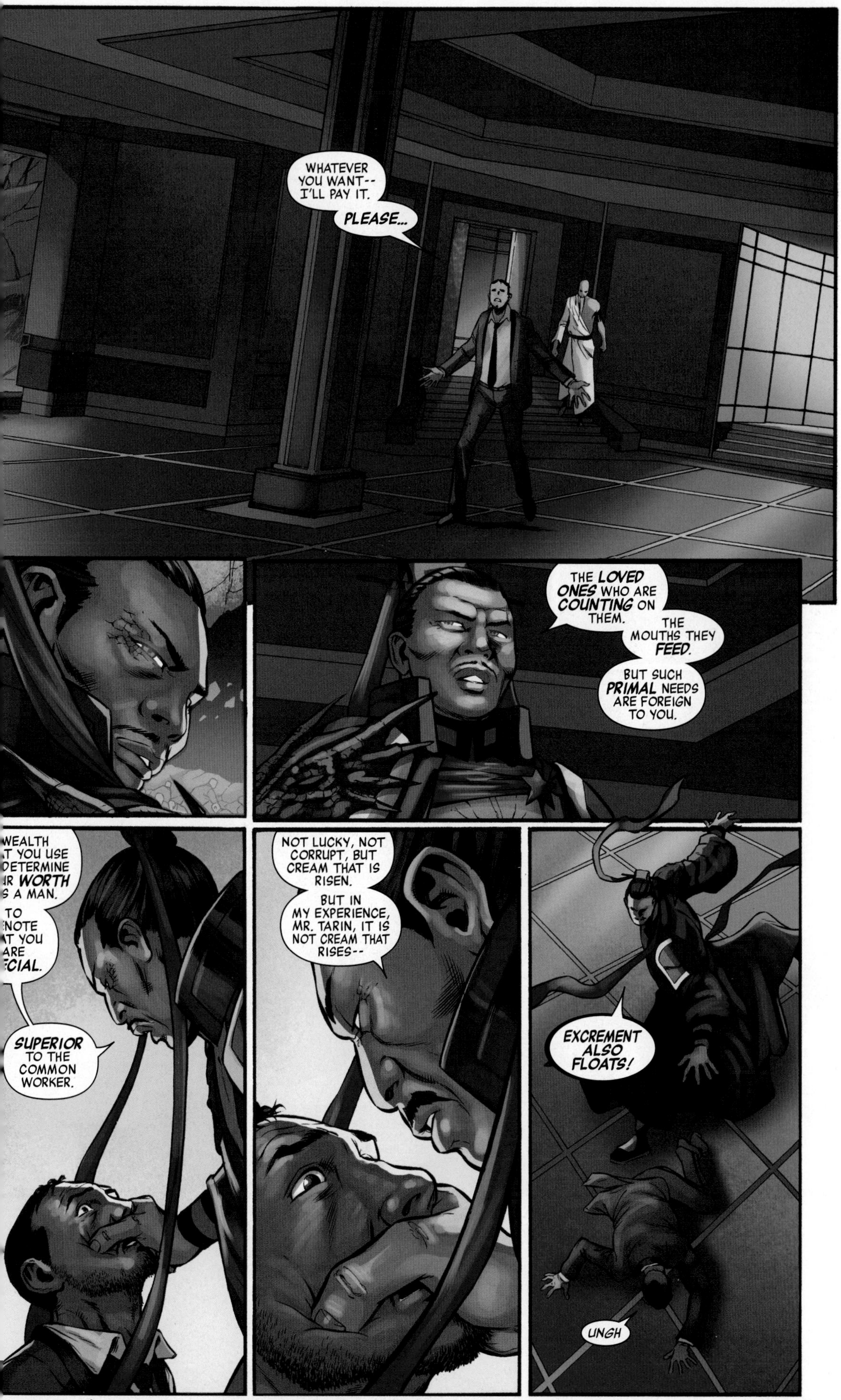
WHATEVER YOU WANT-- I'LL PAY IT.
PLEASE...
THE LOVED ONES WHO ARE COUNTING ON THEM.
THE MOUTHS THEY FEED.
BUT SUCH PRIMAL NEEDS ARE FOREIGN TO YOU.
SUPERIOR TO THE COMMON WORKER.
NOT LUCKY, NOT CORRUPT, BUT CREAM THAT IS RISEN.
BUT IN MY EXPERIENCE, MR. TARIN, IT IS NOT CREAM THAT RISES--
EXCREMENT ALSO FLOATS!
UNGH

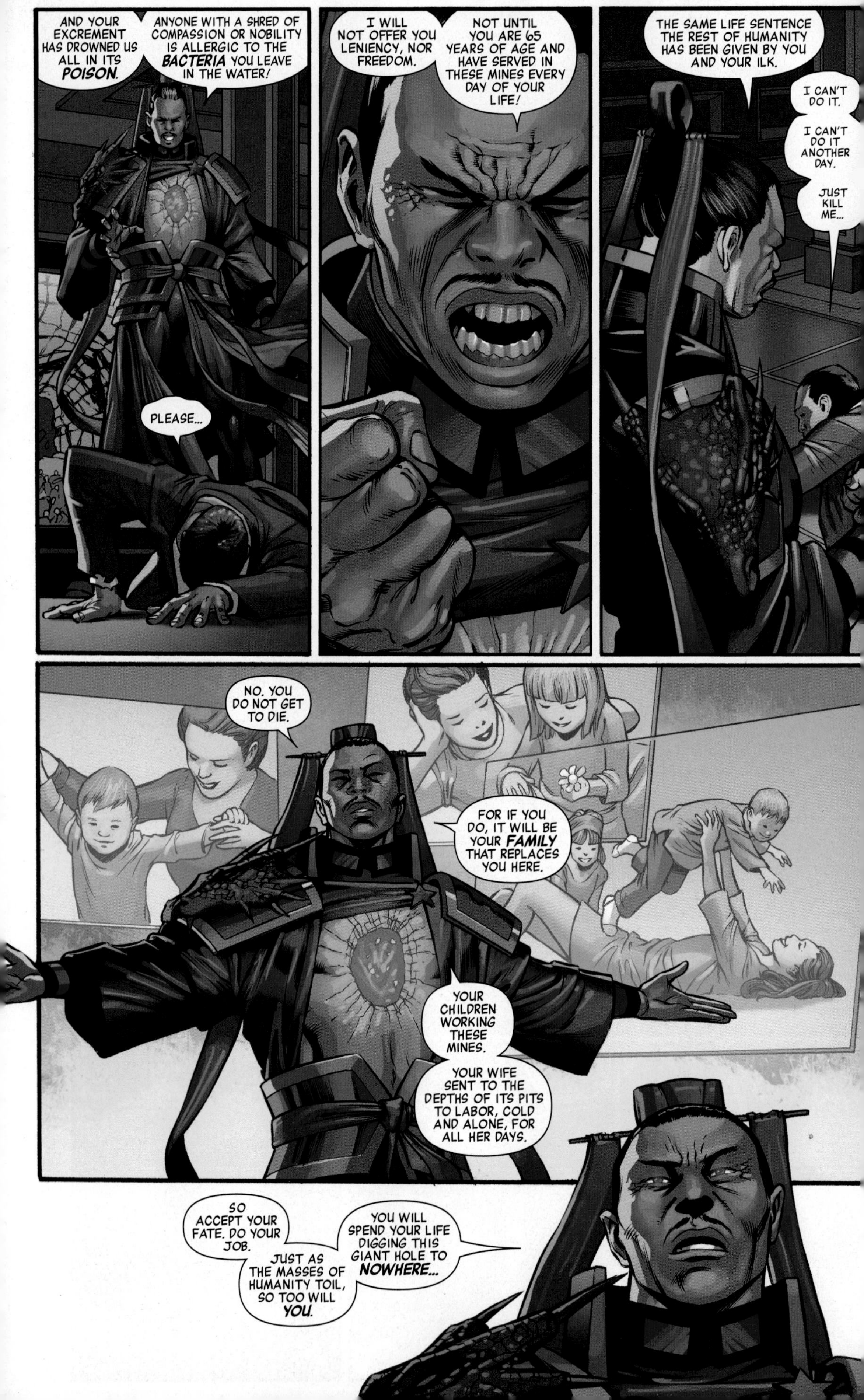
AND YOUR EXCREMENT HAS DROWNED US ALL IN ITS POISON.
ANYONE WITH A SHRED OF COMPASSION OR NOBILITY IS ALLERGIC TO THE BACTERIA YOU LEAVE IN THE WATER!
PLEASE...
I WILL NOT OFFER YOU LENIENCY, NOR FREEDOM.
NOT UNTIL YOU ARE 65 YEARS OF AGE AND HAVE SERVED IN THESE MINES EVERY DAY OF YOUR LIFE!
THE SAME LIFE SENTENCE THE REST OF HUMANITY HAS BEEN GIVEN BY YOU AND YOUR ILK.
I CAN'T DO IT.
I CAN'T DO IT ANOTHER DAY.
JUST KILL ME...
NO. YOU DO NOT GET TO DIE.
FOR IF YOU DO, IT WILL BE YOUR FAMILY THAT REPLACES YOU HERE.
YOUR CHILDREN WORKING THESE MINES.
YOUR WIFE SENT TO THE DEPTHS OF ITS PITS TO LABOR, COLD AND ALONE, FOR ALL HER DAYS.
SO ACCEPT YOUR FATE. DO YOUR JOB.
JUST AS THE MASSES OF HUMANITY TOIL, SO TOO WILL YOU.
YOU WILL SPEND YOUR LIFE DIGGING THIS GIANT HOLE TO NOWHERE...

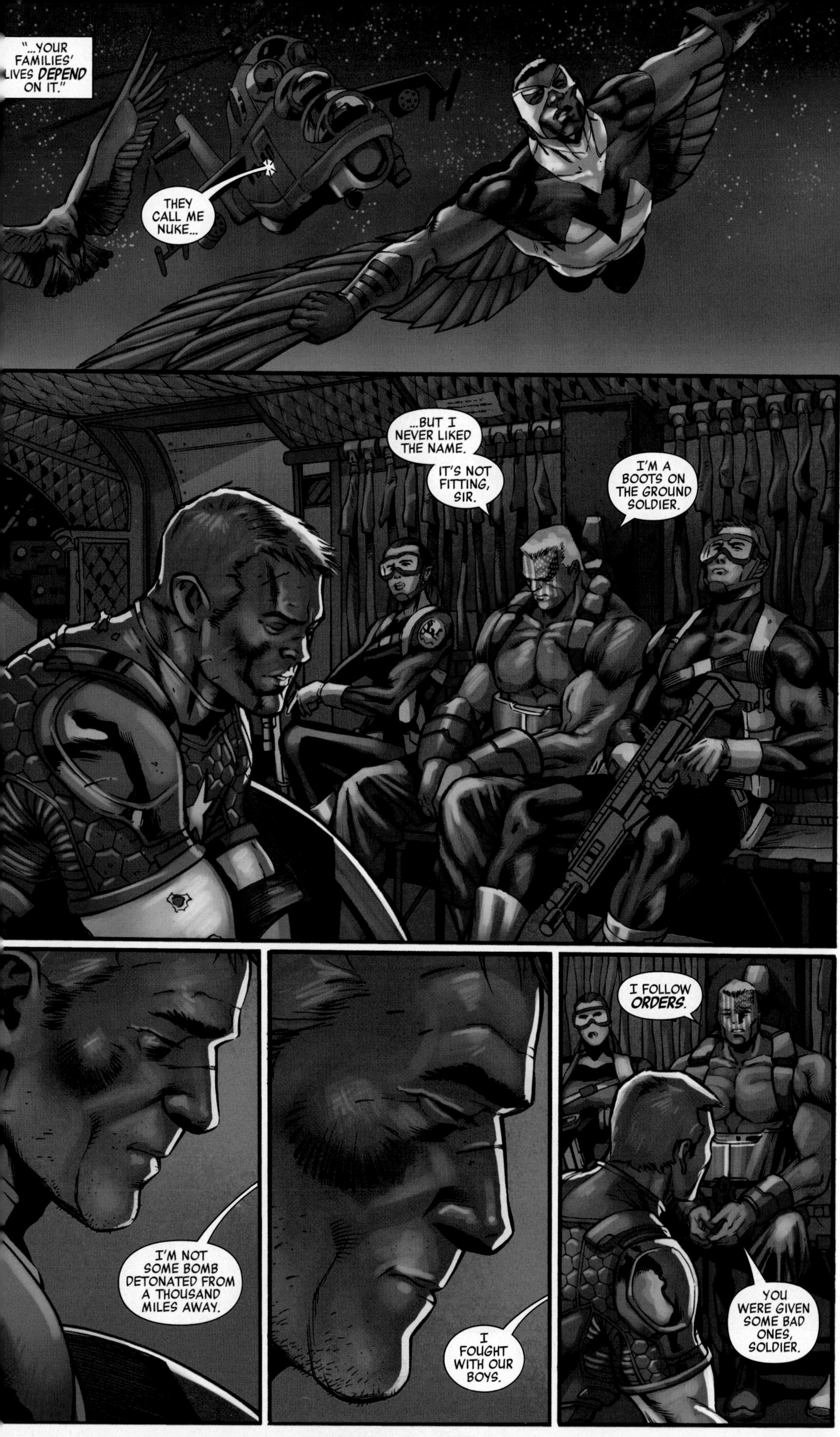
"...YOUR FAMILIES' LIVES DEPEND ON IT."
THEY CALL ME NUKE...
...BUT I NEVER LIKED THE NAME.
IT'S NOT FITTING, SIR.
I'M A BOOTS ON THE GROUND SOLDIER.
I'M NOT SOME BOMB DETONATED FROM A THOUSAND MILES AWAY.
I FOUGHT WITH OUR BOYS.
I FOLLOW ORDERS.
YOU WERE GIVEN SOME BAD ONES, SOLDIER.

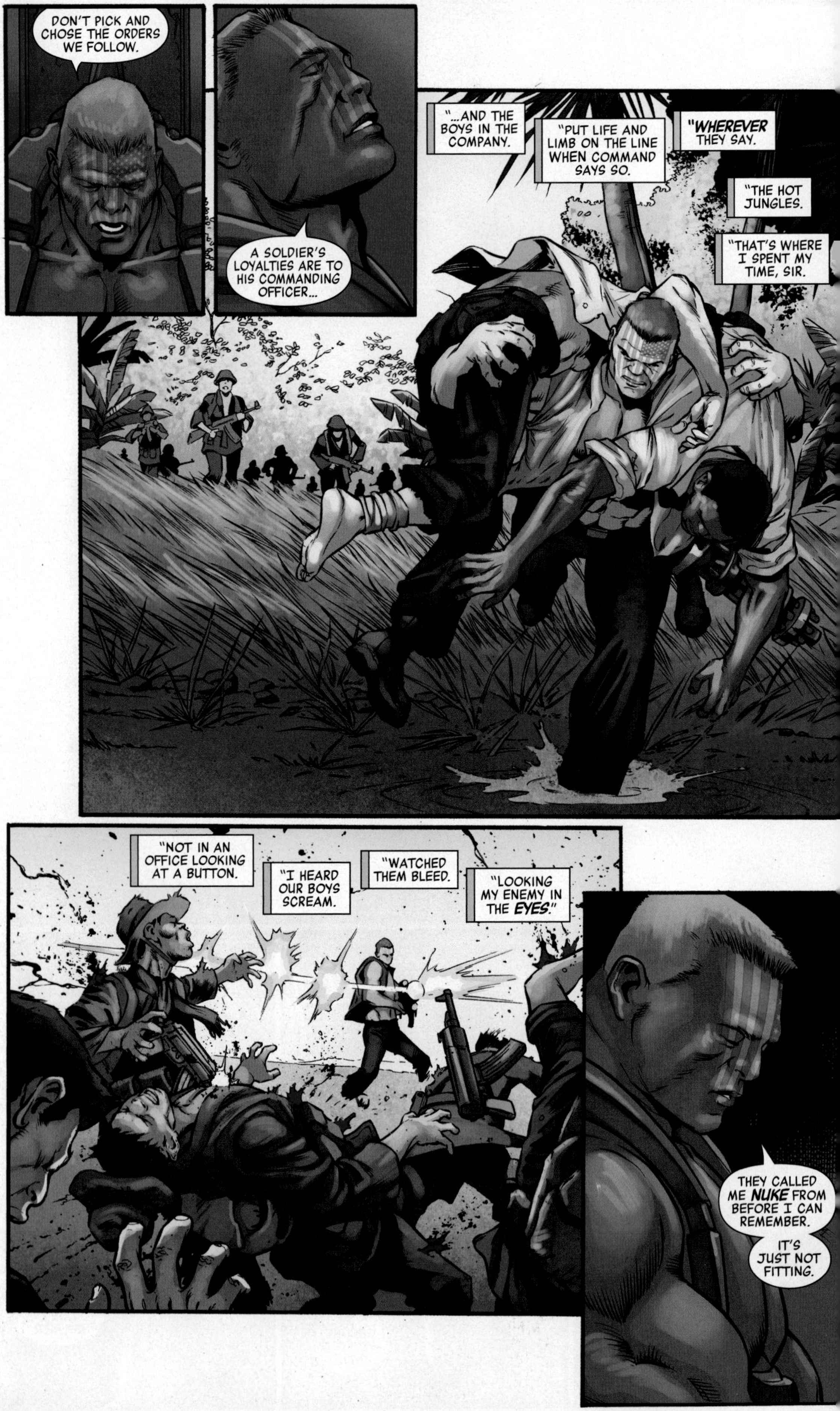
DON'T PICK AND CHOSE THE ORDERS WE FOLLOW.
A SOLDIER'S LOYALTIES ARE TO HIS COMMANDING OFFICER...
"...AND THE BOYS IN THE COMPANY.
"PUT LIFE AND LIMB ON THE LINE WHEN COMMAND SAYS SO.
"WHEREVER THEY SAY.
"THE HOT JUNGLES.
"THAT'S WHERE I SPENT MY TIME, SIR.
"NOT IN AN OFFICE LOOKING AT A BUTTON.
"I HEARD OUR BOYS SCREAM.
"WATCHED THEM BLEED.
"LOOKING MY ENEMY IN THE EYES."
THEY CALLED ME NUKE FROM BEFORE I CAN REMEMBER.
IT'S JUST NOT FITTING.

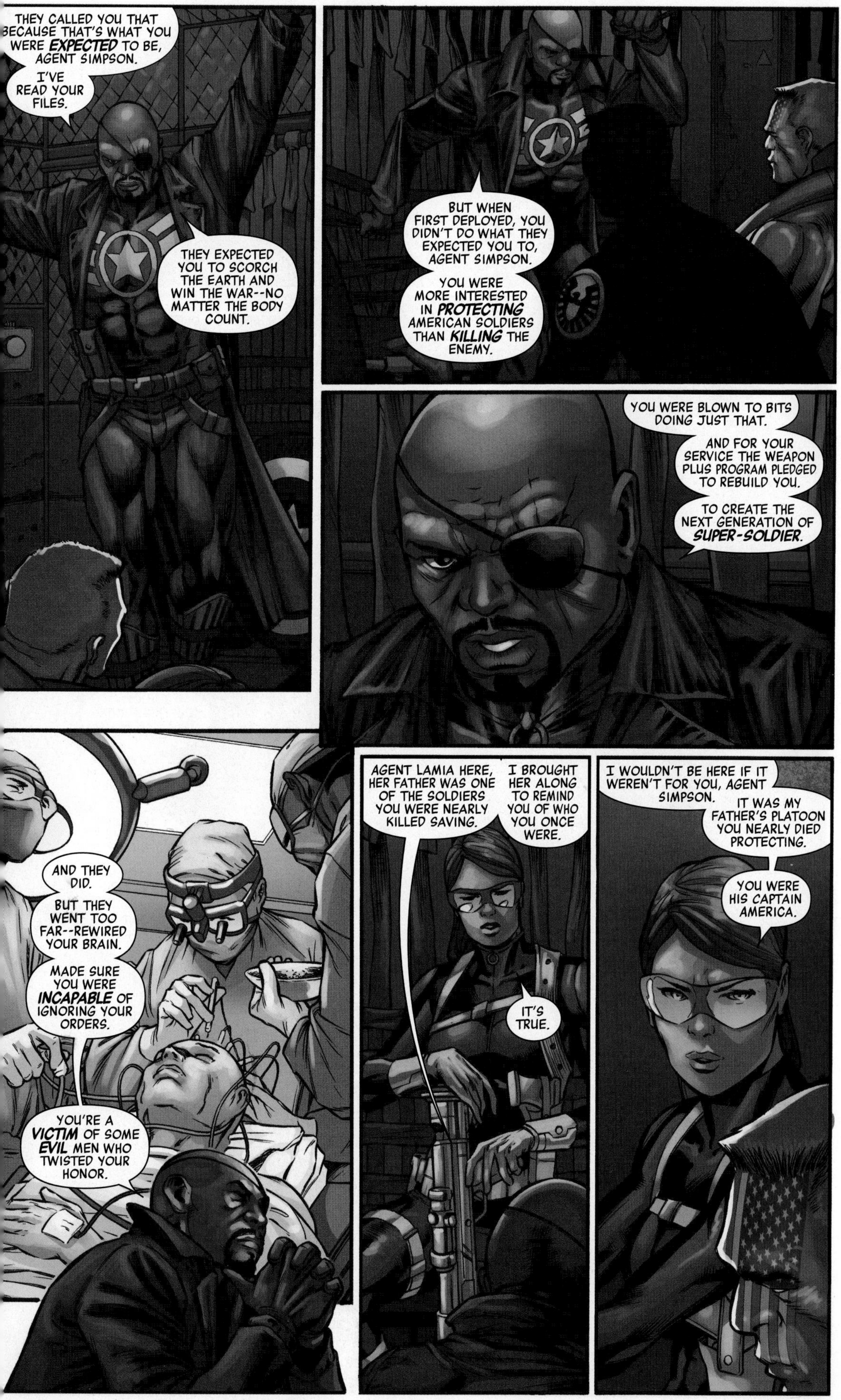

THEY CALLED YOU THAT BECAUSE THAT'S WHAT YOU WERE EXPECTED TO BE, AGENT SIMPSON.
I'VE READ YOUR FILES.
THEY EXPECTED YOU TO SCORCH THE EARTH AND WIN THE WAR--NO MATTER THE BODY COUNT.
BUT WHEN FIRST DEPLOYED, YOU DIDN'T DO WHAT THEY EXPECTED YOU TO, AGENT SIMPSON.
YOU WERE MORE INTERESTED IN PROTECTING AMERICAN SOLDIERS THAN KILLING THE ENEMY.
YOU WERE BLOWN TO BITS DOING JUST THAT.
AND FOR YOUR SERVICE THE WEAPON PLUS PROGRAM PLEDGED TO REBUILD YOU.
TO CREATE THE NEXT GENERATION OF SUPER-SOLDIER.
AND THEY DID.
BUT THEY WENT TOO FAR--REWIRED YOUR BRAIN.
MADE SURE YOU WERE INCAPABLE OF IGNORING YOUR ORDERS.
YOU'RE A VICTIM OF SOME EVIL MEN WHO TWISTED YOUR HONOR.
AGENT LAMIA HERE, HER FATHER WAS ONE OF THE SOLDIERS YOU WERE NEARLY KILLED SAVING.
I BROUGHT HER ALONG TO REMIND YOU OF WHO YOU ONCE WERE.
IT'S TRUE.
I WOULDN'T BE HERE IF IT WEREN'T FOR YOU, AGENT SIMPSON.
IT WAS MY FATHER'S PLATOON YOU NEARLY DIED PROTECTING.
YOU WERE HIS CAPTAIN AMERICA.

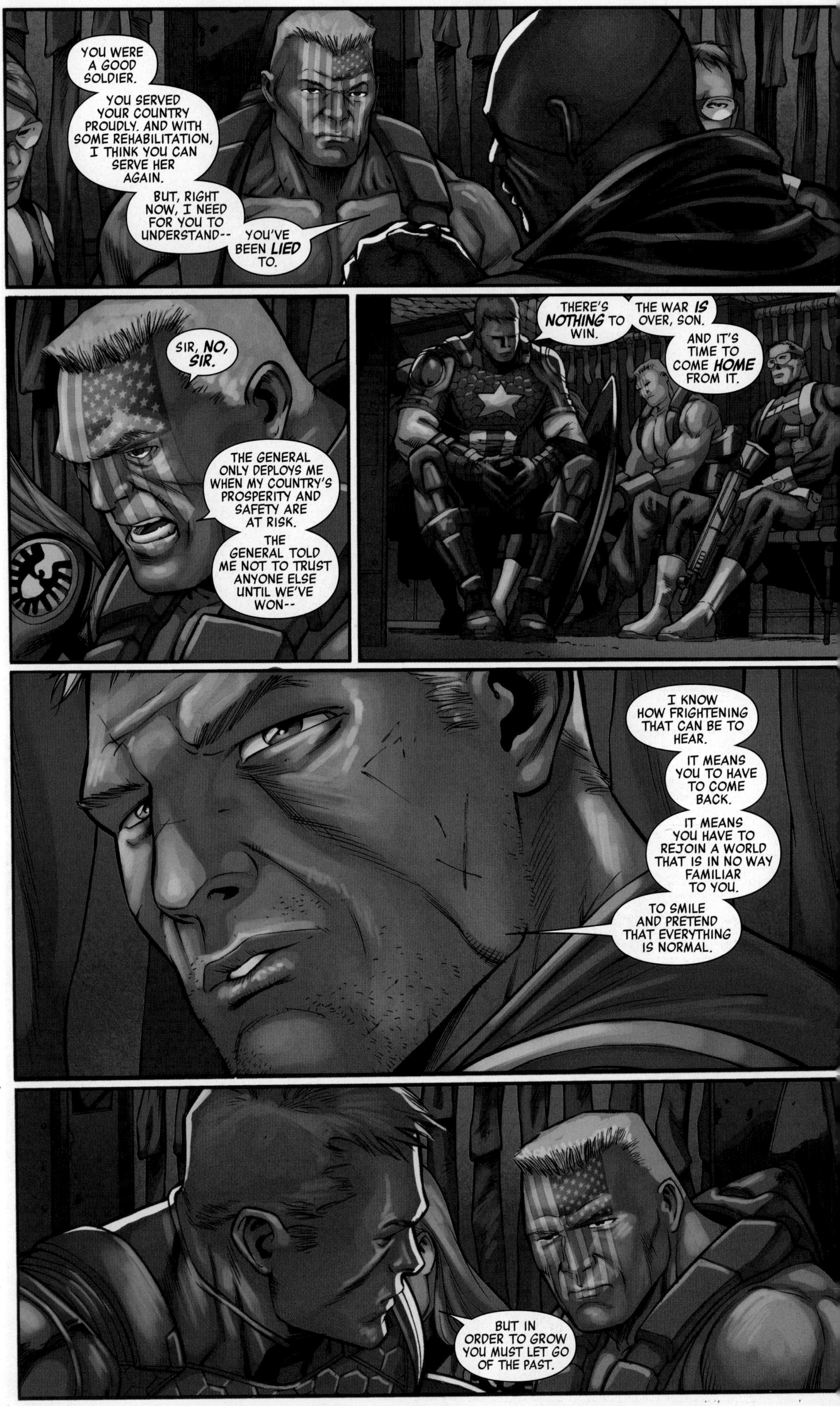

YOU WERE A GOOD SOLDIER.
YOU SERVED YOUR COUNTRY PROUDLY. AND WITH SOME REHABILITATION, I THINK YOU CAN SERVE HER AGAIN.
BUT, RIGHT NOW, I NEED FOR YOU TO UNDERSTAND--
YOU'VE BEEN LIED TO.
SIR, NO, SIR.
THE GENERAL ONLY DEPLOYS ME WHEN MY COUNTRY'S PROSPERITY AND SAFETY ARE AT RISK.
THE GENERAL TOLD ME NOT TO TRUST ANYONE ELSE UNTIL WE'VE WON--
THERE'S NOTHING TO WIN.
THE WAR IS OVER, SON.
AND IT'S TIME TO COME HOME FROM IT.
I KNOW HOW FRIGHTENING THAT CAN BE TO HEAR.
IT MEANS YOU TO HAVE TO COME BACK.
IT MEANS YOU HAVE TO REJOIN A WORLD THAT IS IN NO WAY FAMILIAR TO YOU.
TO SMILE AND PRETEND THAT EVERYTHING IS NORMAL.
BUT IN ORDER TO GROW YOU MUST LET GO OF THE PAST.

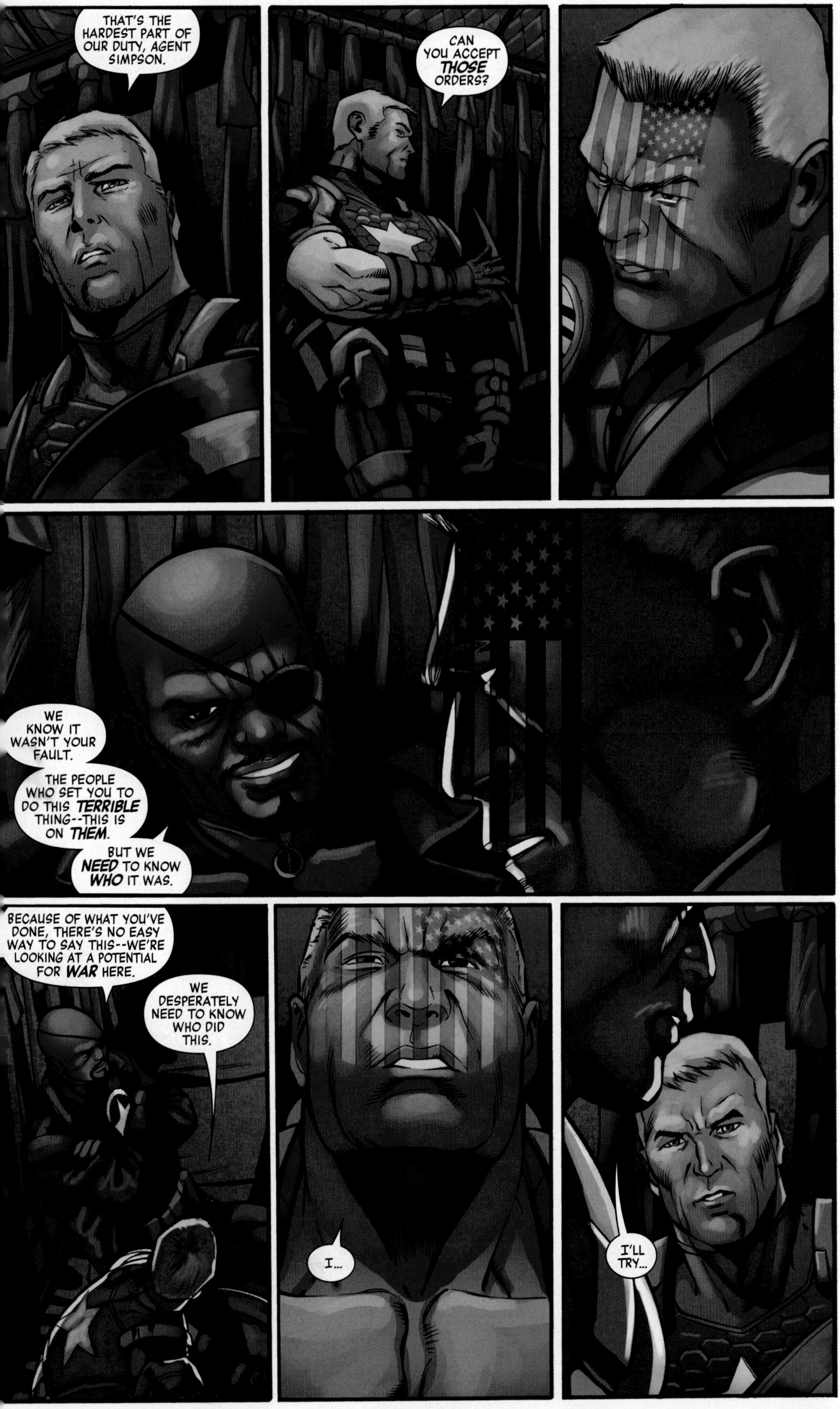
THAT'S THE HARDEST PART OF OUR DUTY, AGENT SIMPSON.
CAN YOU ACCEPT *THOSE* ORDERS?
WE KNOW IT WASN'T YOUR FAULT.
THE PEOPLE WHO SET YOU TO DO THIS *TERRIBLE* THING--THIS IS ON *THEM*.
BUT WE *NEED* TO KNOW *WHO* IT WAS.
BECAUSE OF WHAT YOU'VE DONE, THERE'S NO EASY WAY TO SAY THIS--WE'RE LOOKING AT A POTENTIAL FOR *WAR* HERE.
WE DESPERATELY NEED TO KNOW WHO DID THIS.
I...
I'LL TRY...

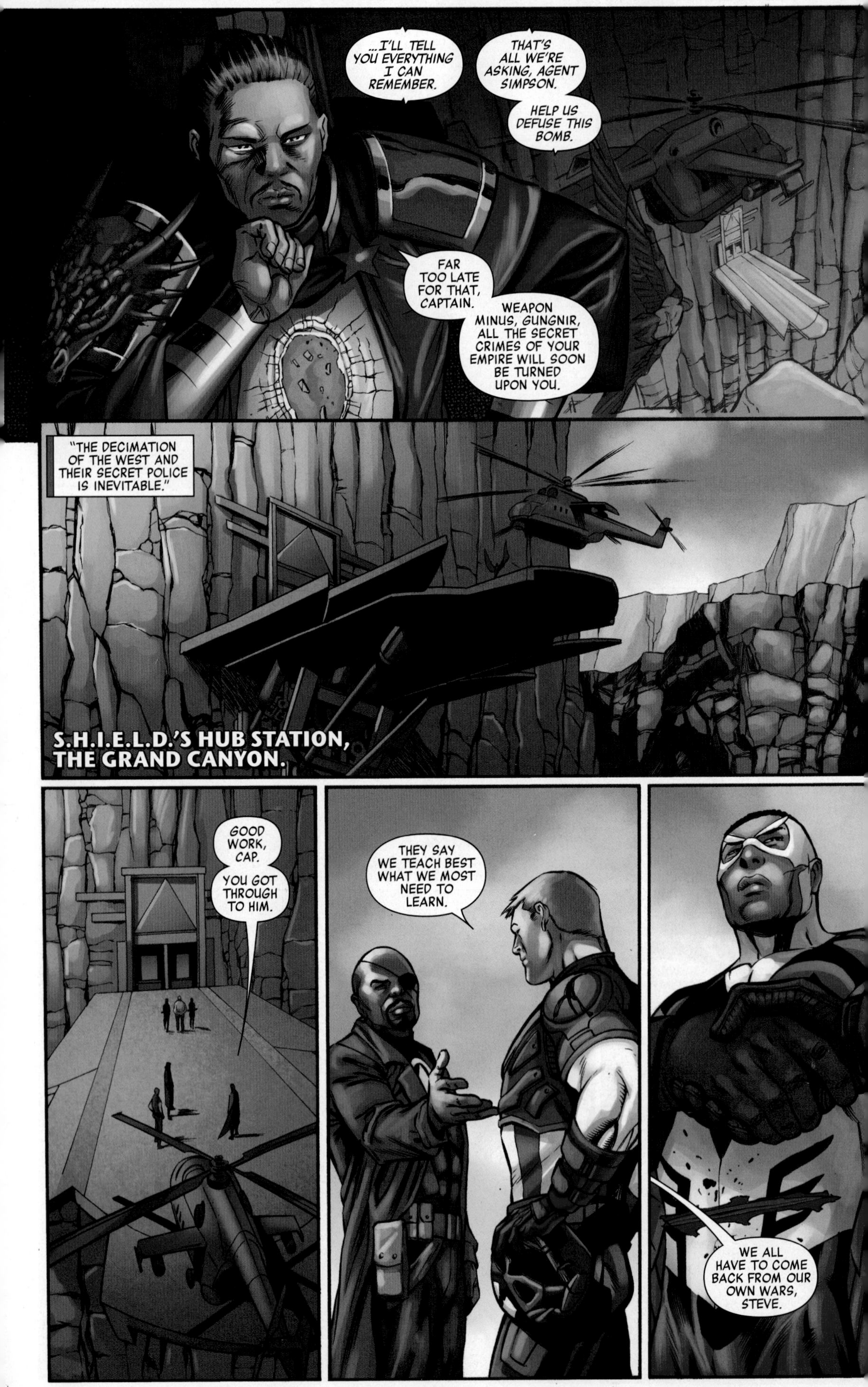
...I'LL TELL YOU EVERYTHING I CAN REMEMBER.
THAT'S ALL WE'RE ASKING, AGENT SIMPSON.
HELP US DEFUSE THIS BOMB.
FAR TOO LATE FOR THAT, CAPTAIN.
WEAPON MINUS, GUNGNIR, ALL THE SECRET CRIMES OF YOUR EMPIRE WILL SOON BE TURNED UPON YOU.
"THE DECIMATION OF THE WEST AND THEIR SECRET POLICE IS INEVITABLE."
S.H.I.E.L.D.'S HUB STATION, THE GRAND CANYON.
GOOD WORK, CAP.
YOU GOT THROUGH TO HIM.
THEY SAY WE TEACH BEST WHAT WE MOST NEED TO LEARN.
WE ALL HAVE TO COME BACK FROM OUR OWN WARS, STEVE.

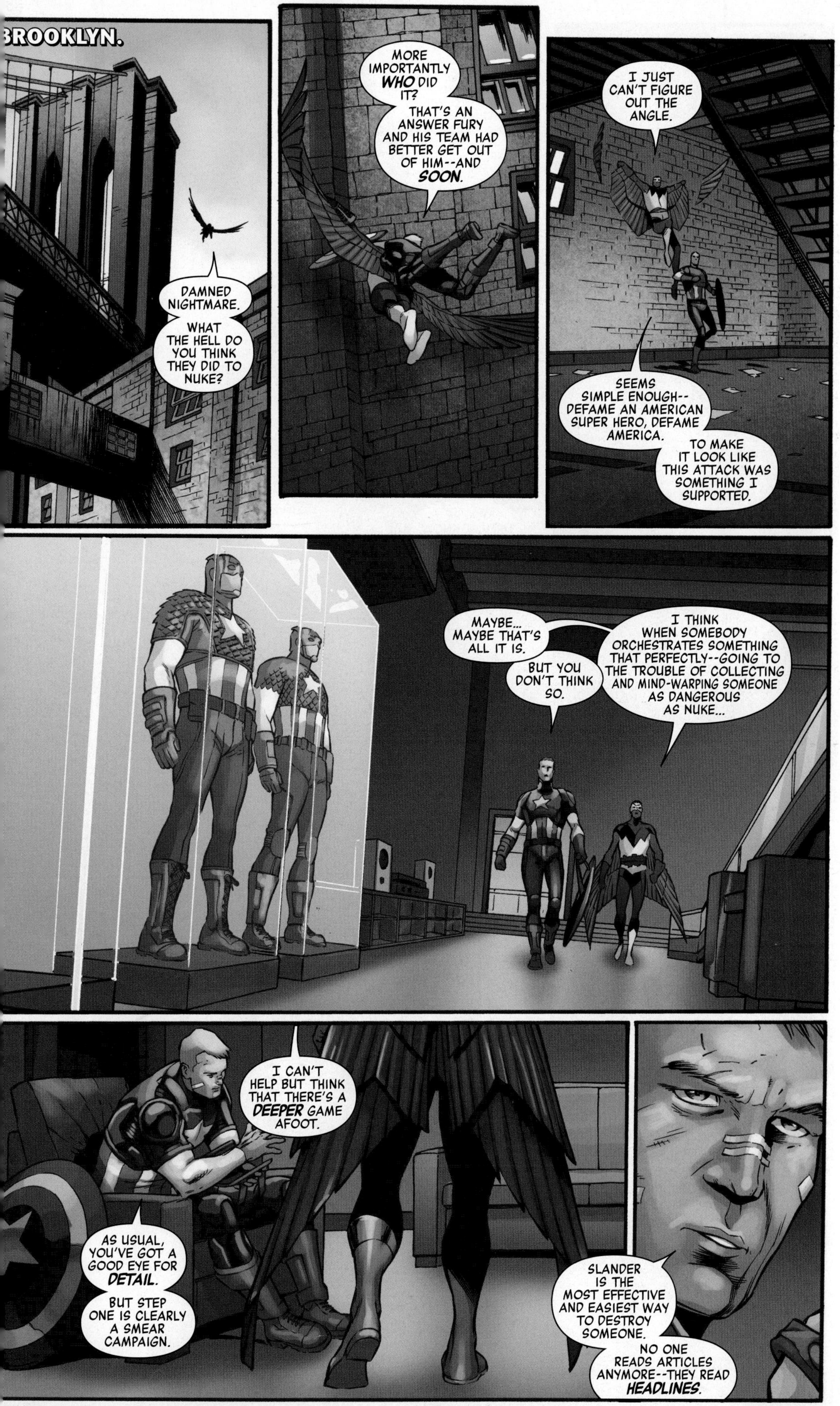
BROOKLYN.
DAMNED NIGHTMARE.
WHAT THE HELL DO YOU THINK THEY DID TO NUKE?
MORE IMPORTANTLY WHO DID IT?
THAT'S AN ANSWER FURY AND HIS TEAM HAD BETTER GET OUT OF HIM--AND SOON.
I JUST CAN'T FIGURE OUT THE ANGLE.
SEEMS SIMPLE ENOUGH--DEFAME AN AMERICAN SUPER HERO, DEFAME AMERICA.
TO MAKE IT LOOK LIKE THIS ATTACK WAS SOMETHING I SUPPORTED.
MAYBE... MAYBE THAT'S ALL IT IS.
I THINK WHEN SOMEBODY ORCHESTRATES SOMETHING THAT PERFECTLY--GOING TO THE TROUBLE OF COLLECTING AND MIND-WARPING SOMEONE AS DANGEROUS AS NUKE...
BUT YOU DON'T THINK SO.
I CAN'T HELP BUT THINK THAT THERE'S A DEEPER GAME AFOOT.
AS USUAL, YOU'VE GOT A GOOD EYE FOR DETAIL.
BUT STEP ONE IS CLEARLY A SMEAR CAMPAIGN.
SLANDER IS THE MOST EFFECTIVE AND EASIEST WAY TO DESTROY SOMEONE.
NO ONE READS ARTICLES ANYMORE--THEY READ HEADLINES.

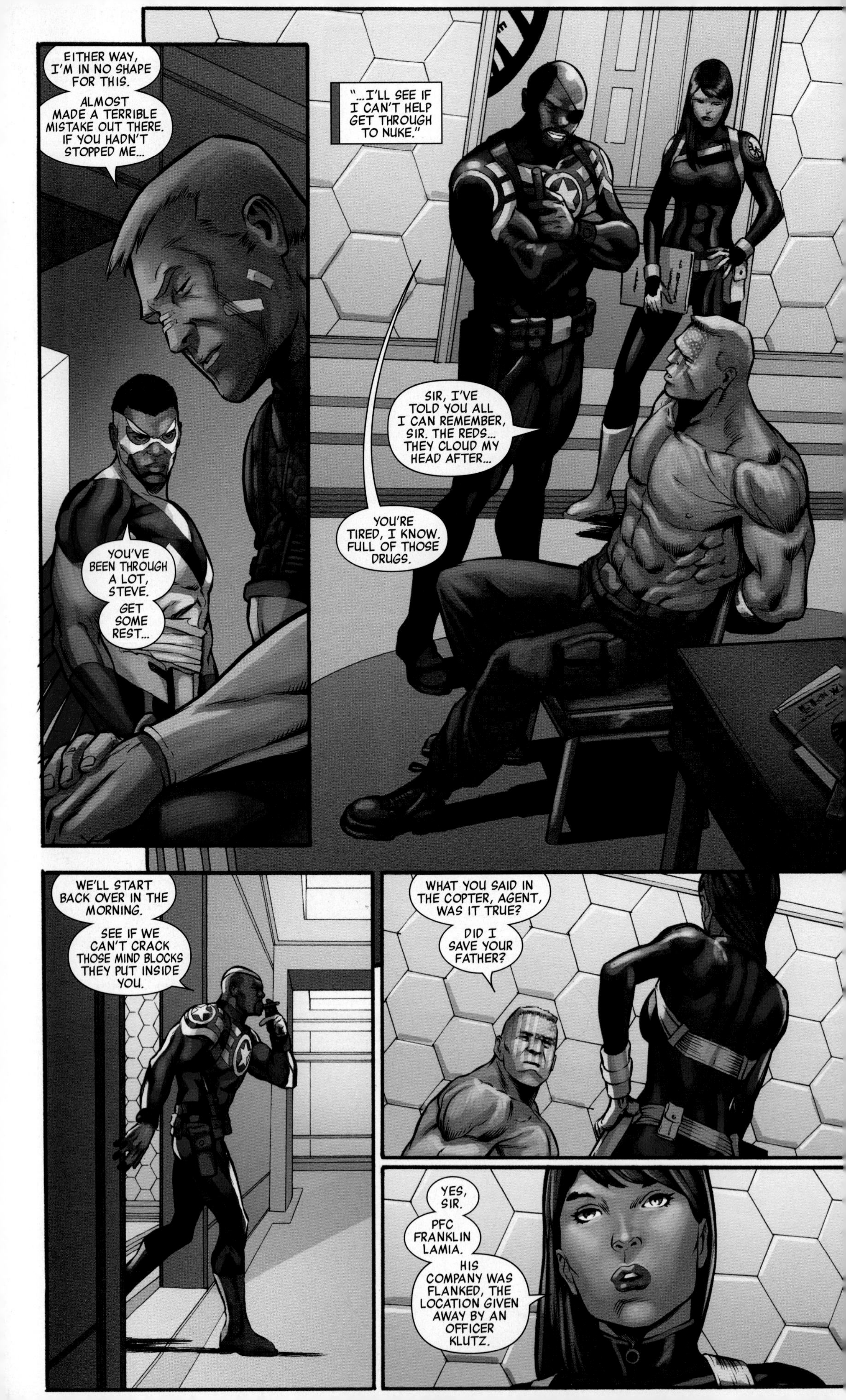
EITHER WAY, I'M IN NO SHAPE FOR THIS.
ALMOST MADE A TERRIBLE MISTAKE OUT THERE. IF YOU HADN'T STOPPED ME...
YOU'VE BEEN THROUGH A LOT, STEVE.
GET SOME REST...
"...I'LL SEE IF I CAN'T HELP GET THROUGH TO NUKE."
SIR, I'VE TOLD YOU ALL I CAN REMEMBER, SIR. THE REDS... THEY CLOUD MY HEAD AFTER...
YOU'RE TIRED, I KNOW. FULL OF THOSE DRUGS.
WE'LL START BACK OVER IN THE MORNING.
SEE IF WE CAN'T CRACK THOSE MIND BLOCKS THEY PUT INSIDE YOU.
WHAT YOU SAID IN THE COPTER, AGENT, WAS IT TRUE?
DID I SAVE YOUR FATHER?
YES, SIR.
PFC FRANKLIN LAMIA.
HIS COMPANY WAS FLANKED, THE LOCATION GIVEN AWAY BY AN OFFICER KLUTZ.

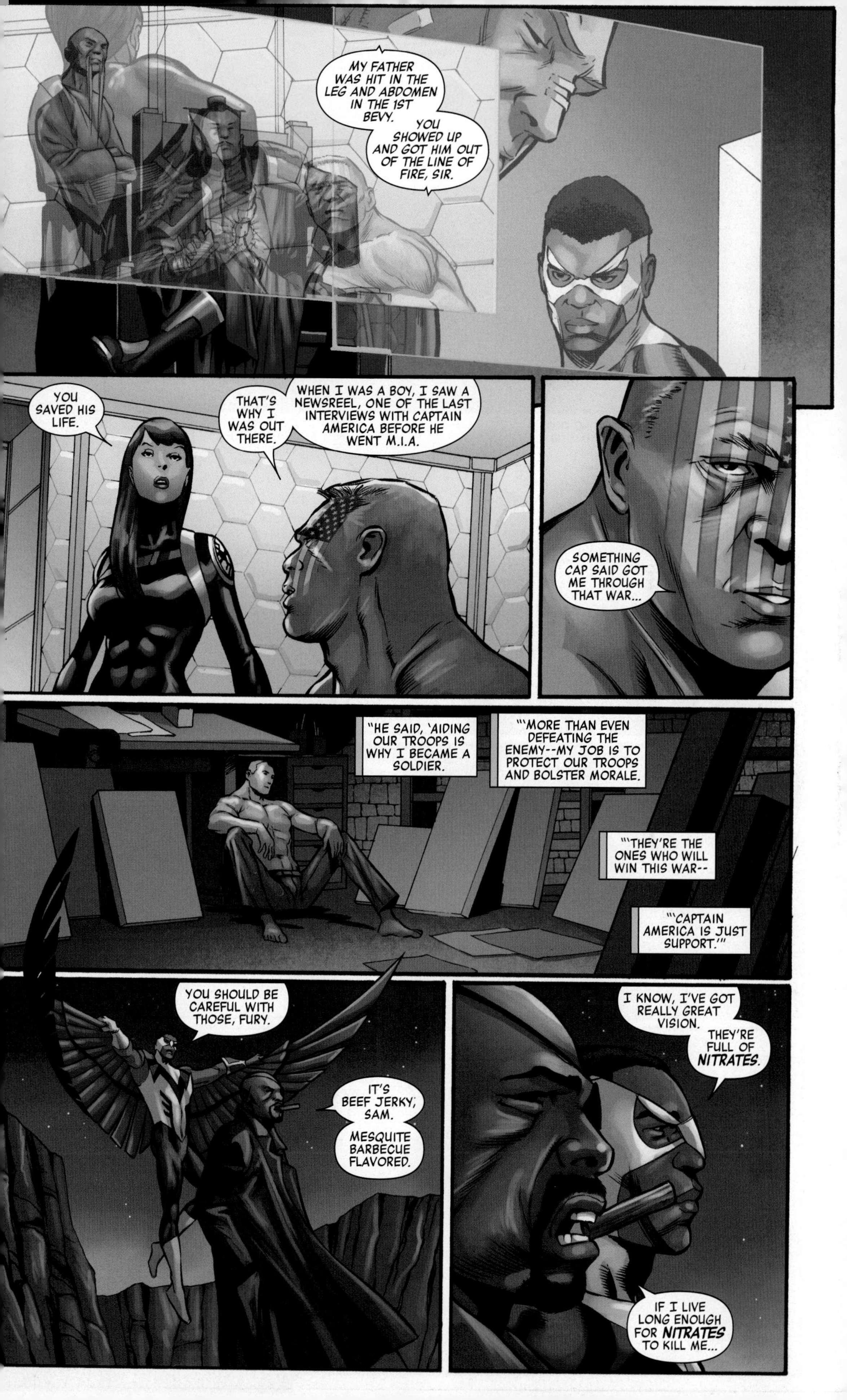
MY FATHER WAS HIT IN THE LEG AND ABDOMEN IN THE 1ST BEVY.
YOU SHOWED UP AND GOT HIM OUT OF THE LINE OF FIRE, SIR.
YOU SAVED HIS LIFE.
THAT'S WHY I WAS OUT THERE.
WHEN I WAS A BOY, I SAW A NEWSREEL, ONE OF THE LAST INTERVIEWS WITH CAPTAIN AMERICA BEFORE HE WENT M.I.A.
SOMETHING CAP SAID GOT ME THROUGH THAT WAR...
"HE SAID, 'AIDING OUR TROOPS IS WHY I BECAME A SOLDIER.
"'MORE THAN EVEN DEFEATING THE ENEMY--MY JOB IS TO PROTECT OUR TROOPS AND BOLSTER MORALE.
"'THEY'RE THE ONES WHO WILL WIN THIS WAR--
"'CAPTAIN AMERICA IS JUST SUPPORT.'"
YOU SHOULD BE CAREFUL WITH THOSE, FURY.
IT'S BEEF JERKY, SAM.
MESQUITE BARBECUE FLAVORED.
I KNOW, I'VE GOT REALLY GREAT VISION.
THEY'RE FULL OF NITRATES.
IF I LIVE LONG ENOUGH FOR NITRATES TO KILL ME...

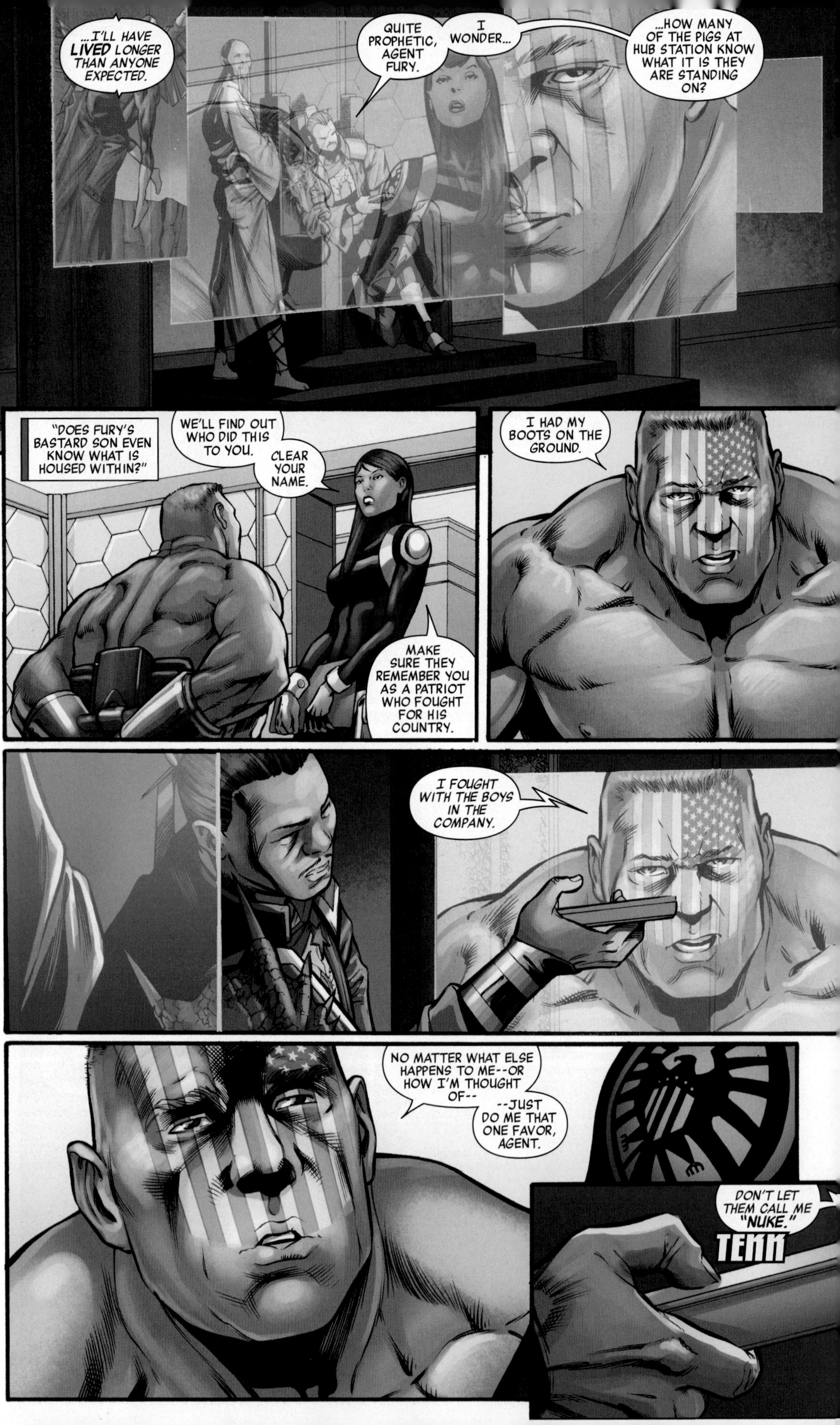
...I'LL HAVE LIVED LONGER THAN ANYONE EXPECTED.
QUITE PROPHETIC, AGENT FURY.
I WONDER...
...HOW MANY OF THE PIGS AT HUB STATION KNOW WHAT IT IS THEY ARE STANDING ON?
"DOES FURY'S BASTARD SON EVEN KNOW WHAT IS HOUSED WITHIN?"
WE'LL FIND OUT WHO DID THIS TO YOU.
CLEAR YOUR NAME.
MAKE SURE THEY REMEMBER YOU AS A PATRIOT WHO FOUGHT FOR HIS COUNTRY.
I HAD MY BOOTS ON THE GROUND.
I FOUGHT WITH THE BOYS IN THE COMPANY.
NO MATTER WHAT ELSE HAPPENS TO ME--OR HOW I'M THOUGHT OF--
--JUST DO ME THAT ONE FAVOR, AGENT.
DON'T LET THEM CALL ME "NUKE."
TEKK

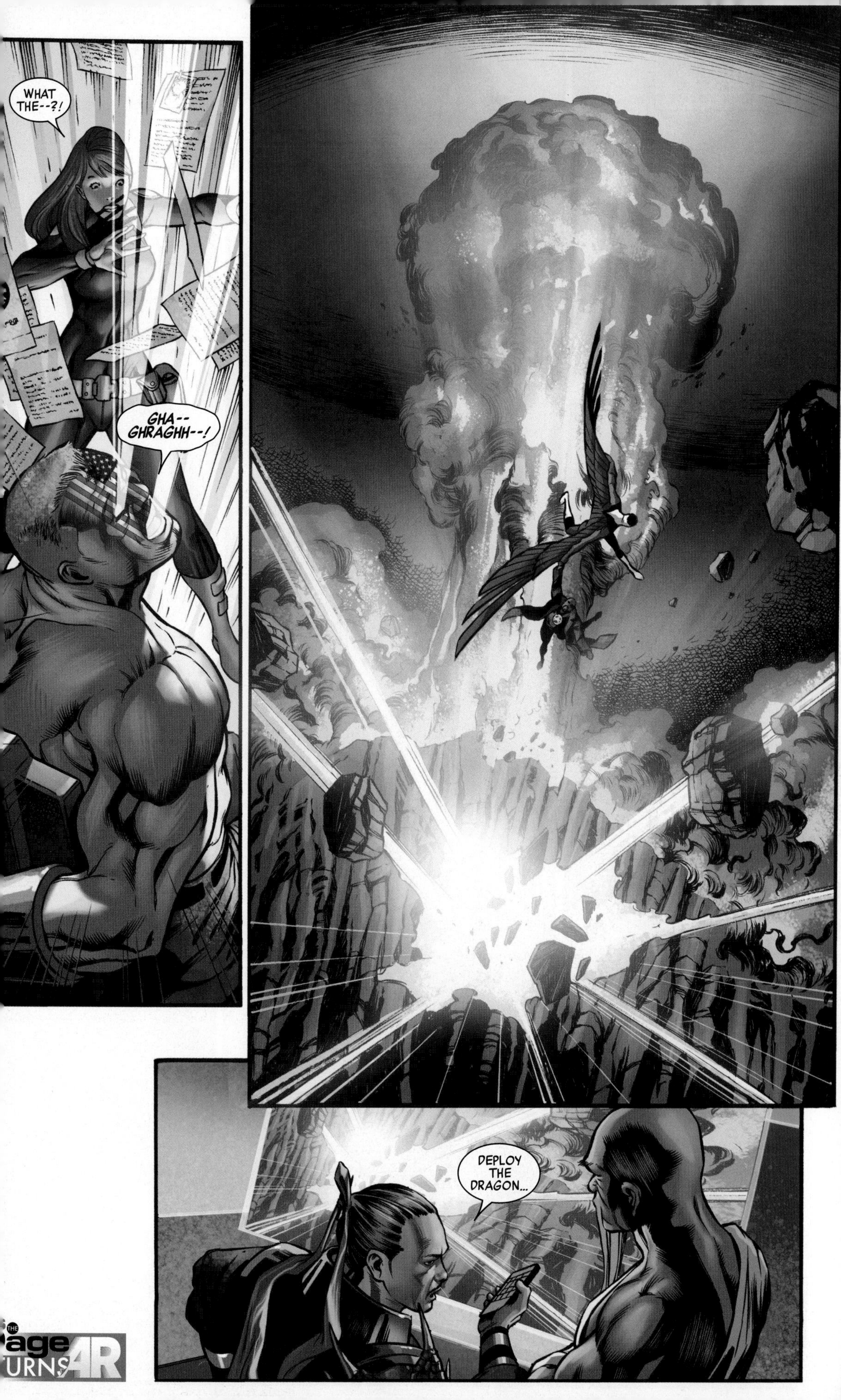
WHAT THE--?!
GHA-- GHRAGHH--!
DEPLOY THE DRAGON...

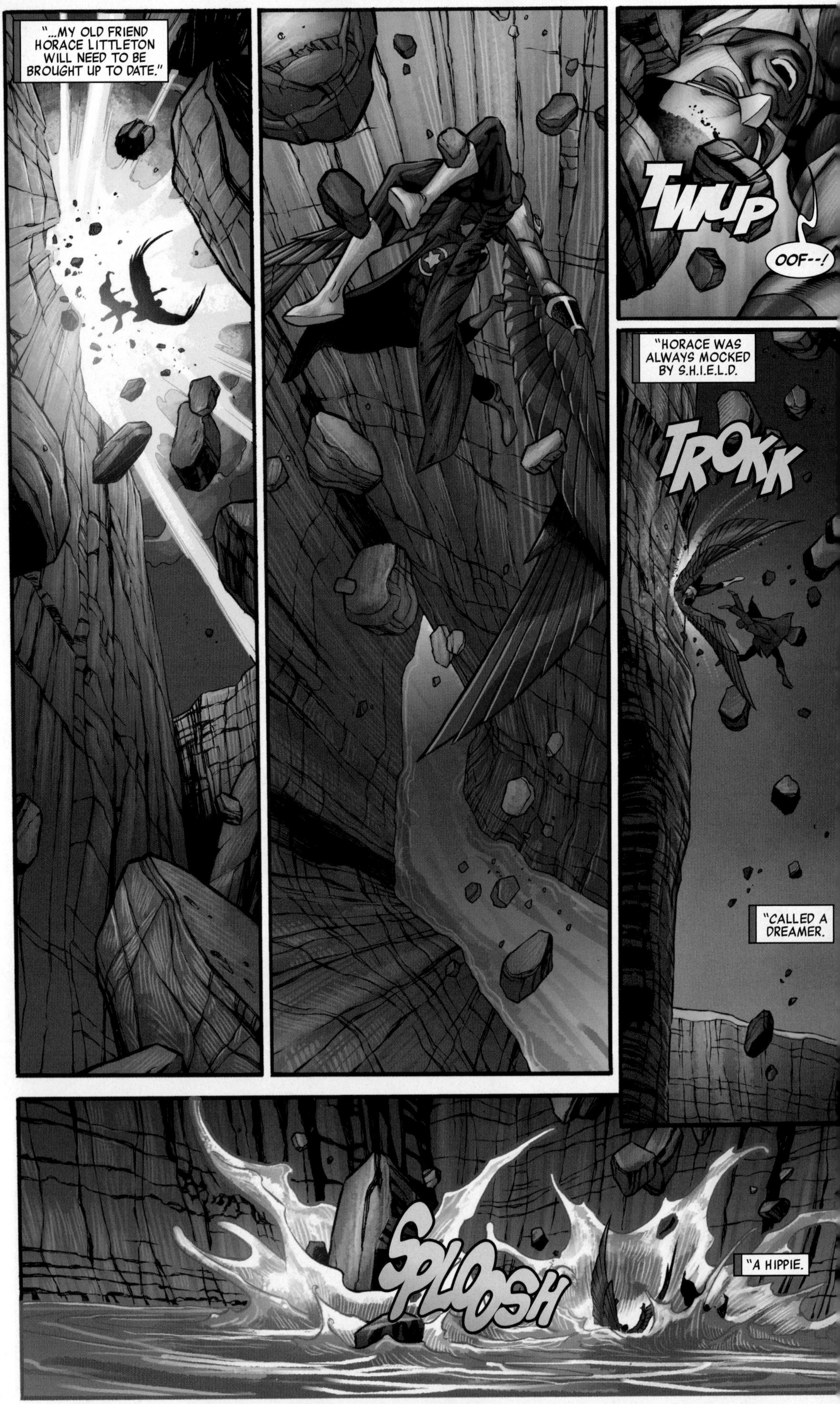
"...MY OLD FRIEND HORACE LITTLETON WILL NEED TO BE BROUGHT UP TO DATE."
TWUP
OOF--!
"HORACE WAS ALWAYS MOCKED BY S.H.I.E.L.D.
TROKK
"CALLED A DREAMER.
SPLOOSH
"A HIPPIE.

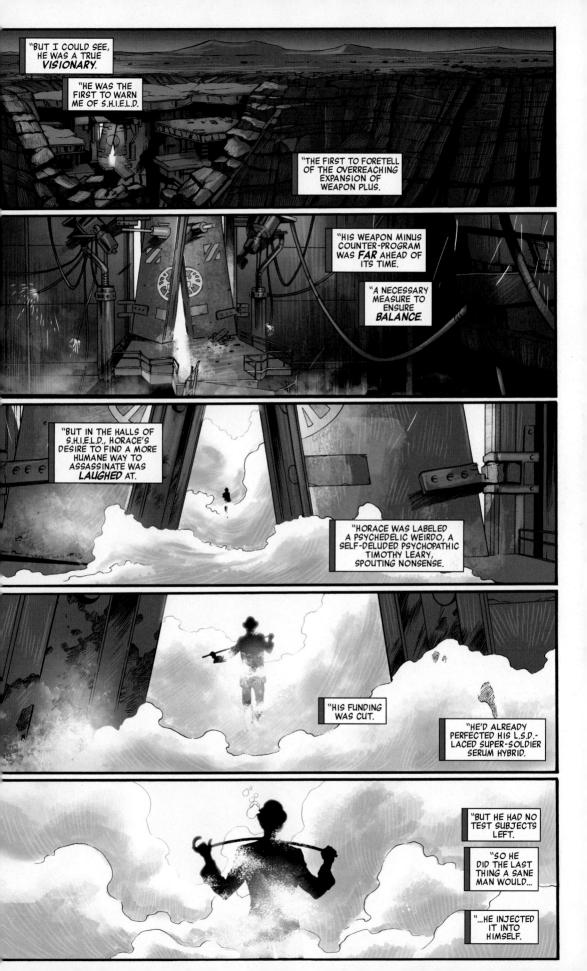

"BUT I COULD SEE, HE WAS A TRUE **VISIONARY.**

"HE WAS THE FIRST TO WARN ME OF S.H.I.E.L.D.

"THE FIRST TO FORETELL OF THE OVERREACHING EXPANSION OF WEAPON PLUS.

"HIS WEAPON MINUS COUNTER-PROGRAM WAS **FAR** AHEAD OF ITS TIME.

"A NECESSARY MEASURE TO ENSURE **BALANCE.**

"BUT IN THE HALLS OF S.H.I.E.L.D., HORACE'S DESIRE TO FIND A MORE HUMANE WAY TO ASSASSINATE WAS **LAUGHED** AT.

"HORACE WAS LABELED A PSYCHEDELIC WEIRDO, A SELF-DELUDED PSYCHOPATHIC TIMOTHY LEARY, SPOUTING NONSENSE.

"HIS FUNDING WAS CUT.

"HE'D ALREADY PERFECTED HIS L.S.D.-LACED SUPER-SOLDIER SERUM HYBRID.

"BUT HE HAD NO TEST SUBJECTS LEFT.

"SO HE DID THE LAST THING A SANE MAN WOULD...

"...HE INJECTED IT INTO HIMSELF.

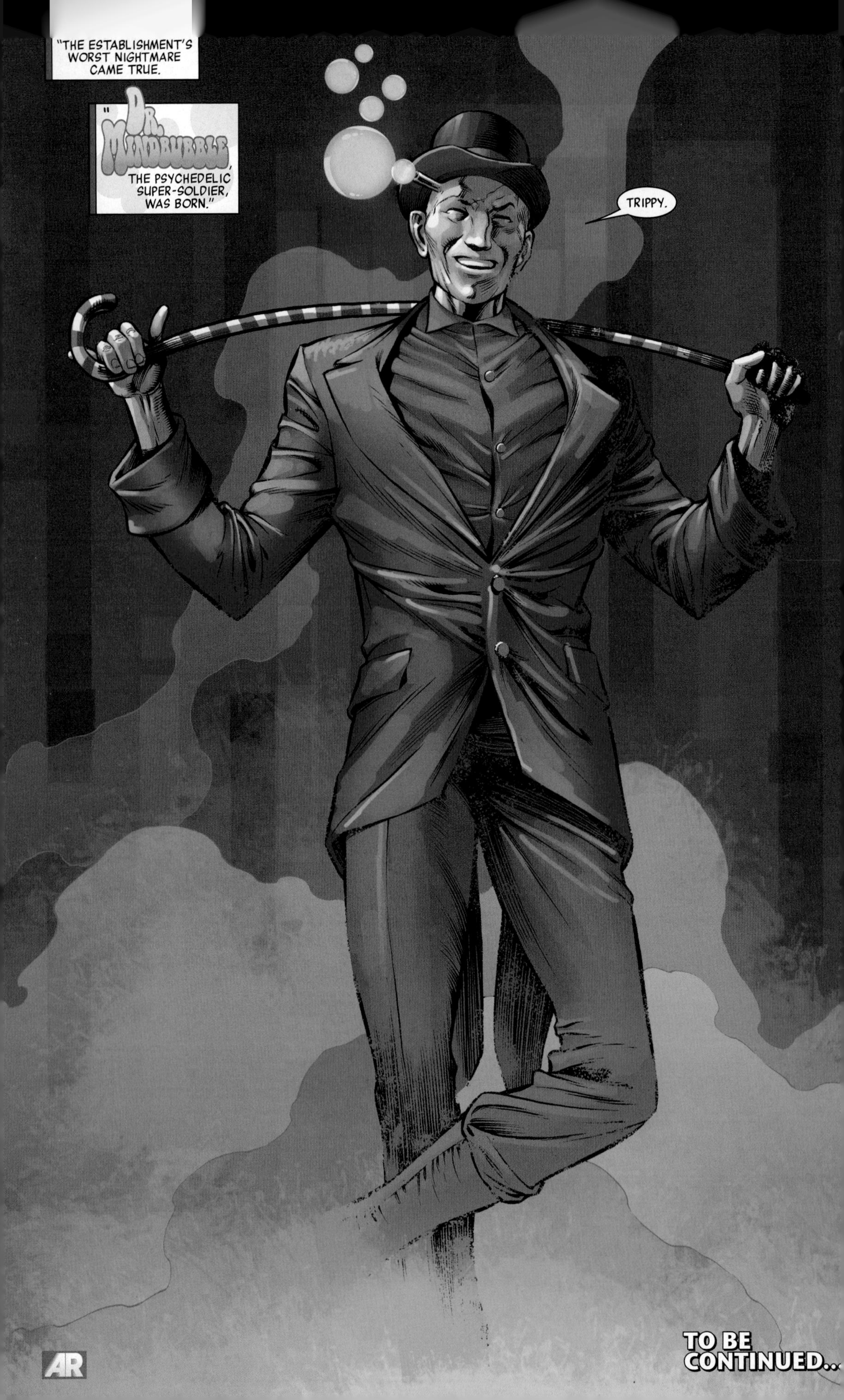
"THE ESTABLISHMENT'S WORST NIGHTMARE CAME TRUE.
"DR. MINDBUBBLE, THE PSYCHEDELIC SUPER-SOLDIER, WAS BORN."
TRIPPY.
TO BE CONTINUED...
AR

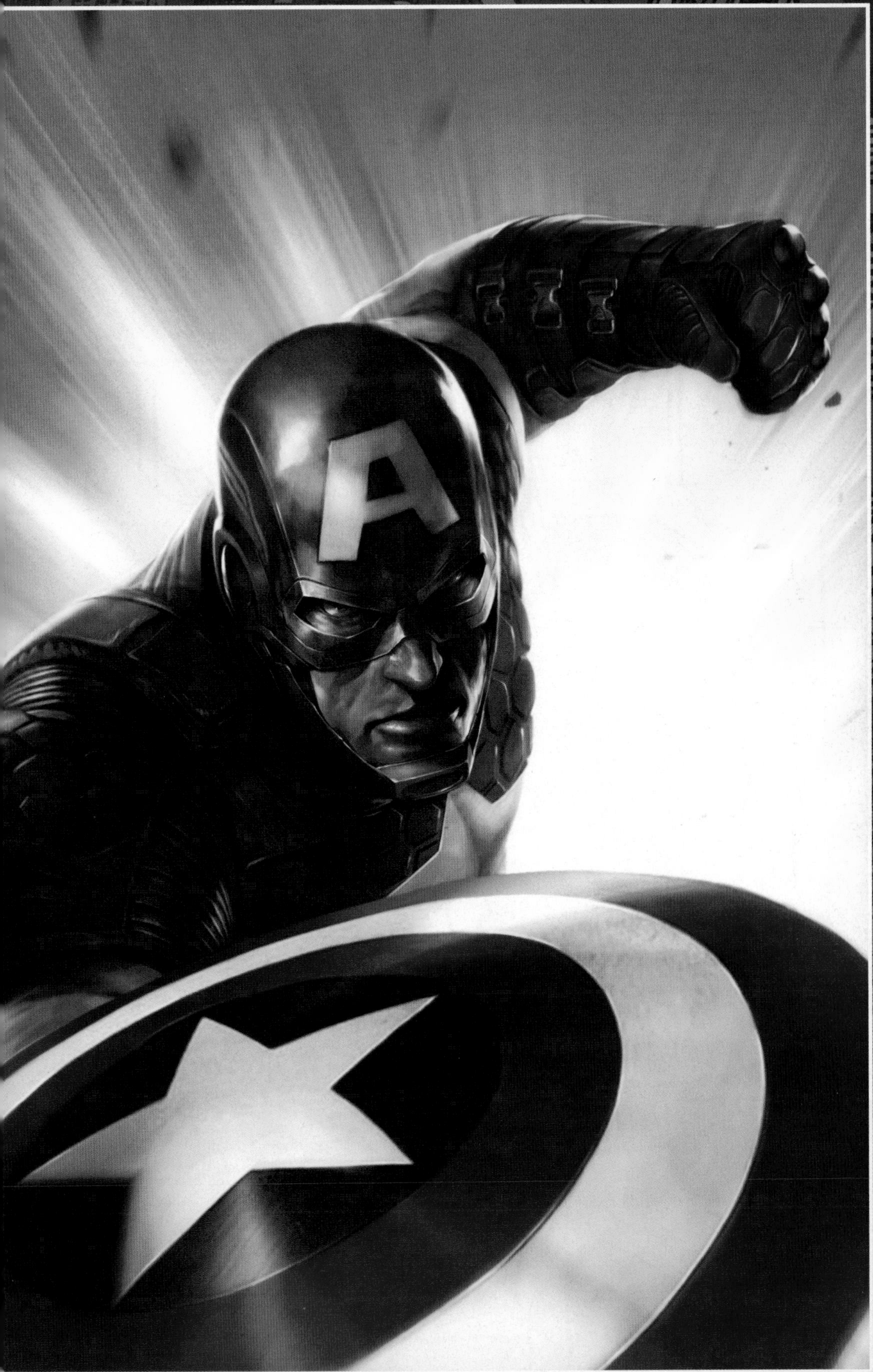

#15 VARIANT BY FRANCESCO MATTINA

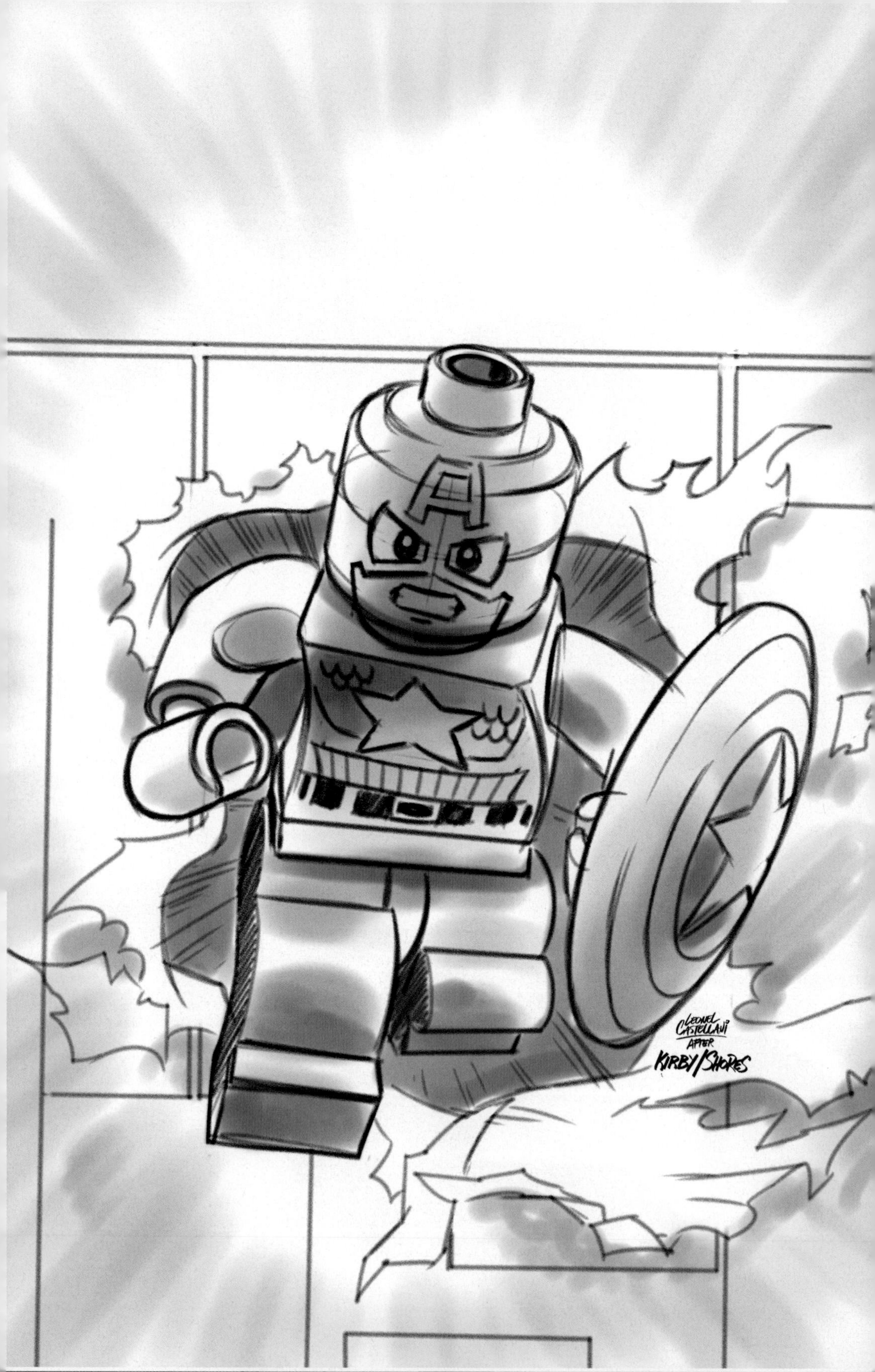
LEONEL CASTELLANI AFTER KIRBY/SHORES

#12 LEGO SKETCH VARIANT BY LEONEL CASTELLANI

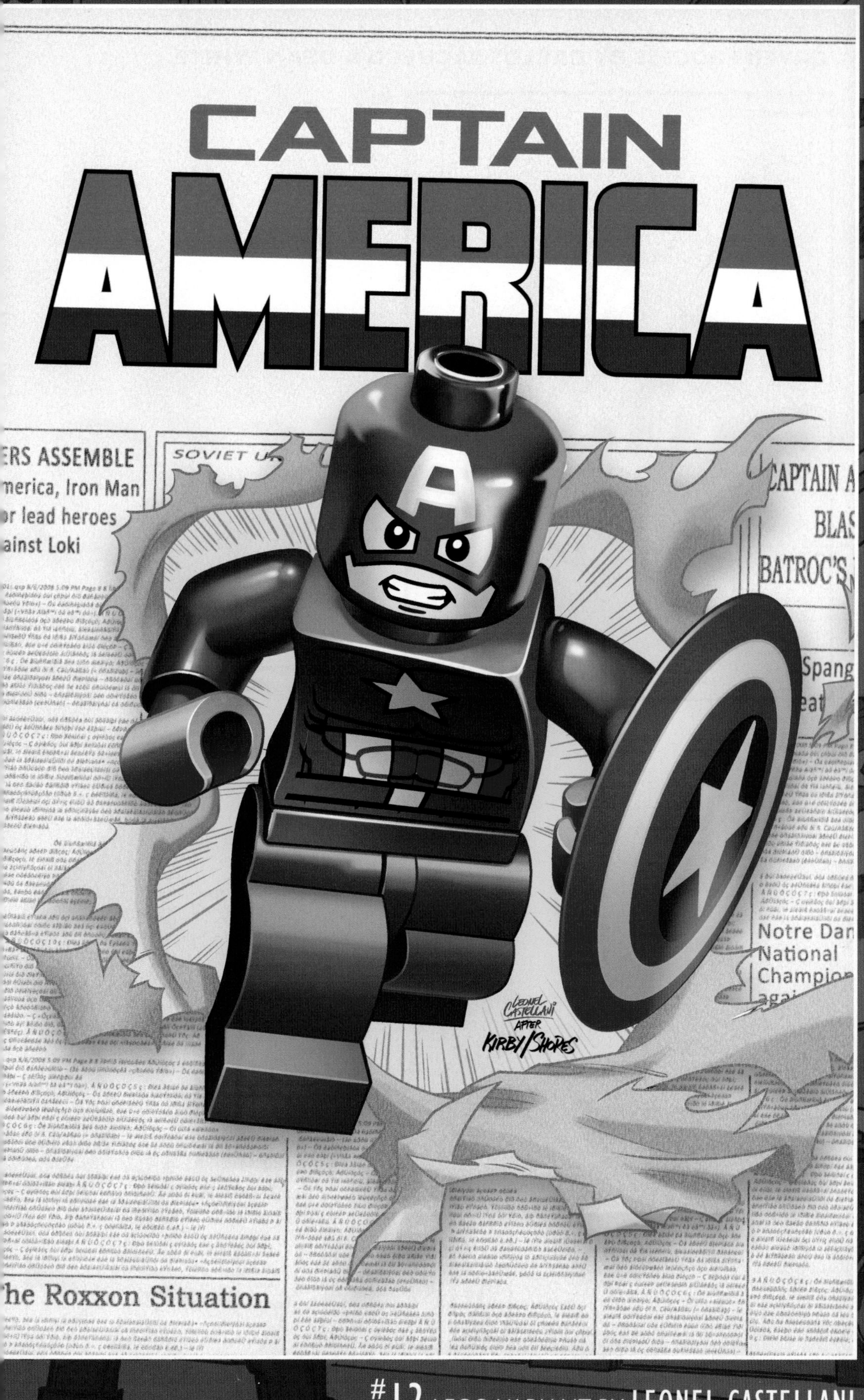
CAPTAIN
AMERICA
ERS ASSEMBLE
merica, Iron Man
or lead heroes
ainst Loki
SOVIET U
CAPTAIN A
BLAS
BATROC'S
Spang
eat
Notre Dan
National
Champion
he Roxxon Situation
LEONEL CASTELLANI AFTER KIRBY/SHORES

#12 LEGO VARIANT BY LEONEL CASTELLANI

COVER PROCESS BY CARLOS PACHECO & DEAN WHITE

#11

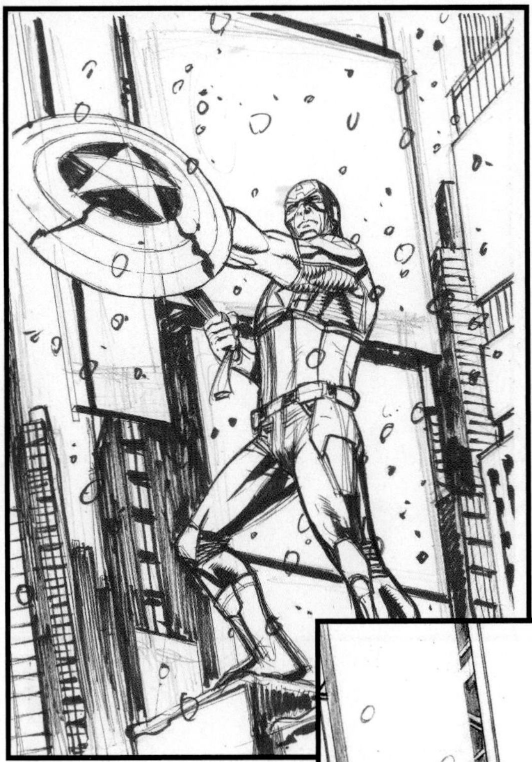

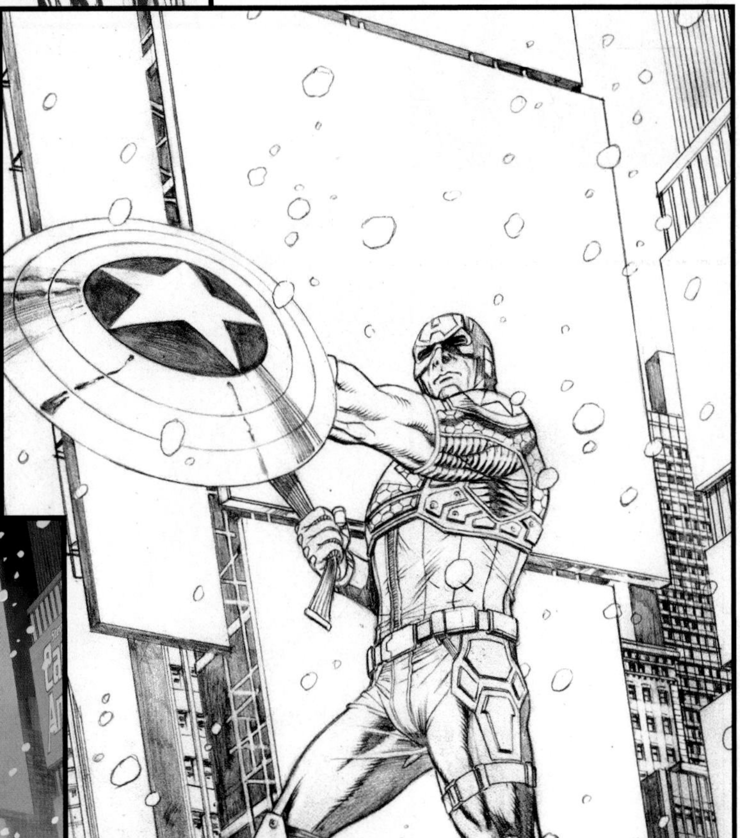
PACHECO-13

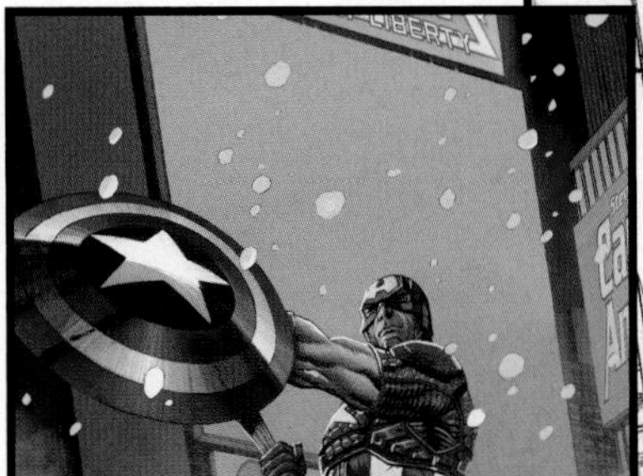

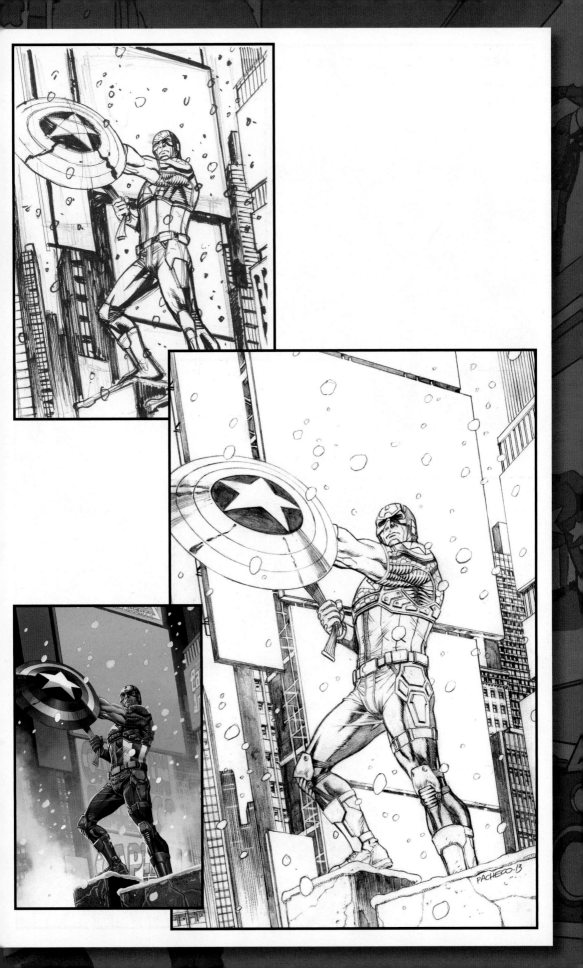

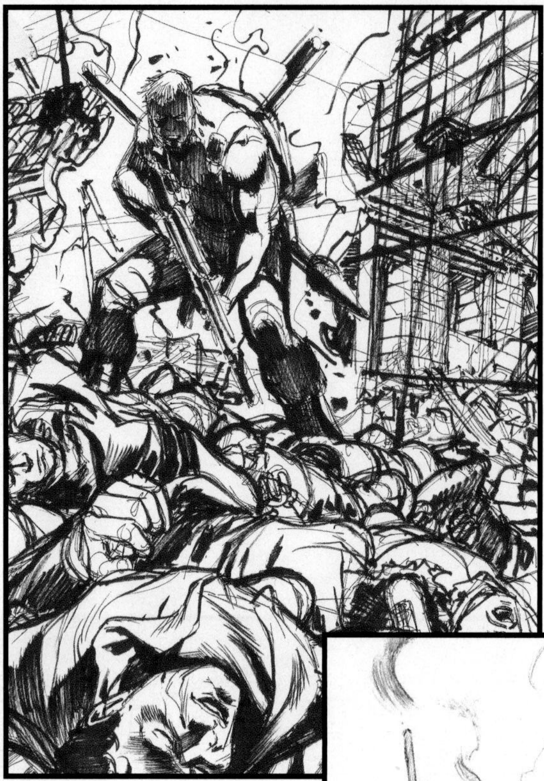

#12

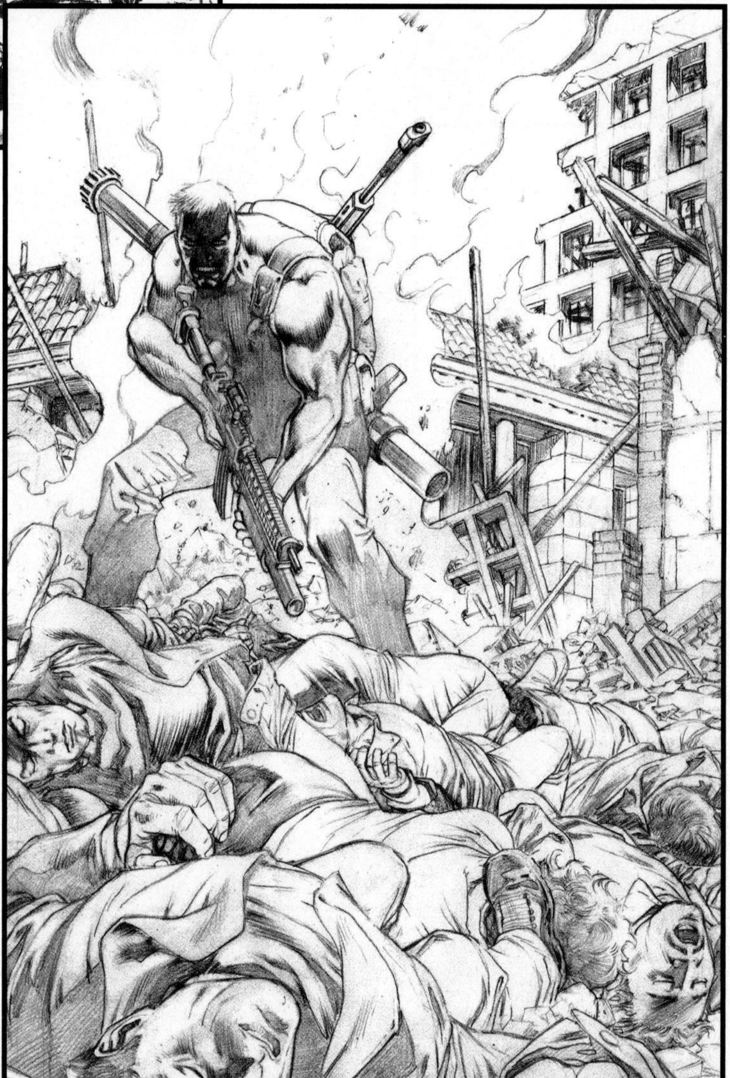

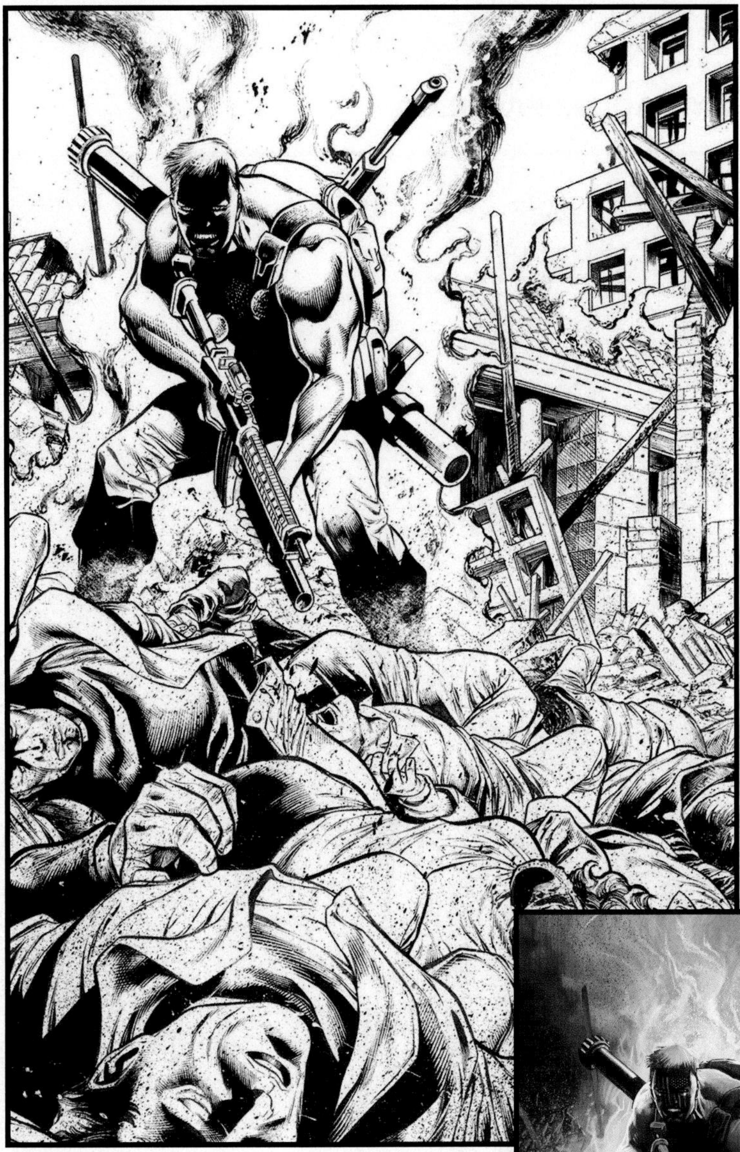

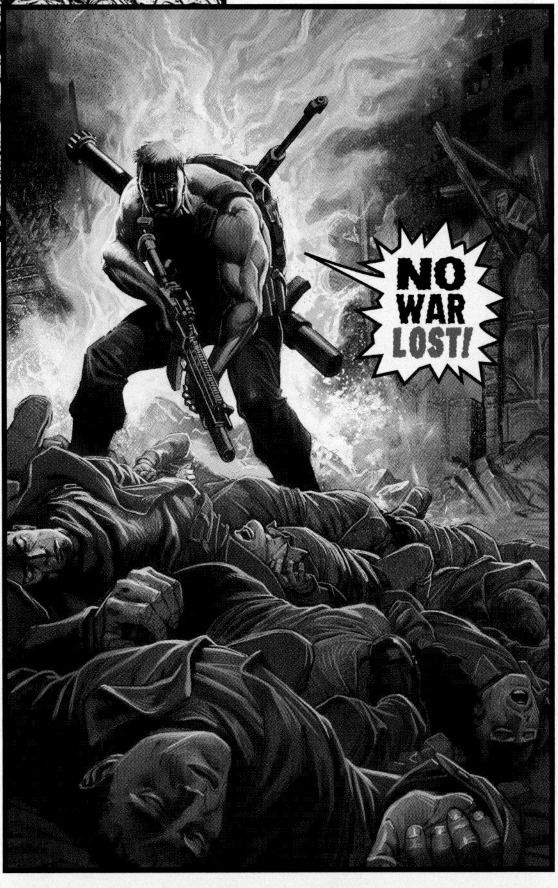
NO WAR LOST!

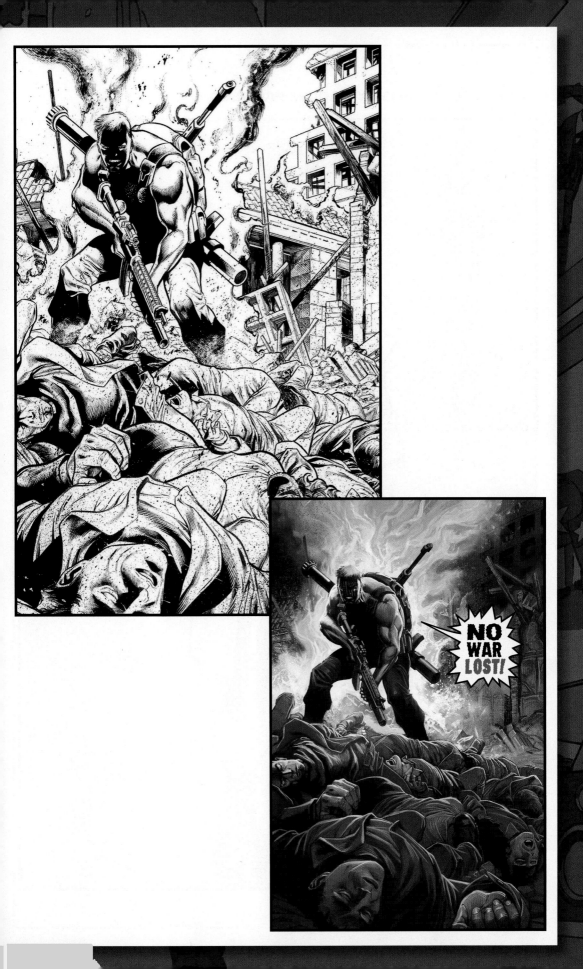

IRON NAIL DESIGNS BY CARLOS PACHECO

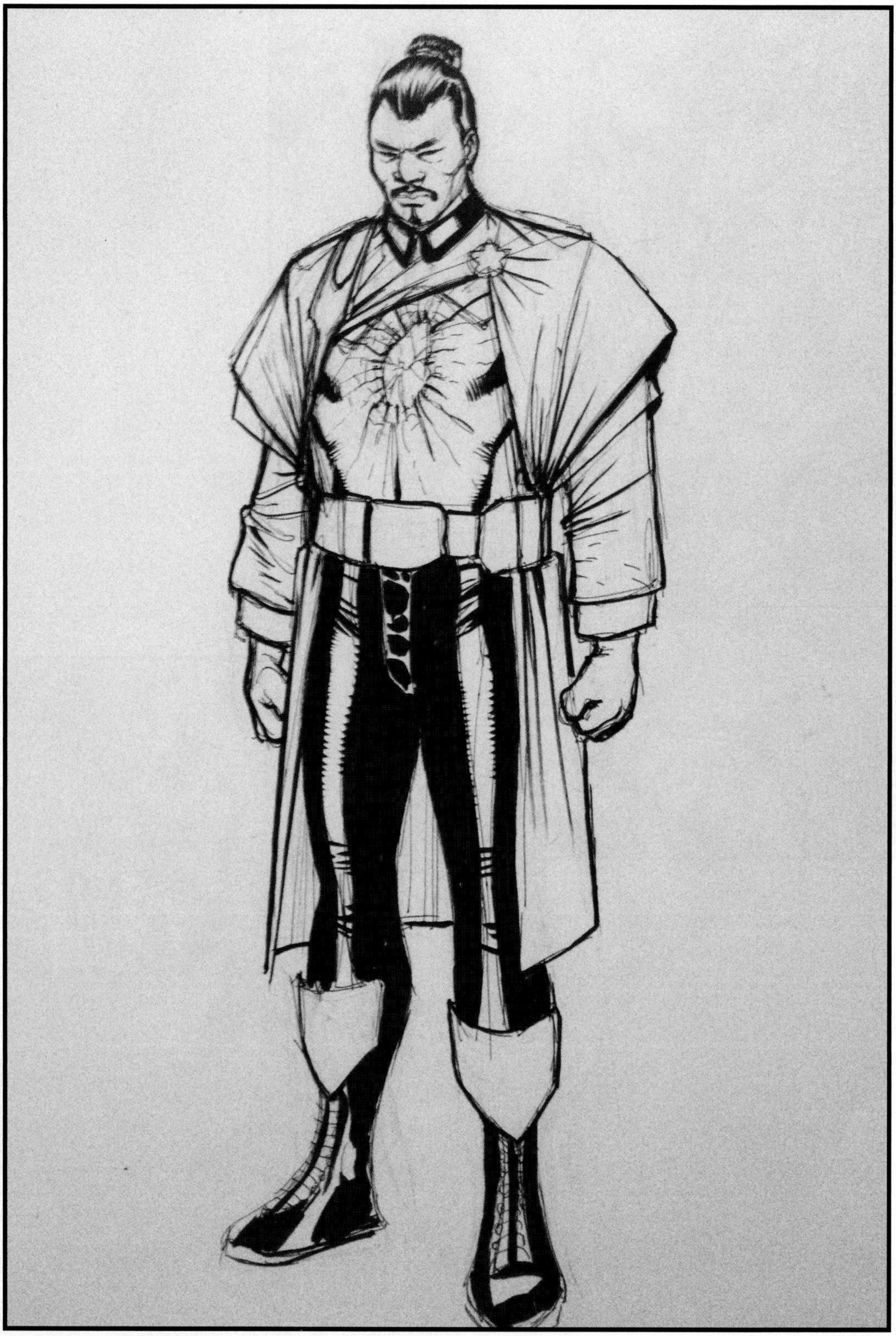

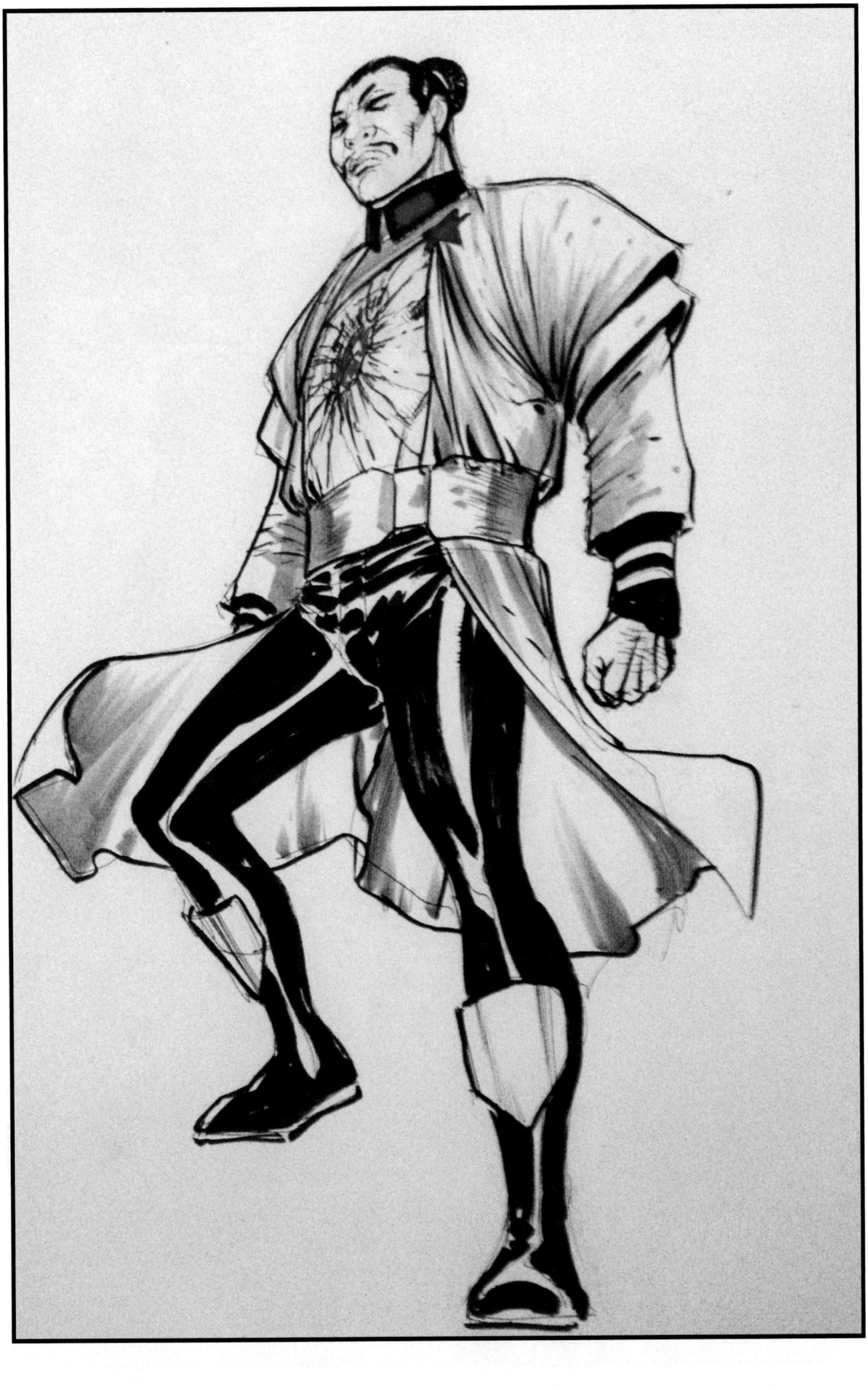

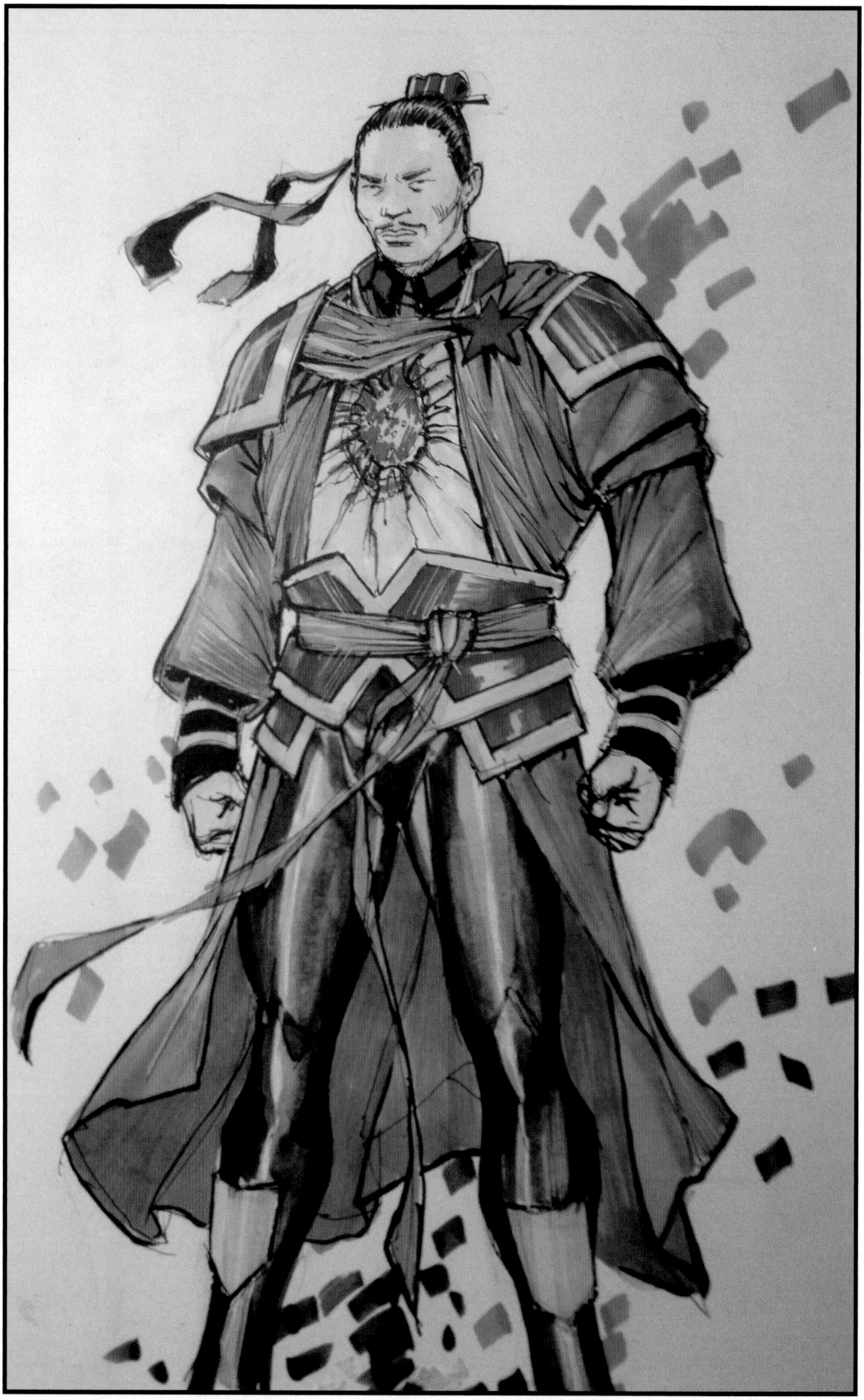

CAPTAIN AMERICA #11
script by RICK REMENDER
pencils by CARLOS PACHECO • inks by KLAUS JANSON

PAGE 1

1 - OPEN ON A FLASHBACK - NY - 1935: Steve's mom is dying, Very sick, SHE SITS IN THE KITCHEN, IN A BLANKET. Behind her STEVE and the DOCTOR talk. Steve is a young man here, early teens, thin, weak looking, very poor.

SEE ISSUES 1-3 FOR REFERENCE OF THE ROGER'S HOME FORM THIS ERA.

DOCTOR

I'm sorry, Steve.

2 - IN ON STEVE, now turning and looking at his Mom as the doctor clearly gives him bad news. Steve's face is sad. The doctor is offering his sympathies.

DOCTOR

There's nothing left I can do for her.

3 - The doctor is putting his hat on, Steve still looking at his mother. Steve is shattered, fighting tears.

4 - The doctor leaves, young Steve approaches from behind his Mother and puts a hand on her shoulder.

STEVE

Mom…

SARAH ROGERS

On top of everything else you've been through.

5 - STEVE'S POV - Sarah puts her hand on top of Steve's hand as she turns and looks up at us/Steve. She looks sick, thin, pale, and dying but she still manages a big reassuring smile.

SARAH ROGERS

It isn't fair for you to have to deal with this

PAGE 2

1 - CUT TO - NOW - SHIELD LAB - STEVE ROGERS IN A HIGH-TECH SHIELD LAB - CAP is on an angled lab table, one side is BRUCE BANNER, on the other is HANK PYM, both are operating on Cap. Cap has his shirt off revealing his bare chest, and the terrible scar in the center of it where he cut the Zola face out of his own chest. He's covered in scars, scabs, wounds, blood, dirt--he's been through hell.

SARAH ROGERS

"But how you do will define you."

BRUCE BANNER

Bleeding on the upper right abdomen under control.

HANK PYM (BG)

Good, this giant hole in his chest isn't.

Bio circuitry everywhere--need the synaptic welders to clean it off.

SARAH ROGERS (CAP)

You've been so strong, Steve…

2 - CUT TO - FLASHBACK: Sarah Rogers is bundled in a blanket on the couch now, very sick. Steve is entering the living room with some steaming soup in a bowl.

SARAH ROGERS

…but I know you're terribly frightened.

STEVE

Stop, Mom. You need to rest.

SARAH ROGERS

Leaving you all alone…

But I know you'll find your way.

3 - Sarah and Steve sit on the couch, she's looking him in the eyes, smiling. Steve has set the soup on the table in front of her.

SARAH ROGERS

That's the gift of this place, the unyielding spirit of a free people.

Optimism is the American state of being.

No matter the calamity, we remain surefooted, confident of tomorrows return…

4 - CUT TO - NOW - STEVE ROGERS IN A HIGH-TECH SHIELD LAB - HIS CHEST IS BEING OPERATED ON BY BANNER, it's a mess, scarred up badly, puss and blood. This is the injury Steve got when he cut the Zola screen out of his chest.

SARAH ROGERS (CAP)

"…It's why we came here, Steve.

"It's what we wanted for you."

BRUCE BANNER

These tendrils are fused to his nervous system, Pym.

PYM

Take your time.

5 - CUT TO - FLASHBACK: Steve's mom is dying. Very sick. She sits up, looking at her son in the eyes.

SARAH ROGERS

Never allow this challenge, this grief, to defeat you, Steve.

Get past this and no matter what life throws at you-- you'll overcome it.

PAGE 3

1 - On Steve, weeping, holding his Mother's trembling hand.

SARAH ROGERS

In order to grow you must let go of the past.

STEVE (WEAK/WAVY)

Mom... please...

SARAH ROGERS

Inside that small frame is a big strong heart.

A good man.

2 - CUT TO - NOW - STEVE ROGERS IN A HIGH-TECH SHIELD LAB - Pym is sealing up the chest wound with a high tech gizmo. Banner helping.

SARAH ROGERS (CAP)

"A strong heart will take you further than any physical strength.

"A strong heart means you'll never quit...

3 - Pym injects a strange red liquid into Steve's chest.

SARAH ROGERS (CAP)

"...You'll always maintain the optimism of this great nation."

PYM

Okay, I'm in.

This should locate and destroy any of the foreign tissue.

SARAH ROGERS

"You can't be stuck here..."

4 - CUT TO - FLASHBACK: Steve's mom is leaning forward now to look her boy in the eyes.

SARAH ROGERS

Life is too short to allow yourself to become trapped in one chapter.

You learn what you can, you stand up, and you move forward.

STEVE

How can I go forward without you?

5 - She smiles so warmly at him. Tears streaming down both of their faces now. Her eyes are full of pride for her skinny and sickly son.

SARAH ROGERS

My love is in you, angel.

No matter where you go...

PAGE 4

ALL PAGE WIDE PANELS

1 - CUT TO - MOM'S FUNERAL - SNOWY DAY - STEVE'S ALONE, IN AN INEXPENSIVE SUIT OF THE ERA. ALL HIS FAMILY IS DEAD. NO ONE ELSE AT THE FUNERAL.

SARAH ROGERS (CAP)

"I'll always be in your heart."

2 - ON YOUNG STEVE, watching the casket be

lowered. Alone, his family is dead. This skinny kid will face the world alone. He holds a flower. He weeps.

3 - CUT TO - INT. SHIELD HUB - CAP is being operated on, another wound sewn shut by Pym. He is in bad shape.

BANNER

He's been through hell. I'm frankly surprised he survived.

PYM

Think about whom you're talking about.

BANNER

Yeah, but even for him, I know Steve's strong, but this…

4 - CUT TO - THE FUNERAL - STEVE DROPS A FLOWER ON THE CASKET.

BANNER (CAP)

"…I don't know how he stood up after taking this kind of a beating."

5 - PULL UP AND OUT - YOUNG STEVE WALKS AWAY. The snow drifts down as his mother is buried.

BANNER (CAP)

"Where does any one man get that kind of courage?"

PAGE 5

1 - CUT TO - EXT. SHIELD LAND BASE THE HUB - DAY - WE SAW THIS BASE IN UNCANNY AVENGERS #1, it is buried in the side of a dessert canyon's red rock.

MARIA HILL (INSIDE)

Twelve years?!

2 - INT. SHIELD HUB - LATER - CAP is cleaned up now, shaven, sitting up in a medical bed, on one side is BRUCE BANNER, on the other is HANK PYM, both are caring for Cap. In front of Cap is MARIA HILL, listening to his incredible story. Cap has his shirt off revealing his bare chest, and the multiple places he's wrapped up in gauze, it's crazy, the man has been through Hell. He's COVERED IN BAND AIDS AND GAUZE.

CAPT. AMERICA

As best as I can tell.

Yes.

HANK PYM

The carbon date testing I ran on the uniform confirms it.

3 - MARIA HILL GETS CLOSE, looking closely at the cleanly shaven and fixed up Steve Rogers face, looking for wrinkles.

MARIA HILL

You haven't aged.

CAPT. AMERICA

I hadn't noticed.

4 - On Banner and Pym, they mess about with holographic controls and high tech doo-dads, instruments connected to Steve, doing his vitals etc.

BRUCE BANNER

A super-soldier serum affect we never thought much about.

HANK PYM

Congratulations Steve. It appears you don't age.

(CONT'D)

5 - Maria turns to Banner and Pym.

MARIA HILL

The Zola infection?

BRUCE BANNER

Erased it and the bio circuits welded to his nervous system.

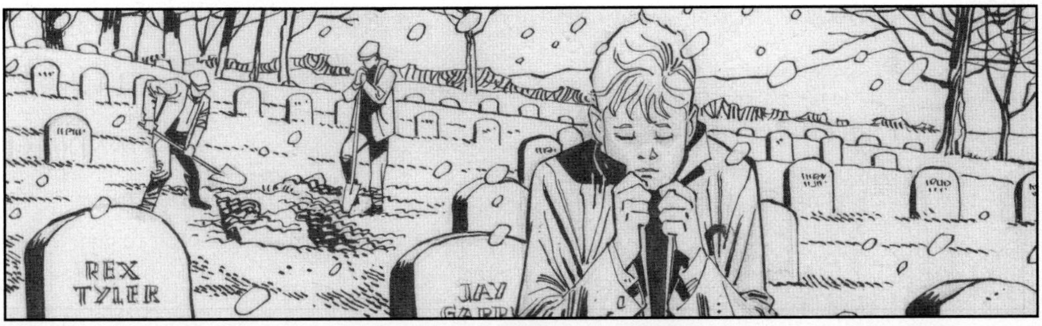
REX TYLER

PYM

He gets a clean bill. Physically anyway.

6 - ON MARIA HILL, TROUBLED, LOOKING UP.

MARIA HILL

Captain, about Agent Carter, I have to ask…

We need to be certain there wasn't any chance of survival?

7 - Steve looks down, silent. EVERYONE IS SILENT.

PAGE 6

1 - Maria places a caring hand on Cap's arm, she smiles warmly at him.

MARIA HILL

I'm sorry, but we needed to be sure.

My deepest condolences.

CAPT. AMERICA

No need to apologize, Maria.

MARIA HILL

Twelve years… I can't even imagine what you've been through.

2 - On Steve, lost in thought, a million miles away.

MARIA HILL (OP)

I want to keep you close, for observation.

MARIA HILL (OP)

So you can talk to someone about it all, about Sharon…

3 - Steve looks away, lost in thought.

4 - SAME SHOT - STEVE LOOKS UP AND FORCES A SMILE. Pretends he's okay all of a sudden.

CAPT. AMERICA

I'll feel better fulfilling my duties, Commander Hill.

Getting back to it.

5 - On Maria, very worried.

MARIA HILL

Of Course, Captain.

I didn't mean to suggest otherwise…

6 - Maria walks out of the room.

MARIA HILL

And don't worry, Steve. Consider this top level classified.

Highly. None of this leaves the room.

HANK PYM

Zip.

BRUCE BANNER

Zilch.

PAGE 7

1 - CAP TURNS TO BANNER. They can all tell he's hurt, but he acts strong.

CAPT. AMERICA

Where's Jet?

BRUCE BANNER

She proved… less than amicable. Rude even.

CAPT. AMERICA

Where is she now?

2 - CUT TO - EST. SHIELD INTERROGATION ROOM - MODERN NICK FURY stands calmly, JET BLACK is in shackles, chained to the floor. She is still wearing her battle costume, she is still battle worn from issue 10's climax.

BRUCE BANNER

"With the only equally as disagreeable person I know.

Who isn't gamma irradiated anyway."

NICK FURY

I don't like to dance around things, Jet.

You see, here, adult people, you waste their time-- they just move on.

If I move on, you move to a jail cell, remember?

3 - On Jet, evil, smiling coldly at Nick, she is top lit to add noir mood.

NICK FURY (OP)

I don't know much about where you come from, not yet I do not, but here on Earth--oh, it's a busy world.

We all have lots to be doing.

4 - Two shot - Nick paces, Jet looks straight ahead.

NICK FURY

Now, Captain America vouched for you, promised you'd be forthcoming.

You're lucky. Cap's a high value advocate here.

NICK FURY

Your Father, on the other hand, is among the very worst human beings that this planet has ever produced.

5 - Fury leans, fists on the table, getting himself closer to Jet.

NICK FURY (STROKED)

So, before I sign off on granting THE DAUGHTER OF ARNIM ZOLA access to MY WORLD--I'm going to know a BIT about her.

SFX

KLAMM

PAGE 8

1 - NICK FURY LEANS IN CLOSER, getting right in Jet's face.

NICK FURY

And make no mistake--that's where you are now, Princess.

My world.

And my world is a sunny and happy place provided you play by the rules.

If you don't...

2 - Nick turns around picking up a notebook and a pen off of the desk.

NICK FURY

Well, I can make it a dark place full of missed opportunity and grave remorse.

So.

Now...

3 - Nick Fury licks the tip of a pen, he holds a notebook, he's shooting Jet a sly look as he prepares to take notes.

NICK FURY

List your super powers.

Captain America tells me you're a test tube super warrior, a real gifted fighter.

What kind of fighting?

4 - Jet looks up, cold.

JET

Release me and I will show you the might of my TACHYON FU.

My bare skin can read the near future keeping me ahead of any opponent.

5 - Two shot - Jet and Nick.

NICK FURY

Ladies skin can read the future.

That's a pretty great power, Miss Black.

What else?

JET

Infinite Omniscenses.

6 - On Jet, looking up, evil.

JET

I can smell, hear, and even taste things hundreds of miles away.

However, when I'm using any one sense at omni level, all others are turned off.

NICK FURY (OP)

Nothing's perfect.

PAGE 9

1 - Behind Nick we angle on Jet.

FURY

What can you hear? How far can you hear it?

JET

I can an insect on the other side of the world. I can hear and decipher digital transmissions.

I can hear your heart, strong and level.

I can hear the blood flowing inside your brain.

2 - CLOSER ON JET, looking up at Nick Fury, she is deadly, seductive, and clever.

JET

Flowing to the section related to attraction.

3 - CLOSER STILL ON JET, sexy, manipulative, smart as a whip. SMILING.

JET

You tie up women, interrogate and break them down.

You tell yourself its just part of your job, but that's not all, is it?

There's something else, another reason.

4 - CUT TO FURY - A BIT NERVOUS, curious, caught off guard.

NICK FURY

What would that be?

5 - Tight on Jet, looking up, deadly, sexy.

JET

It gets you off.

PAGE 10

1 - CAP ENTERS THE ROOM, breaking the moment, smiling at Nick. Cap looks wounded and tired, but clean and fresh in his all-new Captain America outfit.

CAPT. AMERICA

Hope I'm not interrupting?

2 - Cap would like a word with Jet alone. She is smiling devilishly at Nick Fury who looks angrily at her.

JET

Mr. Fury and I were just getting acquainted.

CAPT. AMERICA

Okay. Come on. We're leaving.

FURY

I'd feel safer if I could spend a few days with her--

3 - Fury leaves. Shooting Jet a cold look. Jet smiles to him warmly.

JET

It was nice meeting you, Agent Fury.

CAPT. AMERICA

She'll be safe with me, Nick. I promise.

FURY

Truth, Steve…

4 - CUT TO - EXT. SHIELD LAND BASE THE HUB - SUNSET - Captain America and Jet flying away from the base in a classic SHIELD FLYING CAR.

FURY (CAP)

"…It isn't her safety I'm worried about."

CAPT. AMERICA

What did you tell him, Jet?

5 - On Cap, driving. Jet sits next to him.

JET

Most everything.

Nothing about Ian.

As we agreed.

PAGE 11

1 - She turns and looks away, lost on the memory of her brother and father.

JET

My family is dead.

JET

Captive in another world where nothing is familiar.

CAPT.

The uncertainty is terrible.

I can remember the feeling.

2 - EXT. OF THE CAR - it rockets over a forested mountain range.

JET

What will happen to me now? Where will I stay?

CAPT. AMERICA

With me.

Until we can get you settled into a normal human life.

We'll get you some help dealing with the trauma.

3 - Steve looks ahead, lost in thought. Jet turns to him, coy, sad.

JET

What about your trauma? Ian, he was a son to you.

I can only imagine the pain. If want to unburden yourself, I'd be willing to listen…

4 - Silent on Steve driving. Close on Cap, dead inside, a man who lost a son. The setting sun outside adds a beauty to this somber moment.

5 - Jet looks out the other side of the window, neither have anything to say.

JET

I prefer the silence as well.

PAGE 12

1 - CUT TO - SKYLINE OF NROSVEKISTAN - AFTERNOON - SNOWING OUTSIDE - THIS IS A FICTIONS EASTERN EUROPEAN NATION that has been through a number of wars. It's in rough shape, very poor. (We saw this nation designed in Venom #1, ask me for ref). It's a winter day, SNOWING OUTSIDE.

LOC CAP

Nrosvekistan

2 - CUT TO - STREET LEVEL - A man fills a stand with produce for sale. Other pedestrians move around, some women shopping, a drunk stumbles, etc.

3 - THE PRODUCE MAN watches as the SHOPPING WOMEN DROP THEIR BAGS IN SHOCK at something they see down the road. We can't see what yet.

NUKE (OP)

Doesn't matter how much good we've done in the region.

4 - THE GROCER TURNS to see NUKE marching calmly down the center of the dilapidated and war torn street of this ravaged city. Nuke is carrying a large duffle bag full with a giant gun, but we don't want to telegraph that here. It's just a big US MILITARY ISSUE DUFFLE BAG full of something.

NOTES: Agent Simpson: Codenamed Nuke. Project Rebirth. NUKE: skin contains several kinds of plastics. Doesn't burn. Is tough. Skeleton and muscles, only part human. Sergeant Simpson.

NUKE

You still hate us.

5 - PULL OUT WIDE - The citizens all around the street stop and look at the crazy American. Nuke, cold, walking and looking straight ahead. Snow drifts down. Everyone is curious about this.

NUKE

Hate our freedom.

Hate our values.

Hate our God.

PAGE 13

1 - Nuke stops in the center of town and drops the large duffel bag. A man leads a think old horse pulling half of a VW Bug. Another shopkeeper comes out of his shop. People are sanding and listening to this crazy man.

NUKE

Our boys gave their lives here.

Our boys died defending you people from yourselves.

2 - Nuke puts a hand in a pouch on his belt.

NUKE

Those who survived came home forgotten.

No parades.

3 - Nuke looks in his hand to see three pills, red, white and blue.

NUKE

They call what happened here a loss for the U.S.

4 - On his face - He tosses the pills in his mouth.

NUKE

"A war we rushed into and lost."

5 - Nuke grimaces, gritting his teeth, like a junkie who just got a fix.

SFX (BY TEETH)

KKRICHH

6 - Nuke stands tall at attention, his veins are popping out. His face is clenched.

NUKE

But we don't lose.

War here just went on pause--YOU HEAR ME?!

PAGE 14

1 - Nuke is enraged, standing at attention, screaming like Henry Rollins, red in the face, neck bursting with veins. People are scared now, beginning to move away.

NUKE (STROKED/BIG)

THE WAR ISN'T OVER!

You thought we cut and run back home?!

Left our boys to rot for nothing?!

2 - He bends over, reaching back into the duffle bag.

NUKE

That's not American.

3 - NUKE pulls out a GIANT 80S ACTION HERO STYLE MACHINE GUN. The ostentatious kind we saw in PREDATOR.

NUKE

We finish what we start.

We clean our own dishes.

4 - IMPACT - NUKE OPENS FIRE AT US, big classic Nuke hate on his face, opening up in to civilian population off panel.

NUKE

And we don't lose wars.

SFX

BRAKKA-BRAKKA-BRAKKA-

PAGE 15

1 - CUT TO - CAPTAIN AMERICA'S BASE HOME - CLOUDY EVENING - CAP'S FLYING SHIELD CAR HOVERS, IT IS APPROACHING HIS HOME. This base is new, so design it to last. Simple looking red brick apartment building or warehouse in BROOKLYN.

LOC CAP

Brooklyn

CAPT. AMERICA

2 - CLOSER ON THE EXT. BUILDING - FLYING CAR ENTERS A WALL THAT IS A HOLOGRAM FIELD allowing the car to pass right into the building.

CAPT. AMERICA

Hold on.

Don't worry, the wall is a--

JET

Hologram.

3 - INT. CAP'S GARAGE - THE FLYING CAR IS LANDED, Jet and Cap getting out. We see his other vehicles here, the Cap motorcycle and some jet packs on the wall that stark made for him. They are designed like his new outfit.

JET

I can see.

4 - JET FOLLOWS CAP, they walk through the garage, towards the entrance to the main room.

JET

This is your home?

CAPT. AMERICA

It was.

PAGE 16-17

1 - DOUBLE PAGE WIDE IMPACT EST. INT. OPEN PLANNED HOMEBASE OF CAPTAIN AMERICA. All around them in this rustic, open planned room is CAP'S OWN PERSONAL MUSEUM. WWII memorabilia, his various shields, framed images of him with Various ages of the Avengers. Grab one team shot form each of the most famous teams from each decade. The room is plastered with relics, pictures of Cap with Bucky for the bond drive, propaganda images of Cap and Torch, A big war time poster of the Invaders rushing into action, newspaper clippings from the era etc. In the center of the room is an old dusty boxing ring, punching bag, etc. This is like CAPTAIN AMERICA'S BATCAVE, an old and dusty gym/museum.

CAPT. AMERICA

A million years ago.

2 - He silently shows Jet her new home. She looks at all the old WWII Cap memorabilia, toys, war bond posters, lunch boxes, decoder rings, all kinds of Cap memorabilia.

JET

These proclamations of past victories, they are important to you?

CAP

Yes.

3 - Cap stops and looks at the big image of him leading the Invaders in WWII.

CAP

They used to be.

4 - Steve walks on, towards his desk. He walks past his memories, walls covered, a room full of his WWII memorabilia. The room is plastered with relics, pics, newspaper clippings etc.

JET

When I think of Father and Ian I feel a pained longing...

CAPT. AMERICA

Mourning.

5 - STEVE STOPS AT HIS OLD DESK. It's an old WWII era wooden desk, on it we see an old picture of Steve with the original Nick Fury and another of Sharon Carter. CAP'S ANSWERING MACHINE IS BLINKING.

CAPT. AMERICA

Grief at the loss of someone you cared for.

6 - CLOSE ON THE ANSWERING MACHINE:

CAPT. AMERICA

MISSED CALL: SHARON CARTER

PAGE 18

1 - Cap ignores it, turns to Jet; she is looking around at the wall full of Cap memories and memorabilia.

CAPT. AMERICA

I don't know what the future holds, Jet. But I'm here for you.

I'm going to help you put together a new life.

2 - Jet turns away, frightened, worried.

JET

What if I prefer my old life?

CAPT. AMERICA

My mother once told me, "In order to grow you must let go of the past."

That's just what you'll have to do.

3 - Jet looks at Steve like he's a hypocrite.

JET

Are you lecturing me about letting go of the past while standing in your shine to it?

4 - SAME SHOT - SHE THEN TURNS TO LOOK AT THE MUSEUM OF CAP AL OVER THE WALL NEXT TO THEM.

5 - PULL WAY BACK WIDE - JET AND CAP STAND LOOKING AT THIS LARGE ROOM FULL OF CAP memorabilia; posters, framed newspaper articles, old shields, pictures of the Invaders, pictures of Steve with Nomad, with Sharon, With Bucky, With the Avengers from all the most famous eras. Newspaper article is framed: Daily Bugle: Torch kills Hitler. War is over. Bucky's original costume is dressed on a mannequin. Nomad's in on another. This is a museum of the life and times of Captain America.

CAPT. AMERICA

I see what you mean.

PAGE 19

1 - CUT TO - ROOFTOP OF CAP'S BUILDING/ BASE - IT'S BEGUN TO RAIN - Steve and Jet on the rooftop of his building, Brooklyn all around them. Grey clouds swirl. There is a pile of stuff in front of them, we can't see it; it's silhouetted.

2 - CLOSER ON JET AND CAP LOOKING DOWN at SOMETHING WE CAN'T SEE YET. Cap looks calm and at peace.

3 - Cap turns and looks at Jet, he's looking for reassurance.

JET

Go on.

4 - Cap looks back down, the rain has really picked up now.

5 - Cap lights a match.

6 - Cap holds the match up, looking at it, thinking.

PAGE 20

EVEN SIZED PAGE WIDE HORIZONTAL PANELS

1 - STEVE DROPS THE MATCH IN THE PILE OF ALL THE MEMORABILIA WE SAW IN HIS BASE. IT'S ALL IN A BIG PILE IN FRONT OF HIM. MAYBE IT'S PILED IN A COUPLE OF METAL GARBAGE CANS. WHATEVER SELLS IT BEST. HE'S BURNING HIS PAST.

2 - FRONT ON CAPTAIN AMERICA AND JET, ILLUMINATED BY THE FIRE, standing in front of the pile of burning boxes of old photos and stuff.

3 - PULL OUT - CAPTAIN AMERICA AND JET, ILLUMINATED BY THE FIRE, standing in front of the pile of burning boxes of old photos and stuff.

4 - PULL OUT FURTHER - RAIN COMING DOWN, the fires builds, growing hirer, fighting the rain. Steve repeats something his mom taught him.

5 - PULL OUT FURTHER STILL, WE'RE VERY WIDE AND FAR NOW, all we see are the silhouettes of the skyline and one building with a small fire burning in the rain. A black plume of smoke drifting upwards.

6 - A PANEL SIZED WHITE SPACE FOR STORY TITLE/CREDITS: FIRE IN THE RAIN

#13 LAYOUTS BY NIC KLEIN

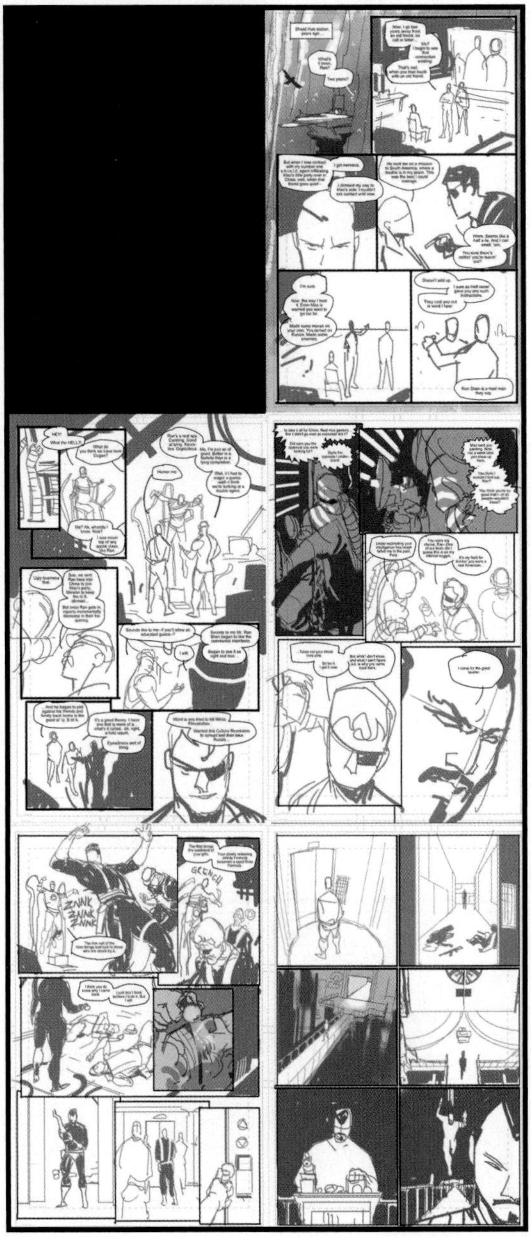

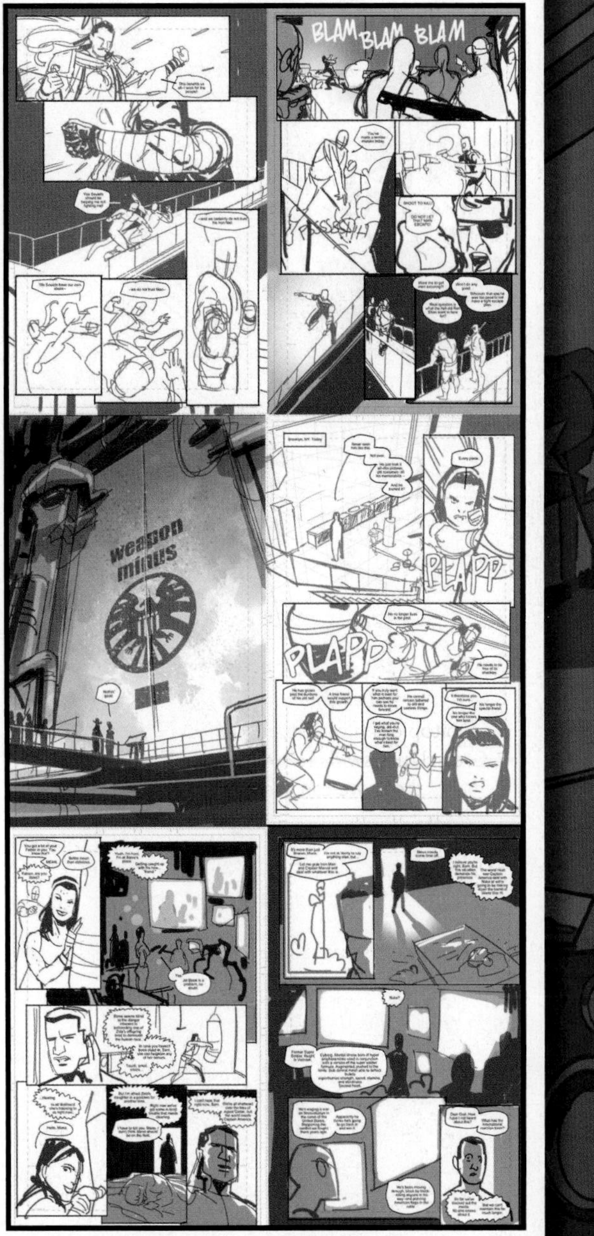
BLAM BLAM BLAM
weapon minus
PLAPP
PLAPP

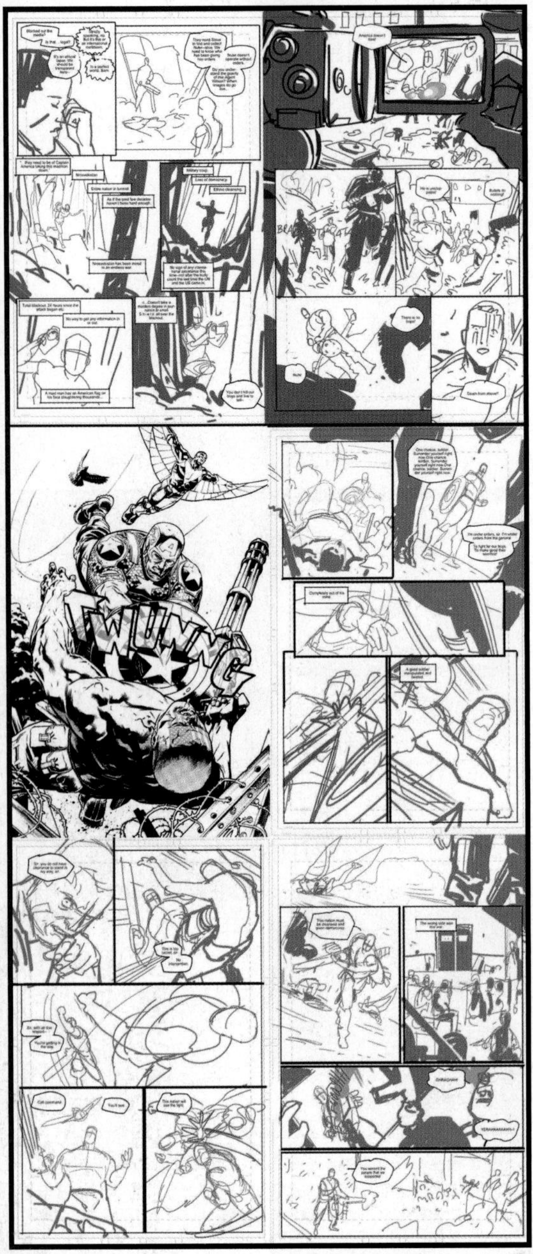

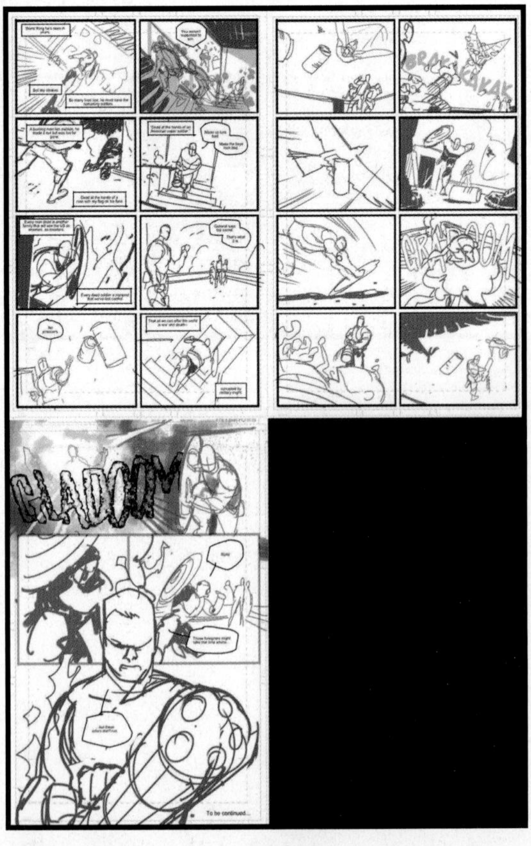
GLADOOM
To be continued...

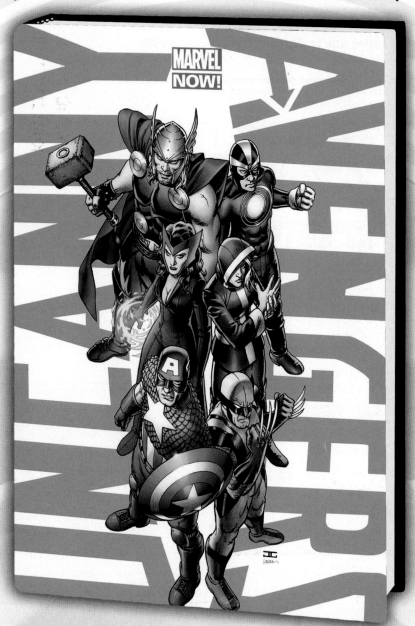

UNCANNY AVENGERS VOL. 1: THE RED SHADOW
WRITTEN BY RICK REMENDER • ART BY JOHN CASSADAY
978-0-7851-6603-0 • DEC130776

MARVEL AR AUGMENTED REALITY

MARVEL AUGMENTED REALITY (AR) ENHANCES AND CHANGES THE WAY YOU EXPERIENCE COMICS!

TO ACCESS THE FREE MARVEL AR CONTENT IN THIS BOOK*:

1. Locate the AR logo within the comic.
2. Go to Marvel.com/AR in your web browser.
3. Search by series title to find the corresponding AR.
4. Enjoy Marvel AR!

*All AR content that appears in this book has been archived and will be available only at Marvel.com/AR – no longer in the Marvel AR App. Content subject to change and availability.

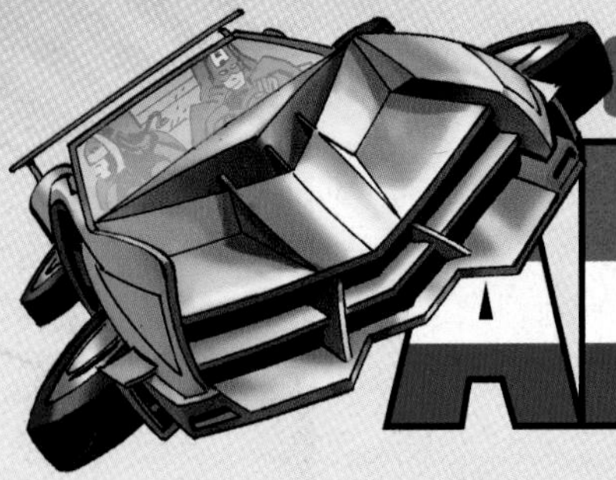

CAPTAIN AMERICA AR INDEX